Parish Registers
of
Prince George Winyah Church

Georgetown
South Carolina

1815-1936

By

Brent H. Holcomb

HERITAGE BOOKS
2019

HERITAGE BOOKS

AN IMPRINT OF HERITAGE BOOKS, INC.

Books, CDs, and more—Worldwide

For our listing of thousands of titles see our website
at
www.HeritageBooks.com

Published 2019 by
HERITAGE BOOKS, INC.
Publishing Division
5810 Ruatan Street
Berwyn Heights, Md. 20740

Copyright © 1996 Brent H. Holcomb
SCMAR
Columbia, South Carolina

Library of Congress Catalog Card Number: 96-69420

International Standard Book Number
Paperbound: 978-0-7884-5884-2

CONTENTS

INTRODUCTION

The seven parish registers extant from the colonial period of South Carolina have all been published in some form. Four of these registers were published serially in the *South Carolina Historical and Genealogical Magazine* in the early part of this century. The other registers (St. Philip's, Prince Frederick Winyah, and St. Thomas and St. Denis) have been published in book form. Prince George Winyah parish was established in 1721 from St. James Santee Parish and its bounds were stated to be "to the South-West on Santee River and to the North-East on Cape Fear River, to the Eastward on the Ocean and to the Westward as far as it shall be inhabited by his majesty's subjects." In 1734 the Parish of Prince Frederick Winyah was taken from Prince George. Information from Dalcho's *Historical Account of the Protestant Episcopal Church in South-Carolina* (1820) indicates that the parish was frequently vacant of a clergyman. Some of the earliest entries in the Prince Frederick Winyah register beginning in 1713 probably are properly of Prince George. The extant register of the Parish of St. James Santee (1758-1788) contains vital data on many residents of Prince George Winyah parish. (A book of the St. James Santee Parish is in progress.) It is likely that not register earlier than the one present here was ever kept for Prince George Winyah Parish.

The first known register of Prince George Winyah Parish begins in 1815 and ends in 1916. This original register is presently housed at the South Carolina Historical Society in Charleston, with a microfilm copy available at the South Carolina Department of Archives and History in Columbia. The format of the original register has been followed as closely as possible. Some entries, such as the baptisms from pages 2-53, are spread across two pages, as they are in the original. The burials of elderly persons in the first few decades of this register are for persons who were born in the colonial period.

The second register, included also in this volume, covers baptisms, burials, confirmations, marriages, and lists of communicants 1916-1936. This register remains at Prince George Winyah Church in Georgetown. The memoranda pages following the lists of communicants (beginning on page 115) give us records of events even later. The entries in these registers for slaves, negroes, and free persons of color will be a boon to those interested in African-American history and genealogy. The excellent history of the parish by Sarah Parker Lumpkin, *Heritage Passed On* (1992), complete with illustrations and photographs, makes further accounts unnecessary here.

Since vital records in South Carolina are largely a twentieth century phenomenon, the publication of any record containing records of births, marriages, and deaths prior to that time is important. The Prince George Winyah registers are even more important because of the loss of records in Georgetown District for the ante-bellum period. As we approach the twenty-first century, we are realizing that nineteenth century and early twentieth century records are gaining importance. Reliable oral sources for that period are now almost totally gone. It is an honor to have brought this information to publication, and my appreciation goes to Miss George Townsend, Mrs. Sarah Parker Lumpkin, and Mr. Arthur Doyle for their help and encouragement in this project. My thanks goes also to the Archives committee of Prince George Winyah for their cooperation in this project, especially for providing me copies of the registers from which to work.

Brent Howard Holcomb
June 7, 1996

Art work by John C. Dennis, Spartanburg, South Carolina

	Time	Place of Wedding
names of		
Ceo... 11		Charleston
John W. Shackelford & Elizabeth S. Tail	24	Georgetown
Stephen Ford & Nellie Walter	25	Black River Smith
Thomas Loughton Smith Fraser & Isabella Wakefield May 1		Charleston
John ... Greenborough &		Georgetown

The Number of Marriages }
within the last year } 5

Marriages in 1817	Time	Place of Wedding
Marcus & Rose (free people	April	Georgetown
Dr Henry Denson & Hannah C Waldo	May 14	Do
John Lewis & Sarah Williamson	Decb 25	Do
Joey servant of Mrs Smith & Amey of Wm E Alston	Do 28	Do

Marriages in 1818	Time	Place of Wedding
Joseph Sessions & Martha Mary Wilson	August 1	Georgetown
John Gordon & Jane M Burgis	Novemb 19	Williamsburgh
Joseph W Allston & Sarah Prior	Decb 15	Georgetown
Dr James Doughty & Sarah B Pawley	17	Do
Thomas Fry & Mary Broderick	31	Do

Marriages in 1819	Time	Place of Wedding
Henry A Middleton & Harriet Kinloch	January 20	Kensington, near
James C Coggeshall & Margaret Prior	28	Georgetown
Charles Munnerlyn & Hannah Shackelford	May 13	Do
John White Capt of ... Emely & Jane Hayes	Novr 8	Winyaw Bay
Francis Lance & Elizabeth Ball	Do 18	Charleston
James Maggott & Nancy Mosely (people of Color	Dec 16	George
John Porter & Esther Torrner	Do Do	Do

Marriages in 1820	Time	Place of Wedding
Isaac Caw & Sarah B Wilson	May 18	Georgetown
John Shackelford & Mary Godfrey	Decr 19	Do
George Baxter & Nancy Johnson (people of Color	Dec 21	Do

Marriage page from original register

BAPTISMS

Wednesday March 1815. baptized in St. Michaels church Charleston 2 children of my brother and sister, Daniel & Sarah L. Huger. Names of the children. Daniel & Elizabeth Roper. Sponsors for Daniel were the Father & Miss Charlotte Huger. Sponsors for Elizabeth Roper were the Mother, Miss Elizabeth Motte & John G. Lance.

Sunday April 30. baptized in private at the house of the Father, Emma Boome, daughter of John & Nancy Holmes. Child dangerously ill.

Baptized in private, very ill son of Thomas & ____ Crafts.

Sunday May 21st. preached at St. James Santee (near Peach Tree) and baptized in the church the following negroes fourteen in number belonging to Miss Eliza Bowman: Phoeby, Cinna, David, Peter, Judith, Pino, Willoughby, Miby, June, Priscilla, Adam, Jack, Sarah, Caterina.

Monday 22d May in the same parish baptized in private at the house of Mr. Joseph Logan (there being no clergyman in the parish or near) 3 children. One, son of Mr. Logan, by the name of Joseph Elisha. The second, Ann Dupre, daughter of David & Mary Gaillard. The third. Jane Catherine, daughter of John & Martha Dutart.

Wednesday 31st May. Preached at the church at Statesburg and baptized the son of Honble. Judge James by the name of George Edmund. Sponsors were the Parents.

Friday July 14th. baptized in Charleston in private being very ill, Margaret, a negro child belonging to Mrs. Cochrane.

Friday 22d September, baptized in Charleston _____ daughter of James Gordon, a mulatto man. The child was sick.

BAPTISMS REGISTERED IN THE YEAR 1815 by the Revd Mr Lance:

Names	Parents Names	When born
Thomas William	Thomas & Anna B. Henning	July 24
Eliza Ashby	William & Eliza Shackelford	February 19

BAPTISMS REGISTERED IN THE YEAR 1816 by the Revd Mr Lance:

Henry Allston	Richard & Mariah Shackelford	July 1st 1815
Isaac John	Isaac & Ann Course	
Elizabeth Blythe	John & Eliza Tucker	
Edmund	Dr. Edmund & Susannah Tucker	
Thomas	Captn. Harry & Brooks	
Benjamin	Benjamin & Ann Eliza Lincon (people of color)	
James Rees	George & Sarah Ford	
Benjamin Foissin	Benjamin F. & Hannah Shubrick Trapier	January 29, 1813
James Heyward	Do Do	November 24, 1814
Mary Ouldfield	Robert & Maria Heriot	September 1, 1814
Sibby	Female Servant belonging to Miss Bowman	
Duncan	Duncan & _____ McPhale	
	Female Servant of Mrs. Margaret Ford	
James Withers	Dr. Willis & Leonora Wilkinson	
Samuel Isaac	Thurston	
Isaac Daniel	George & _____ Mitchell (people of color)	
Jimmy	Servant of Mr. John Tucker	

Total number baptized - 16.

BAPTISMS REGISTERED IN THE YEAR 1817 by Revd Maurice H. Lance:

Names	Parents Names	When born
Caroline Matilda	& Eliza Norman	
Sarah Esther	Thomas & Mary Allston Carr	
Francis	Col. Francis Kinloch & Huger	December 12, 1811
Thomas Pinckney	Do Do	May 4, 1815
Harriott Horry	Do Do	March 17, 1817
Windham Theodosia	Benjamin F. & Hannah Trapier	November 15, 1816
Ann Elizabeth	John W & Elizabeth S. Shackelford	February 9, 1817
Mary Julia	Richard & Maria Shackelford	Do 6, 1817
Francis Shackelford	Thomas & Anna B. Henning	April 11, 1817
George Washington	George Washington & Eliza Heriot	Jany 17, 1817

BAPTISMS REGISTERED IN THE YEAR 1818 by Revd M. H. Lance:

Mary Heriot Brown- field	Robert & Maria Heriot	1818
Mary Taylor	Revd Maurice H. & Anna Maria Lance	March 22d 1818 (Easter Sunday)
Perry	Christopher Gadsden & Matilda Hasell	
Anthony Martin	George & Sarah Ford	
John	John W & Elizabeth Cheesborough	

When Baptized	Sponsors	Place of Baptism
24 December	William Shackelford & Miss Hannah Shackelford	Georgetown
Do	Spencer I. Man & Mrs. E. C Toomer	Do
January 1st	William Shackelford & Mrs. Charlotte Allston	Georgetown
" 19	Adult	Do
February 2d	The Father, Mrs. Blythe & Mrs. Charlotte Allston	Do
" "	John Tucker, Thomas Herriet, & Mr. Geo Herriet	Do
" 22	Private baptism being dangerously ill	Charleston
March 11	Private baptism being dangerously ill	Georgetown
" 22	The Parents	Do
April 19	Wm Windham & B. Foisin Trapier & Mrs. M. E. Keith	
" "	James Heyward, John A. Keith & Miss Maria M. Heyward	
May 14	Private baptism, being at the point of death	Do
" 26	Adult	Do
June 7	Mr. _____ & the Mother	Do
" "		Do
" 11	The Parents	Do
November 10	Adult. Witnesses. Mrs. E. Cogdell & W. W. Trapier	Do
December 17	Private baptism, being dangerously ill	Do
" 22	Adult	Do

When Baptized	Sponsors	Place of Baptism
April 20	Norman & Mr John Shackelford	Georgetown
May 4	Thomas & Mary A. Carr & Miss Sarah B Pawley	Do
Do 11	Benjn Huger, Josep Pyatt & Mary Huger	Do
Do --	Cleland & Francis Kinloch Junr & Harriett Kinloch	Do
Do --	Thomas Pinckney, Elizabeth Lowndes, & Elizabeth Alston	Do
Do 15	Mrs. M. M. Drayton, Mrs. M. E. Keith, W. W. Trapier	Do
Do 23	The parents, and Miss Ann Labruce	Do
June 8	The parents & Miss Mary Allston	Do
Do 20	The parents & John W. Shackelford	Do
August 17	James C. Coggeshall, George Tucker & Miss Jane Thurston	North Island
April 30 Asc. day	John Man Taylor, Mary Huger, Eliza A Gadsden and Sarah L. Huger	Geo Town
May 17	Daniel T. Heriot, Sophia C. Heriot	Do
June 5	The Parents	Do
Decemb. 4	The Parents	Do
January 15th	Anthony B. & Miss Hannah Shackelford, the Mother	Georgetown
April 1st	The Parents	Do
" 16th	Witness Mrs. Wragg	Do
June 27th	Benjn Allston, Dr. Isaac M. Campbell, Mary C. Allston	Do
July 3rd	Private baptism	North Inlet
September 5th		Do Do
December 6th	Private baptism	Georgetown

BAPTISMS REGISTERED IN THE YEAR 1819 by Revd M. H. Lance:

Names	Parents Names	When born
Hannah Martha	John W & Elizabeth S. Shackelford	May 17th, 1818
Virginia	Dr. Willis & Leonora Wilkinson	
Sylvia	Servant of Major Saml Wragg	Adult
Lambert	Revd. M. H. &ʰAnna M. Lance	May 28, 1819
Joseph Blythe	Thomas & Mary Carr	
Maria Sophia	Robert & Maria Heriot	
James	Obadiah & _____ Potter	

BAPTISMS REGISTERED IN THE YEAR 1820 by the same:

Phillis	Servant of Mrs. Esther Cogdell	Adult
Celia	Do Do	Do
Ann Allston	John H & Elizabeth A Tucker	
George	Obadiah & _____ Potter	
Jane E	Do	
Ann Eliza	Do	
Caroline Matilda	Do	
Martha Elizabeth	Thomas & Anna B Henning	
Sarah	John W & Elizabeth S. Shackelford	August 17th '19
Grace	Adult Servant of Dr. George Ford	
Henry Futhey	George Washington & Eliza Heriot	April 25th 1818
	Dr James & Bogle	
	Do & Ditto	
	Do & Ditto	
Charles William	John W. & Eliza Cheesborough	
	Adult Servant of Mr. B. Huger	

BAPTISMS REGISTERED IN THE YEAR 1821 by the same:

Sophia Ellen	George Washington & Eliza Heriot	November 1st 1820
Robert James	Robert & Rebecca Collins	
Rebecca	Do	
Sarah	Do	
Mary Huger	John W & Eliza Cheesborough	
Sarah	Revd. M. H. & Anna M. Lance	September 28, 1820
Charles Vanderhorst	Servant of Mrs. E. Cogdell	
Charlotte Anzey	John & Esther Porter	
Sarah Ford	Thomas & Anna B. Henning	
Jacob Bond I'On	Samuel & Mary A. Wragg	
Joseph	John F. & Martha Pyatt	1820
John Francis	Do	1817
Jinny	Adult Servant of Mrs. M. C. Allston	
Lizette	Do Mrs. Cogdell	
Edmund	Thomas & Mary Carr	
John Wright	John W. & Elizabeth Shackelford	
Hannah Mary	Benjamin F. & Hannah Trapier	

BAPTISMS REGISTERED IN 1822 by M. H. Lance - Rector:

Sarah Ann	Brigs	June 5th 1819
Elizabeth Charlotte	Do	August 21, 1821
William Gibson	James Wallace & Agnes Chambers	December 27, 1818
James Wallace	Do	April 1821
Daniel Hucks	Orphan	
Isabella	Richard & Susannah Nites (colored)	
Caroline	Christopher G. & Matilda Hasell	

When Baptized	Sponsors	Place of Baptism
January 1st	Mrs. Cogdell & Mrs. Thurston Witnesses	Georgetown
Do Do	Do & Do Do	Do
January 2d	John H. Tucker, Mrs. Pyatt & Miss A. Weston	Do
Do 20th	The Parents	Do
Do 20th	Do Do	Do
Do 20th	Do Do	Do
Do 20th	Do Do and Miss C. M. Norman	Do
March 5th	Mr & Mrs. A. B. Shackelford & Miss Ann Shackelford	Do
Do Do	Mr & Mrs. A. B. Shackelford & Mrs. Henning	Do
Do 12th		Do
April 16th	The Parents and Miss Sophia Heriot	Do
Do 19th		Do
Do Do		Do
Do Do		Do
June 9th	Mr & Mrs. Benjn Huger (baptised in private because ill)	
Do Do		Do
	Sophia Heriot & Ellinah Spierin	Georgetown
Decr 21st 1820	The Parents	Do
Do	Do	Do
Do	Do	Do
January 1st 1820	Mr. & Mrs. Richard Shackelford & Mrs. Mary Huger	Do
Do	Dr. John Gough Lance, Mary C. Allston, S. M. Hort	Do
Do	Mrs. Croft	Do
February 4th	The parents & Mrs. ____ Fraser	Do
Do XI	The parents & Mrs. Sarah Ford	Do
March XI	The parents, Jacob Bond I'On, Miss Rothmayler	Do
May 6th	Private baptism	Do
May 20th		Do
May 27th	Mrs. Cogdell	Do
June 3d	Do	Do
June 10th	Thomas Carr & Mrs. Charlotte Allston	Do
August 12th		North Island
Do 19th	Paul T. Keith, Miss E. M. Trapier	North Inlet
Jany 9th	The parents & Miss C. Allston	Parish Church
Do Do	Do & Miss Rothmahler	Do
Do 31st	In private for good & sufficient reason	
Do Do	Do	
March 27th	In private, because ill	
June 2d	The parents & ____ Mitchell	Do
September 22d	The parents & Miss C. Perry	North Inlet

5

Names	Parents Names	When born
	1823	
Esther Jane	Revd. M. H. and Anna M. Lance	June 18th 1822
	Robert & Maria Heriot	
	Do	
Eliza Maria	George Washington & Eliza Heriot	November 7, 1822
John Wragg	Richard & Eliza Shackelford	
John	John & Esther Porter	
Mary Margaret	Banister & Margaret Lester	
Thomasine Maria	Thomas & Anna Miller	
Benjamin Huger	John Harleston &	
	John W. & Elizabeth Shackelford	
Willis Wilkinson	Anthony Bonneau & Jane Shackelford	

	1824	
Hagar	Brodut (colored)	
Elizabeth	Mitchell (wife of George)	
Sarah	Richard & Susannah Nites (people of color)	
Legrand		
Theodore Samuel	Theodore & Elizabeth F. Gourdin	Novbr 28th
Sarah Elizabeth Withers	Isaac & Sarah B. Carr	Decr 8th 1823
John Magill	Thomas & Mary Carr	April 9th 1824
William Henry	Banister & Margaret Lester	

	1825	
Mary Allston	& Allison	
John Wragg	Dr. S. S. & Esther C. Gasque	Decr. 20th 1824
Betsy	Richard & Susannah Nites (people of color)	
Rachel Moor	Henry & Flagg	
Eliza Chesborough	John & Esther Porter	
Hasford	Legrand G. & Mary Walker	March 15, 1825

Baptisms in 1826 Registered by M. H. Lance, Rector, and P. T. Keith, Assistant Minister:

Names	Officiating Clergyman	Parents Names	When born
Thomas William	M. H. Lance	Thomas & A. B. Henning	
Mary Magdaline	M. H. L.		
John William	M. H. L.	John & Sarah Tarbox	April 26th
Elizabeth	P. T. Keith	Jacob & Elizabeth Wayne	
Allen Fort	P. T. K.	Daniel & Rebecca Scott	
Lydia Ann Tyler	P. T. Keith	John & Lydia Craft	July 2nd 1822
John Thomas Davis	P. T. Keith	Do	July 17th 1824
Caroline Thurston	P. T. Keith	Stephen & June Ford	January 18th 1825
Richard Walter	P. T. K.	Stephen & Helen Ford	October 24th 1820

	1827		
William Walter	P. T. Keith	LeGrand G. & Mary E. Walker	Dec 8 1826
Hannah Esther	P. T. Keith	John & Esther Porter	January 18th 1826
Margaret Ann	P. T. Keith	Mrs. & Wm. Cambridge	March 25th 1827
Susan	M. H. Lance	Richard & Susannah Nites	
Wm. Allston	P. T. Keith	Theodore & Elizabeth F. Gourdin	April 4, 1827
Sarah Elizabeth	P. T. Keith	Stephen C. & Hannah B. Ford	Decr. 4th 1826

1823

When Baptized	Sponsors	Place of Baptism
March 5th	Rev. Thos. H. Taylor, Mrs. Pyatt & Miss Julia Huger	Parish Ch.
Do 9th		Do
Do Do		Do
Do Do		Do
April 3d	In private, for sufficient reason	
May 7th	John Porter, I. W. Cheesborough & Mrs. E. Cheesborough	Do
May 18th	Mr. McClenan & the Mother	Do
Novr 16th	His Excellency Gov. Wilson & Lady Nesbit (per alias)	Do
Do 7th		Do
Decr 28th		Do
Do Do		Do

1824

April 4th	Legrand G. & Mary Walker	
Do 15th	Theod. Gourdin, Wm. C. Doughty, Louisa M. Gourdin	
May 16th	The parents	
Decr. 12th	The parents	
Decr. 19th	The parents	

1825

January 29th	At the house of Benjn Allston Esq.	
February 6th	Sally Cohen	Parish Church
April 10th	Mrs. E. B. Rothmahler, Dr. Wragg, Miss W. W. Rothmahler & Miss C. A. Allston	Do
May 1st	Mother, and George Mitchell	Do
Do Do	Henry Flagg, Mrs. Henning & Miss Labruce	Do
Do 8th	The parents & Mr. D. McDowall	Do
November. 6th		Do
1st January 1826		Church
19th March	L. G. Walker	Do
3d May	Child ill, of Methodist parents	House of the parents
6th May	Do	House of the parents
13th May	Do	Private house
17th May	The mother	Church
Do Do	Do	Do
21st May	George Ford, the mother and the Aunt Mrs. Heriot	Do
1st October	R. O. Anderson, J. W. Shackelford, & Mrs. C. K. Anderson	North Island

1827

11th February	Peter W. & Marg.[?] A. Fraser & L. G. Walker	Church
15th April	George Ford, Mrs. Anna B. Henning, Mrs. Wm. Cheesborough	Do
17th April	Child ill	House of parents
4th April	The parents	Church
20th May	R. Ann Gourdin, Samuel Gourdin & Henry Gourdin	Do
23rd Septr	Dr. Wm. R. T. Prior, Miss Martha Vaux & Miss Charlotte Toomer	North Island

Names	Officiating Clergyman	Parents Names	When born

P. T. KEITH RECTOR 1828

Names	Officiating Clergyman	Parents Names	When born
Erasmus Rothmahler	P. T. K.	Shadrach S. & Esther C. Gasque	Dec. 8, 1827
Robert John	P. T. K.	B. & Mrs. Lester	July 3rd 1827
Arnold (colored)	P. T. K.	Elsey (servant of Dr. Wragg)	31st Jany 1818
Walter (colored)	P. T. K.	Do	23rd April 1822
Mary Rebecca	P. T. K.	J. L. E. Easterling & June E.	27th Decr 1827
Mary Helen	P. T. K.	Stephen & Helen Ford	24th Decr 1818
Joseph Wragg	P. T. K.	Stephen & Jane Ford	13th Sept 1827
Edgar Laroche	P. T. K.	Robert & Maria Heriot	25th Nov 1825
Anthony Toomer	P. T. K.	John & Esther Porter	31st Jany 1828

1829

Names	Officiating Clergyman	Parents Names	When born
Archibald James	P. T. K.	Thos L. & Nannette Shaw	Oct 20, 1828
Jane Caroline		John G. & Jane G. North	July 16, 1828
Obadiah Gallevant		Obadiah & Potter	February 7, 1829
Ann LaBruce		Dr. & Mrs. Wm. Prior	January 31, 1829
Mary Catharine LeGrand		LeGrand G. & Mary Walker	December 30, 1828
William Henry		Stephen Charles & Hannah G. Ford	Sept. 19, 1828
Thomas Davis (colored)			
Thomas		John & Hall	
Thisbe (cold)		Richd. & Susannah Nites (cold)	
Magdalen Elizabeth Trapier		John A. & Sarah Keith	July 13, 1829

Baptisms in 1830 Registered by P. Trapier Keith, Rector:

Names	Parents Names	When born
Scipio (colored adult)		
Beetie (Do)		
George Gaillard	George Thos. & Mary Warham Ford	
Mary Ann Margaret	John & M. Hall	March 10, 1819
James Mallan	Do	June 10, 1821
Jane Elizabeth	Do	Sept. 10, 1823
John Kitching	Do	Sept. 25, 1825
Maria Louisa	Thomas & M. Hall	June 29, 1825
Ann Eisenhart	Do	Feb. 9, 1829
Margaret (col. child)		
Banister Smith	Banister & Margaret Lester	Feb. 20, 1830
Joseph Llewellyn	Joseph L. E. & Jane Easterling	March 20, 1830
LeGrand George Walker	Thos. L. & Nannette Shaw	
Susan Magdalen	John M. & Atkinson	Sept. 19, 1829
Esther Ann Caroline	_____ Vernon	
Stephanus	Stephen Charles & Hannah Ford	May 11, 1830

When Baptized	Sponsors	Place of Baptism
10th Feb	Mr. Sam Wragg & the father, Mrs. Ann E. Mitchell & Miss E. Taylor	Church
Do Do	The parents	Do
17th March	Dr. John Wragg	Private house
Do Do	Mr. Peter Cooper	Do
13th April	Mrs. Walker, J. R. Easterling, & wife	Church
27th April	Mr. & Mrs. W. Reese & Mrs. Jane Ford	Do
Do Do	Dr. Wragg, Mrs. W. Reese & the mother	Do
25th May	The father & Robt Heriot Junr. & Miss Sarah Caroline Heriot	Do
16th Novr	Mr. & Mrs. L. G. Walker, Mr. Dozier, Miss C. Toomer & Mrs. Cheesborough	Do
Jan. 18th	LeGrand G. Walker, Wm. Chapman & Miss Magdalen Walker	Church
Jan. 21st	Father and mother & Miss Eliza Emily North	Do
March 29th	James Potter and Miss Susan Gallevant	Do
April 17th	The father, Miss Ann La Bruce & Miss E. M. A. Vaux	Do
April 19th	Mrs. Catharine LaBruce, Miss M. A. LaBruce, Miss M. Walker & Thos. C. Callender	Do
May 24th	A. Dozier, the mother, and Mrs. Esther Porter	Do
July 19th		Do
Sept. 11th	child ill	North Island
Dec. 13th		privt house
Dec. 16th	Miss Anna E. Brown & Maria H. Trapier, W. W. Trapier & E. B. Brown	Church
Feb. 14.	-- Thomas, Sally & Philis (colored)	Church
Do Do	Do	Do
Feb. 28		Do
April 7	Mrs. Cogdell & mother	Do
Do Do	Do	Do
Do Do	Miss E. A. Taylor & Mr. Patterson	Do
Do Do	Mrs. Briggs & Mr. Forsyth	private house
Do Do	The father & Miss Eisenhart	Do
Do Do	Father & Mother	Do
Do Do	Do	Do
April 11	Bettie, Sary & Scipio (col.)	Church
May 23	Dr. Greaves, Elizabeth Gallevant & the mother	Do
May 30	Parents	Do
July 11		Do
Oct. 3	The Parents & Mrs. Steedman	North Island
Nov. 2	Child ill	Parents' house
Dec. 12	Miss E. Vaux & George Thomas Ford	Church

9

Names	Parents Names	When born
	1831	
Sary (cold adult)		
Eliza (cold Child)	Sary	
Phillips (Do)	Do	
Susan (Do)	Do	
Sarah Elizabeth	William R. T. & Martha Prior	Aug. 20, 1830
Henry Berton	R. A. & _____ Sands	Sept. 27, 1830
Frederick (cold adult)		
Cupid (cold adult)		
John (cold adult)		
Anne (cold adult)		
Emma Lovina	Thos & Margaret Hall	Jan 15, 1831
Edwin Henry	John W. & Elizabeth Shackelford	Aug. 3, 1829
Samuel Wragg	Dr. S. S. & Mrs. Esther C. Gasque	Dec. 13, 1830
Moll (cold adult)		
Jack (cold adult)		
Catharine Perry	William & _____ Chapman	
William Henry	Do	
George Ryerson Hendrickson	Dr. S. P. Dunbar & Mrs. D.	
Henry Bicker	Do	
William Fort	Do	
Robert Heriot	Thos Boston and Caroline Clarkson	

Phebe (cold adult) baptized 4th Decr 1831 in Church. Witnesses Scipio, Thomas, Beetie, Sally (all colored)

Baptisms in 1832 Registered by P. Trapier Keith, Rector:

Betsey (colored adult)		
Mary Charlotte	John G. & Jane North	Feb. 21, 1832
Nanette (colored)	Jack & Moll (colored)	

Emma (colored)	Do	
Mary Huger	Thos. L. & Nannette Shaw	Feb. 22, 1832
Archibald William	Peter & _____ Walker	Sept. 16, 1831
Juliet (col. adult)		

1833

Benjamin	Robert F. W. & Adelle Allston	Feb. 25, 1833
Susan Catherine		
Gergereau[?]	John Alexander & Sarah Keith	Jan. 14, 1833
Esther Charlotte	Dr. Shadrach S. & Esther C. Gasque	Dec. 27, 1832
Virginia Caroline	Edward & Mary Thomas	Feb. 1, 1833
Frank (cold.)	Jack & Moll (cold.)	Jan. 31
	Stephen C. & Hannah Ford	
	(adult) Hawkins Mrs.	

When Baptized	Sponsors	Place of Baptism
Jan 26	Patty & Phyllis & Annie	Church
Do Do	Do	Do
Do Do	Do	Do
Do Do	Do	Do
Feb 20	Miss E. Vaux, Mrs. Mary Walker, & Captn. P. E. Vaux	Do
March 13	The Father & Dr. Berton & Mrs. Mary Walker	Do
Do Do	Scipio & Thomas (col) witnesses	Do
Do Do	Do	Do
Do Do	Do	Do
April 6	Phillis & Sary (col) witnesses	Do
April 17	Miss Eisenhart & the father	Private house
April 20	Revd. Mr. Lance & Miss E. Vaux	Church
May 15	Major Samuel Wragg, E. B. Rothmahler, & Mrs. M. A. Wragg	Do
May 22	Scipio & Thomas (cold) witnesses	Do
May 29	Thomas (cold) witness	Do
Do Do	The Parents	Do
Do Do	Do	Do
June 1	Parents	Private house
Do	Do	Do
Do	Do	Do
	Parents & Mr. and Mrs. Robert Heriot	North Island

1832

March 25	Witnesses: Salley, Thomas Scipio (col)	Church
May 2	Mr. & Mrs. Benjn Allston, Miss Robertson, Miss Mary Pettigru	Private house (chd. unwell)
May 20	Moll, Scipio, Frederick, Thomas (all cold.)	Church
Do Do	Do	Do
May 27	The Parents	Do
	The Parents and Miss	Do
Dec 9	Thomas (cold)	Private house (very ill)

1833

April 14	Joseph W. & R. F. W. Allston & Mrs. Mary Pyatt Jones	Church
May 5	Mrs. Susan C. Brown, Mrs. Esther C. Gasque, & Mr. Benjn. F. Trapier	Do
Do Do	Mrs. Charlotte Mitchell, Mrs. Mary I. Simons, & Mr. Harris Simons	Do
May 26	Miss Elizabeth Vaux, Miss Eugenia Thomas & Revd. P. T. Keith	
June 2	Thomas, Charles & Mother (cold.)	Do
		North Island
	Mrs. Gallivant, Mrs. Percy (witnesses)	Church

1834

Names	Parents Names	When born
Louise Gibert	John G. & Jane North	11 Nov '33
Albert (cold.)	Louisa a free woman of color	11 or 13 yrs of age
Maria Reese	Stephen & Jane Ford	

1835

William Benjamin	Asa & _____ Palmer	6 yrs of age
Robert	Robert F. W. & Adelle Allston	31 Dec 1834
William Alston	James G. & Mary Ann Henning	11 Feb 1835
Harris Simons	S. S. & Esther Gasque	26 Aug 1834
Eugene Albert	Edward & Mary Thomas	7 Nov 1834
Harry (col)	Jack & Moll, servants of Mrs. Keith	24 Feb 1835
George Robert (col)	Duffee & Phebe (col)	
Henry (col)	_____ & Rose	

1836

George Warren (col)	Inglis (col)	April 1, 1835
Francesca Louisa	Anthony L. Mariano	March 28, 1826
Elizabeth	Anthony L. & Maria N. Mariano	March 20, 1831
Maria Ellen	Do	Dec. 20, 1832
Martha Georgiana	Stephen C. & Hannah Ford	Nov. 10, 1831
John Cheesborough	George T. & Mary W. Ford	March 7, 1835
Henry Benjamin (col)	Harriet (col., servant of Mrs. I. Carr)	Jan 1836
James	James G. & Mary Ann Henning	Dec. 21, 1836

1837

William Henry	Captn. & Mrs. Jones
Tober (col)	Cuffee & Phebe (col) servants of Mrs. Keith

1838

Samuel Withers	Dr. Saml. P. & Mrs. Dunbar	Oct. 19, 1835
Emerina	Samuel & ---- Marsh	
Martha Helen	Stephen C. & Hannah B. Ford	19 July 1837
Charlotte Frances	Robt. F. W. & Adelle Allston	23 Nov 1837
Sarah Ford	Mr. ----- & Jane Cowling	26 Aug 1837
Scipio (col)	Scipio & Binkey (col). servants of Mrs. Keith	

1839

Willis Wilkinson	Paul Trapier & Anna B. Keith	4 Apr 1839
Ellen (col)	Jack & Moll (servants of Mrs. Keith)	
Robert (col)	Scipio & Binky (Do)	

1834

When Baptized	Sponsors	Place of Baptism
January 1	Mrs. Louise Porcher, Miss Harriet Petigru &	Private house
	Mr. Phil. J. Porcher	child feeble
March 30th	Peter Tryall, Henry & ____ (col)	Church
		private house child ill

1835

March 28		private house child ill
Do 29	John G. North, P. Trapier Keith & Mrs. Jane North	Church
April 3	Col. Arthur Hayne, W. B. Pringle, & Mrs. Mary Alston	Do
April 16	John A. Keith, John G. North, Mrs. Jane North	Do
April 29	John G. North, S. S. Gasque, & Mrs. Jane North	Do
May 10	Peter Tryall & the parents (all col)	Do
May 17	Peter Tryall, Scipio, & Amy (all col)	Do
May 31	Charles Thomas (col. all)	Do
Do Do	Elias & Lucy Smith (all col.)	Do

1836

April 20		private house child ill
May 22	The Father & Stepmother	Church
Do Do	The Parents	Do
Do Do	Do	Do
May 29	Mrs. Ann Henning, Mrs. Isaac Carr, & James G. Henning	Do
Do Do	Stephen C. Ford, the Father, Mrs. H. Ford & Mrs. A. Hening	
Do Do	Peter Tryall & Maria (col)	Do
Dec. 31		Child at the point of death

1837

Jan 1st	The Parents	Church
May 28		Do

1838

Jan 10	The mother &	Church
Do. 19		Private (child ill)
Do. 28	Miss Martha E. Henning, Miss Mary	Church
	Helen Ford & J. Reese Ford	
April 11	Mr. & Mrs. T. Henry Lecesne & Mrs. Thos Petigru	Do
Do. 22	The mother, Mrs. Mary Helen Coachman &	Do
	R. O. Anderson	
Do Do	The Father, Newman, and (all col)	Do

1839

May 12	Rev. Paul Trapier, C. G. Memminger &	St. Stephen's
	Mrs. Mary Memminger	Chapel, Charleston
May 19	Thomas & Margarett (col.)	Church
Nov. 10	June & Scipio (col.)	Do

1840

Names	Parents Names	When born
Benjamin Daniel	William H. & Tucker	13 years of age
Sarah Heriot	Charles & Matilda Smith	21 Dec 1839
Martha Selina	John Potts & Elizabeth Ford	
Anna Alice	Do	
Anna Charlotte	John Alexander & Sarah Keith	25 July 1840
(Tennent)		

1841 Robert Theus Howard, Rector

Eliza Ann (col)	_____ & Catharine Pich	3 Sept 1836
Emma Elizabeth (col)	Do	Dec 17, 1838
Junius Wilson	Stephen C. & Hannah B. Ford	
Sarah	_____ McCollough	
Lucy (col)	Slave of Mrs. Gen. Carr	
Anna Glenn	John W. & Mary Coachman	May 13, 1839
Harriet (col)	Slave of Mrs. Carr	
Simon (col)	Slave of Mrs. Carr	
Mary Thomasine	George T. & Mary W. Ford	7 March 1839
Thomas	Do	
Emily Ann	James G. & Emma A. Henning	Jan 26, 1841
Ann Cox	_____ Glenmore	
Sarah (col)	Slave of Miss E. A. Taylor	
Charles (col)	Do	
Ramell Lanceford	D. L. & Anna McKay	Dec. 12, 1838
Binkey (col)	Slave of Mrs. Keith	
Charles (col)	Slave of B. F. Trapier	

1842

Walter Roland	John W. & Mary Coachman	
William Wallace	William W. Harlee & Martha Harlee	July 26, 1841
Ann Eliza	Jonah & Susan Atkinson	April 12, 1838
Louise Catherine	"	Jan. 11, 1840
Charles Steedman	"	March 16, 1841
Robert Thurston Ford	Stephen & Jane Ford	Jan. 25, 1830
Esther Brown Ford	"	Nov. 7, 1835
Margaret F. Ford	"	Dec. 5, 1836
Eliza Jane Ford	"	April 24, 1839
Emily T. Ford	"	Feb. 24, 1842
John Rosa (col)	_____ & Amy Allston (free)	Dec. 29, 1831
Lucy (col)	Slave of Mrs. Keith	Oct. 27, 1841
Martha Emma	James G. & Emma A. Henning	
William James	William & Elizabeth Sparkman	Aug. 6, 1842

1843

Ella Maria	Capt. & Mrs. Christian	Oct. 5, 1831
John Furman	_____ & Mrs. McWilliams	Dec. 31, 1832
Georgianna Catherine	"	Sept. 19, 1835
Goverman Kortright	Revd. Robert Theus & Hester M. Howard	Dec. 4, 1842
Louise Gibert	R. F. W. & Adelle Allston	June 14, 1842
Laura Desaid (col)	Anne Allston	
Frances Maria	Minerva & Samuel Wilmot	Sept. 14, 1842
Francis Green	John W. & Mary Coachmen	
Donella Coachman	Donald L. & Anna McKay	Dec. 13, 1842

1840

When Baptized	Sponsors	Place of Baptism
April 5th	The Father	Church
May 23rd	Miss M. R. Smith, Miss Martha Tucker & Dr. B. B. Smith	Do
June 7th		Do
Do Do		Do
Nov 29th	Mrs. M. E. Keith, Miss S. C. Brown & Rev. P. Trapier Keith	Do

1841

Feb 17, 1841	Peter Tryall, Catharine Pich & Elizabeth Withers	
" "	"	
March 28	Dr. James Sparkman & Mrs. Nevil Ball	
April 6th	R. S. Howard, Mrs. Howard & Miss Lester (witnesses)	
April 7th	Peter Tryall, Ann Allston & Ann Taylor (witnesses)	
April 11, 1841	Frederick W. Ford, Maria Julia Maxwell & Martha Ford	
April 14, 1841	Ann Allston & Catharine Piatt (witnesses)	
"	"	
April 18, 1841	Mrs. Stephen C. Ford, Miss E. A. Taylor & the Father	
"	Mrs. E. Porter, John Porter & the Father	
May 16, 1841	James G. Henning, M. C. Thomas & M. E. Ford	
"	Mrs. Benjamin Allston	
"		
"		
June 2, 1841	Angus N. McKay, Mrs. Harriet M. Allston & Miss A. Gadsden	
" 6, 1841	Tom Allston & Scipio Keith. Witnesses	
" 6, 1841	Tom Allston & Frederick Keith. Witnesses	

1842

Feb. 13, 1842	Dr. James Sparkman & Mr & Mrs. W. Sparkman
March 3, 1842	W. W. Harlee, Rees Ford & Mrs. R. Ford
April 10, 1842	Parents & Mrs. M. A. Atkinson
April 10, 1842	Parents & Miss Ellen Steedman
April 10, 1842	Parents & Miss Mary Louisa Huggins
April 24, 1842	Frederick Ford & Mrs. Jane C. Ford
"	Mrs. Jane C. Ford & Mrs. Esther Ball
"	James Rees Ford & Martha Ford
"	Henry F. Heriot, Elizabeth M. A. Ford, Caroline F. Ford
"	Emily Ford & Mrs. Jane C. Ford
May 22, 1842	Scipio Keith, Amy Taylor & Amy Allston
"	Scipio, Binkey & Amelia
Dec. 12, 1842	Miss Eugenia Thomas, Miss Sarah F. Henning & Father
Dec. 26, 1842	John E. Allston, Walpole Cogdell, Jane Louisa Davis & Mrs. Elizabeth Sparkman

1843

Jan. 4, 1843	Mrs. Christian & Mrs. McWilliams
"	"
"	"
"	"
Feb. 8, 1843	E. B. Rothmahler & Parents
March 1, 1843	Mrs. Pettigru, Mrs. Francis Weston & R. F. W. Allston
March 9, 1843	Witness Anne Allston
May 24, 1843	The Parents
May 28, 1843	Messrs Elijah Coachman, Francis Green & Mrs. S. Ford
May 31, 1843	Mrs. Mary C. Allston, Mrs. Kay & Benn A. Coachman

Names	Parents Names	When born
	1844	
Julia Rose	Dr. Francis S. & Mary Parker	Nov. 29, 1843
Pamela Middleton	William & Elizabeth Sparkman	
Maria Caroline	John P. & Elizabeth Ford	July 8, 1843
June (col)	Scipio & Binkey (slaves of Mrs. Keith)	Aug. 16, 1843
William Rees	James Rees & Martha Elizabeth Ford	Feb. 17, 1844
Edmund Kortright	Robert Theus & Hester Mary Howard	March 27, 1844
Moses (col adult)	Property of Mrs. Lester	
	1845	
Susan Catharine	Dr. E. B. & Elisa Brown	Oct. 6, 1844
Harry (col)	Property of Miss Ann Brown	
Angelina S. Swinton (col)	Gerry & Isabella Pawley	Dec. 11, 1844
James Green	James G. & Emma A. Henning	Feb. 24, 1845
Charles Bannister	J. J. Dickison & Mary Margaret Dickison	Apr. 23, 1845
Anna Henning	James Rees & Martha Elizabeth Ford	July 1, 1845
	1846	
Stephen Ford	John W. & Mary Helen Coachman	Sept. 19, 1845
Frances Blythe	D. L. McKay & Mary Jane McKay	Sept. 4, 1845
Benjamin	Benjamin & Caroline Coachman	Dec. 6, 1845
Thomas Townsend	Samuel & Minerva Wilmot	March 20, 1845
Annie Elizabeth	William & Elizabeth Sparkman	Oct. 12, 1845
Wm Warham Withers	Dr. Alexis & Mrs. Elizabeth Forster	
Ann Manigault)		
Arthur)	Henry A. & Harriet Middleton	
Francis Kinloch)		
Alicia)		
Mary Ann (col)	Scipio & Binkey, belonging to Mrs. Keith	June 5, 1845
Martha Ann (col)	belonging to Miss Brown	"
Harvey Leonidas	Dr. & Mrs. Byrd	
John	George & Mary Ford	Jan. 8, 1846
Catharine Ann	John & Elizabeth Ford	Feb. 2, 1846

When Baptized	Sponsors	Place of Baptism
	1844	

When Baptized	Sponsors	Place of Baptism
Feb. 2, 1844	Mrs. James Rose, Miss Sarah Parker & Dr. Parker	Mansfield B. River
Apr. 7, 1844	Miss Pamela Burgess, Miss Ann Campbell & S. M. Grimke	Geo Town
Apr. 7, 1844	Mrs. B. A. Coachman, Miss P. Burgess & B. A. Coachman	Geo Town
Apr. 21, 1844	Scipio, Febus & Silvy	Geo Town
May 5, 1844	James G. Henning, J. R. Ford & Mrs. S. C. Ford	Geo Town
May 8, 1844	The Parents	Geo Town
June 9, 1844	Witnesses Tom, Betsy Mitchell & J. Tunno	Geo Town

1845

When Baptized	Sponsors	Place of Baptism
Jan. 9, 1845	Mrs. E. A. Porter, Miss C. Toomer & T. Porter	Church G. T.
March 23	Witnesses Tom, Scipio & Jane Brown	Church G. T.
Apr. 13, 1845	Betsy Mitchell, Elizabeth & Richard Knight	Church G Town
May 4, 1845	The Parents & Mr. Edward Thomas	Church G Town
June 1, 1845	The Father & Dr. H. L. & Mrs. Adelaide Bird	Church G. Town
Nov. 26, 1845	The Father & Misses Sarah J. Shackelford & S. F. Henning	Church G. Town

1846

When Baptized	Sponsors	Place of Baptism
Jan. 7, 1846	D. L. McKay, B. A. Coachman & Maria R. Ford	Privately
"	Mrs. May H. Coachman, Miss Regina Coachman & D. L. McKay	Privately
"	John E. Allston, Benjamin Wilson & the Mother	Privately
Feb. 18, 1846	Baptised privately in the night shortly before his death	
March 16, 1846	Mother, Mrs. Davis, Dr. Sparkman & J. R. Ford	Black River
Apr. 8, 1846	Col. A. Belin, Dr. S. Hunt & Mrs. J. W. Wilkinson	Geo Town
Apr. 16, 1846)		Geo Town
")	The Parents Sponsors for the four	
")		
")		
May 10, 1846	Anna Allston, Anna Taylor & Frederick Mitchell	Geo Town
"	Jane & Harry	"
May 31, 1846	The Parents	Geo Town
Oct. 4, 1846	Father, Toomer Porter & Mrs. John Ford	Plantersville
"	Dr. Robert Vaux & wife & Mrs. John Ford	"

1847

Names	Parents Names	When born
John Jackson	Dickison	
Alice	Robert T. & Hester May Howard	Dec. 11, 1846
Edward Thomas	James G. & Emma A. Henning	Jan. 29, 1847
Adeline Blanch	James C. & Elisa Commander	Aug. 25, 1845
Eugene Ringgold	"	Apr. 23, 1847
Olivia Caroline	Benj. A. & Caroline Coachman	
Toomer Porter	Dr. E. B. & Elisa Brown	Apr. 8, 1847

1848

Abby Caroline	Richard & Abby Lathers	March 8, 1848
Olivia)		
Rose)	belonging to Anna Allston (cold)	
Moses	Scipio & Binkey (col) belonging to Mrs. Keith	
John Coachman	Dr. L. & Mary Jane McKay	March 13, 1848
Martha Clara	James Rees & Martha E. Ford	1847
Mary Hannah	Dr. Joseph M. & Ann Elisa Simmons	Sept. 23, 1846
Hasford	Hasford & Mary E. Walker	July 24, 1848

1849

Ben Allston	William H. & Charlotte Trapier	Sept. 9, 1848
James Rose	Dr. Francis S. & Mary Parker	Oct. 25, 1848
Joseph Charles	Dr. E. B. & Elisa Brown	Dec. 15, 1848
Samuel Williams	Robert & Sarah Fraser	Dec. 4, 1847
George Thomas)	Stephen & Jane Ford	Sept. 4, 1843
Stephen)		
Arthur Orlando	Jonah & Susan Atkinson	May 1847

1850

Leila	Dr. L. H. & Adelaide Byrd	Oct. 7, 1849
Mary Coachman	Col. D. L. & Mary Jane McKay	Oct. 25, 1849
Sarah Jane	Benjamin A. & Caroline Coachman	June 24, 1849
Florence Henning	Gen. W. W. & Martha Harlee	July 2, 1848
Annie	Dr. John F. & Hannah Lesesne	Jan. 5, 1849
Legrand Guerry	Hasford & Mary C. Walker	Apr. 28, 1850
Horace Sherwood	Samuel & Minerva Wilmot	Nov. 23, 1849
Robert Lovett	Robert & Sarah Fraser	Oct. 20, 1849
Hess Seaman	Robert T. & Hester Mary Howard	July 30, 1850

1847

When Baptized	Sponsors	Place of Baptism
March 28, 1847	Mrs. Lester, J. G. Henning & E. B. Rothmahler (wit)	Church
Apr. 18, 1847	Mrs. Fogartie, Miss Ann Fogartie & the Father	GeoTown Church
May 30, 1847	The Father, Edward Thomas & Miss Eugenia Thomas	Church
June 3, 1847	Mr. & Mrs. Henning, Mrs. Porter & Mrs. Eliza Commander	Church
June 3, 1847	Gen. Commander, Mr. J. J. Dickison & Mrs. R. Fraser	Church
Dec. 21, 1847	The Parents & Miss Sarah Ford	Church
Dec. 26, 1847	Col. D. L. McKay, Frederick Ford & Miss A. Brown	Church

1848

Apr. 20, 1848	The Parents	Church
May 7, 1848	Anna Allston & Mother	Church
"	"	"
"	Parents	"
May 21, 1848	John E. & Peter Bacot Allston & Miss S. Jane Coachman	Residence
June 4, 1848	Mrs. James G. Henning, Miss A. Gadsden & W. W. Shackelford	Black River
June 5, 1848	Mrs. Evans, Mrs. Jones & the Father	Privately
Nov. 12, 1848	Mr. & Mrs. John Labruce & W. W. Walker	Privately

1849

Jan. 1, 1849	Mrs. Elizabeth Trapier, Paul H. Trapier, Jr., F. Pyatt	Church
Jan. 9, 1849	The Parents & Mr. James Rose	Black River
May 1, 1849	Mrs. D. Lesesne, Messrs. John H. Tucker & G. Ford Junr.	Church
May 27, 1849	The Parents	Church
June 7, 1849	Miss Maria Ford, Frederic W. & Jos. W. Ford	Black River
Aug. 28, 1849	The Mother, Miss Magdalen & Samuel T. Atkinson	Priv

1850

Feb. 10, 1850	The Parents & Mrs. Richard Dozier	Church
Feb. 17, 1850	Mrs. Wm. Sparkman, Miss M. A. Nicholson & W. W. Shackelford	Private
Jan. 13, 1850	Miss A. I. Gadsden, Mrs. R. M. Allston & Father	Church
Feb. 27, 1850	J. G. Henning & wife & Miss S. Henning	Church
May 1, 1850	The Parents	Sampit
May 26, 1850	Mrs. Mortimer, B. H. Wilson, Joshua Ward	Church
May 26, 1850	The Parents	Church
June 2, 1850	The Parents	Church
Dec. 15, 1850	Mr. & Mrs. B. H. Wilson & Miss S. Henning	Privately

1851

Names	Parents Names	When born
Elizabeth Jane Dozier, wife of Richard Dozier		July 16, 1826
Esther Ann	Dr. E. B. & Elisa Brown	Apr. 7, 1851
Charles Julian	Dr. George & Matilda Heriot	June 3, 1845
Thomas	C. Logan	
James Logan	G. N. & C. Merriman	Nov. 3, 1849

BAPTISMS REGISTERED BY ROBERT T. HOWARD 1852

William J. Howard	(Adult)	
Ella (colored)	Slave of Mrs. Sue Carr	
Hess Howard	W. R. F. & Martha Prior	Jan. 11, 1852
Rachel)	Slaves of Mrs. Sue Carr	
Frances)		
Helen Frederine	Benjn. A. & Caroline Coachman	March 18, 1852
James	James Rees & Martha Elizabeth Ford	Aug. 1, 1852
Lydia (col)	Slave of James G. Henning, Esquire	

1853

Richard Oliver Bush	(Adult)	Sept. 9, 1815
Caroline Amelia "	"	Apr. 27, 1816
Richard Oliver	Richard O. & Caroline Amelia Bush	Oct. 31, 1844
Charles Henry	"	Dec. 26, 1846
Caroline Elizabeth	"	Feb. 9, 1850
Jane McGowan	Donald McGowan & Jane Stuart	Jan. 1, 1852
James Madison	James Wm. & Elisa Commander	Jan. 8, 1850
Benjamin Oscar	"	March 7, 1852
Emeline (col)	Scipio & Binkey, slaves of Mr. Keith's	
John Henry Allston (col)	Lavinia, Slave of Mrs. Gen. Carr	
William Prior	Richard Green & Sarah E. White	May 20, 1853
Henry Seaman	Robt. T. & Hess May Howard	May 14, 1853
Alice (col)	Louisa, property of Mrs. S. Carr	

1854

John Shackelford	James G. & Emma A. Henning	Nov. 3, 1853
Stephen Charles	James Rees & Martha E. Ford	Sept. 19, 1853
John Toomer	A. T. & S. Magdalen Porter	Jan. 8, 1854
Benjamin Foissin	B. F. & Julia Trapier	Nov. 8, 1853
Sarah Ann Willis	Wm. I. & Elisa Ann Munro	Aug. 18, 1840
Elisa Rebecca	"	Aug. 7, 1847
Franklin Pierce	Richard O. & Caroline Amelia Bush	March 1853

1851

When Baptized	Sponsors	Place of Baptism
March 19, 1851	Witnesses. Mrs. B. H. Wilson & Susan Atkinson	Church
June 1, 1851	John A. Keith, Mrs. George Ford & Mr. Keith	Church
June 4, 1851	Mr. John H. Tucker, Mrs. Ben Tucker	Church
Sept. 1, 1851	G. N. Merriman & wife	Privately
"	"	"

1852

Jan. 30, 1852	His wife & Mrs. King	Private
March 17, 1852	Witnesses: Jane Tunno & Hay Sciven	Church
Apr. 25, 1852	Robt. T. Howard & wife & Mrs. S. E. White	Church
May 23, 1852	Anna Allston, Jane Brown & Dick	Church
June 6, 1852	S. T. Atkinson, Mrs. M. H. Coachman & Mrs. A. R. Mitchell	Church
Dec. 26, 1852	Miss Sarah Ford, Mr. Francis S. Holmes & Jos. Ford	Church
Feb. 27, 1853	Witnesses: Jane Tunno, Anna Allston & Hay (or Hary)	Church

1853

March 1, 1853		Private
"		" (very ill)
"	The Parents	"
"	"	"
"	"	"
" 9, 1853	The Parents	Private
" 17, 1853	The Father, A. T. Porter & Mrs. Brown	Church
"	"	"
May 15, 1853	Adam, Judy & Binkey	"
" 22, 1853	Adam & Lucy with the Mother	"
Dec. 11, 1853	Dr. & Mrs. Prior & B. H. Wilson	Church
"	Henry I. Seaman & Wife & Jos Lee Howard	"
" 21, 1853	Mary King, the Mother & Thos Jefferson	Privately

1854

Jan. 15, 1854	J. G. Henning, W. W. Shackelford & Virginia E. Thomas	Church
"	T. R. Ford, W. W. Ford & Mrs. Hannah Ford	"
Feb. 26, 1854	Samuel T. Atkinson & Mr. & Mrs. Glennie	"
March 26, 1854	Rev. Mr. Keith, James H. & Miss E. Trapier	Church
April 13, 1854	The Father, Mother & Mrs. Bush	"
"	"	"
"	R. O. Bush, Wm. T. Munro & Mrs. Munro	"

1854 [continued]

Names	Parents Names	When born
William (col)	Slave of John P. Ford	
Paul Horry	William H. & Charlotte I. Trapier	Oct. 7, 1852
John Franklin	Richard & Elizabeth Dozier	Oct. 2, 1847
May Elizabeth	"	Nov. 5, 1853
Thomas Hun (col))	Laura Allston	June 12, 1852
James)		June 25, 1854
Catharine Vaux	Dr. R. G. & Sarah E. White	July 18, 1854
Alexander Grant (col)	Joe & Lydia Parker	
Richard Alden	B. A. & Caroline Coachman	Dec. 12, 1853
Jane	W. W. & Hess Shackelford	July 13, 1854
Mary Leighton	Jos. B. & Joanna Pyatt	Apr. 20, 1854

1856

Names	Parents Names	When born
Florence Adelle	Paul & Hannah Tamplet	March 25, 1855
Emily	Mrs. S. T. Atkinson (adult)	
John	Dr. R. G. & Sarah E. White	March 3, 1856
Anna Henning	W. W. & Hess Shackelford	March 24, 1856
Archibald James	A. I. & May Shaw	
Andrew	Richard & Louisa Cains	Feb. 29, 1844
Agnes F.	"	Sept. 11, 1846
Francis B.	Richard & Louisa Cains	Jan. 12, 1849
Edmund Alston	"	March 1, 1851
Louisa Elizabeth &		
Carolina (twins)	"	Apr. 13, 1854
John Thomas	William H. & Sarah Rebecca Cains	Feb. 23, 1853
William Richard	"	March 15, 1855
Elizabeth Jane Richardson		Aged about 40 years [stricken]
May Josephine)	J. W. & Elizabeth J. Richardson	
Alethia[?] Eugenia)		
Franklin Augustus)		
Joseph Leander)		
Emily Leighton	Richard O. & Caroline A. Bush	June 10, 1856
Emily Bonneau	Samuel & Emily Atkinson	Sept. 22, 1856
Anna Johnson	Slave of Mrs. Carr (infant)	
Elisa Pogas	Slave of Mrs. Brown (infant)	
Ann Elizabeth	George & Elisa Catharine Eldred	Feb. 8, 1856

1854 [continued]

When Baptized	Sponsors	Place of Baptism
Apr. 19, 1854	Ambro Vereen & Scipio Keith, witnesses	Privately
Apr. 26, 1854	Miss Hannah Trapier, Rev. Mr. Keith & J. H. Trapier	Church
June 21, 1854	The Father & Mr. & Mrs. Sherman	Privately
"	The Mother & Mr. & Mrs. Sherman	"
Sept. 3, 1854	Mr. E. Waterman & Anna Allston	Privately
"		
Nov. 26, 1854	Mrs. Catharine Vaux, Miss Jo. Prior & Mr. White	Church
"	Scipio Keith, Anna Allston	"
Dec. 10, 1854	B. A. Coachman, Mr. Leighton & Miss M. Ford	"
"	Miss Emily Thurston, Mrs. G. W. Coachman & J. T. Ford	"
Dec. 26, 1854	Mrs. Alice Ann Rutledge, Mrs. Catharine Labruce & Dr. A. Hasell	Privately

1856

March 26, 1856	Jno. Thamplet, Mrs. Isaac Carr & Miss S. Ford	Church
Apr. 16, 1856	Mrs. B. H. Wilson & S. T. Atkinson, witnesses	Privately
May 4, 1856	J. G. Henning, Benj. White & Miss A. White	Church
May 4, 1856	J. G. Henning, Mrs. Rees Ford & Miss S. Henning	Church
May 25, 1856	B. H. Wilson & wife & Thomas Shaw	Private
June 15, 1856	The Father & Step Mother	North Inlet
"	"	"
June 15, 1856	"	North Inlet
"	"	"
"	"	"
"	The Parents	"
"	The Parents	"
Aug. 6, 1856		Private
Aug. 10, 1856	A. J. Shaw & wife & Mrs. Gallivant	Church
"	"	"
"	A. J. Shaw & R. T. Howard & Mrs. Gallivant	"
"	"	"
Sept. 16, 1856	The Parents	Privately
Sept. 26, 1856	Mr. W. W. Shackelford, Mrs. Prior & Mother	Privately
Nov. 18, 1856	Adam Dunmore & Louisa	Church
"	" & Catharine	"
Nov. 18, 1856	The Parents	Privately

1857

Names	Parents Names	When born
Sarah Henning	James Rees & Martha Elizabeth Ford	Sept. 29, 1856
May Alene	B. A. & Caroline Coachman	Dec. 13, 1856
Lucien	Dr. E. B. & E. C. Brown (service by Rev. A. T. Porter) Apr. 2, 1857
Caroline	Slave of Mrs. Gen. Carr	About 19 years old
Sarah	"	" 16 "
Anna	"	" 8 "
Phoebe	Slave of A. J. Shaw, Esquire	
Martha	"	
David	"	
Edward	"	
Enoch	Slave of B. H. Wilson, Esquire	
Arthur Edward	John & Anna Tamplet	June 28, 1853
Alice Bonneau	"	Nov. 3, 1855
Robert Lee	Rev. R. T. & H. M. Howard	Feb. 7, 1857
Jessie Minnie	Paul & Hannah Tamplet	Nov. 30, 1856

1858

Henry (col)	Slave of Mrs. James Smith	Aged 22
Theodore Herbert	Dr. A. M. & Elizabeth Forster	Apr. 21, 1857
Israel (col)	Slave of Mrs. B. Trapier	
Mary Elizabeth	Col. F. W. & Sarah Heriot	March 20, 1858
Mary Julia	Samuel T. & Emily Atkinson	Nov. 25, 1857
Edward Percy	Edward Parker & Theodora Caroline Guerard	Apr. 21, 1858
Willis Wilkinson	W. W. & Hess Shackelford	Apr. 27, 1858
Katharine Seaman	R. T. & H. M. Howard	May 21, 1858
Ella	Samuel T. & Emily Atkinson	Dec. 26, 1858

1859

Caroline White	Joseph & Gabriella Johnson	May 14, 1858
John Ford	Paul & Martha S. Fitssimmons	Jan. 28, 1859
Margaret	Slave of Mrs. Waterman	
Henry	Paul & Hannah Tamplet	May 8, 1859
John Paul	Jno & Anna Tamplet	July 3, 1859

1860

Elizabeth Shackelford	James Rees & Martha E. Ford	June 12, 1859
Hannah Mary	Dr. R. G. & S. E. White	July 16, 1859
Ephraim (col)	Slave of Mrs. Gen. Carr	Jan. 1860

1857

When Baptized	Sponsors	Place of Baptism
Jan. 25, 1857	W. A. Henning, Mrs. W. W. Shackelford & Miss A. M. Ford	Church
Feb. 1, 1857	Misses S. J. Coachman, A. G. Coachman & Father	Church
Apr. 29, 1857 Privately	Rev. A. T. Porter & Wife	
May 6, 1857	Annette & Ella	Church
"	"	"
"	"	"
May 24, 1857		"
"		"
"		"
"		"
"		"
May 28, 1857		
"	The Parents & Mrs. Isaac Carr	Privately
"	"	"

1858

Jan. 22, 1858	Witnesses: Hay Screven, Jane & Grace	Privately
March 10, 1858	A. M. Forster, A. H. Belin & Miss Caroline Withers	Church
Apr. 4, 1858	Witnesses: Ambro, Tom Jefferson & Scipio	Church
Apr. 6, 1858	Mrs. Isaac Carr, Mrs. D. Sparkman & Tom Ford	Black River
May 5, 1858	B. H. Wilson, Mrs. E. Atkinson & Miss M. Atkinson	Church
May 6, 1858	William Huger, S. T. Gaillard & Mrs. S. R. Barnwell	Black River
May 30, 1858	Mrs. Maria R. Thurston, J. Rees Ford & F. W. Ford	Church
Nov. 7, 1858	Mrs. Mary Shaw, Mrs. H. M. Howard & Dr. Wm. Prior	Church
Dec. 27, 1858	Mrs. B. H. Wilson, Miss A. E. & S. T. Atkinson	Privately

1859

Jan. 2, 1859	The Parents & Miss Elisa Johnson	Church
March 4, 1859	Miss Elisa Ford, J. R. Ford & Father	Private
Apr. 27, 1859	Harry Screven, Alonzo & Moll, witnesses	Private
July 3, 1859	The Parents	Privately, ill
July 12, 1859	The Parents	Privately, ill

1860

Jan. 11, 1860	Mr. J. G. Henning & Miss S. Lucas & Mrs. Jno. H. Read	Church
Jan. 15, 1860	James R. Ford, Misses Hannah Trapier & A. E. Prior	Church
Feb. 26, 1860	The parents	Church

Names	Parents Names	When born
Alice	Dr. A. M. & Elizabeth Forster	Sept. 19, 1859
May Nanette	A. J. & Mary E. Shaw	Jan. 31, 1860
Emily Harrington	Leighton	
Lee Thurston	W. W. & Hess Shackelford	Oct. 15, 1860
Martha Florence	W. Soulby & Hannah Esther Nurse	Apr. 16, 1859
Lindsay Scott	"	Aug. 5, 1860
Samuel) (col)	Mrs. Isaac Carr	
Georgie)		
Sarah Leapear	Ashby	March 31, 1860
Mary Walter	Glennie & Anna Glen Heriot	Nov. 1861
Emily Ravenel	W. W. & Hess Shackelford	Nov. 15, 1861
John Arthur	Dr. A. M. & E. Forster	Dec. 28, 1863
Sarah Ann	W. & C. J. Mayrant	Apr. 21, 1864

1865 by Revd. Alex'r Glennie

Edward Nowell	John Francis & Harriet Nowell Pyatt	March 29, 1865
Willm. Richardson	Wm. Horry & Kate Drayton Mayrant	Sept. 17, 1865
Elizabeth Matilda	Adult: David Henry & Eleanor Elizabeth Smith	Nov. 3, 1851

When Baptized	Sponsors	Place of Baptism
March 7, 1860	Mrs. Withers & Parents	Church
Apr. 29, 1860	C. J. Simonton, Mrs. Joshua Ward & Miss V. Thomas	Church
May 29, 1860	Mr. Leighton, Miss K. Gliddon & Miss Bull, wit.	Privately
Dec. 10, 1860	Mrs. Eliza Heriot, & Messrs David Jennings & E. Thurston	Privately
	Mrs. Prior, Mrs. Nurse & Dr. R. G. White	Church
	Miss A. E. Prior, Mrs. A. J. Shaw & Father	
Sept. 22, 1861		
Apr. 3, 1862	Mrs. Howren [?] & Mother	Privately
	Mrs. M. H. Coachman, Ramell McKay & Dr. J. R. Sparkman	
	Mrs. E. E. Thurston, Joseph Ford & Dr. W. C. Ravenel	
May 22, 1864	The Parents & F. Forster	
May 22, 1864	W. E. Richardson, Miss H. Drayton & Mrs. S. H. Mayrant	

1865

When Baptized	Sponsors	Place of Baptism
Dec. 3, 1865	J. F. Pyatt, Jos. B. Pyatt, Mrs. Pearson	Church
Jan. 21, 1866	Dr. Prior, Majr. Richardson, Mrs. Mayrant	Church
Apr. 29, 1866	Dr. Forster, Mrs. Forster, Mrs. Prior	Church

[From entries at the beginning of the register] "Baptisms by Revd. Robt. T. Howard, not entered under date."

Children of Dr. Richard G. & Sarah E. White:
Anna Josephine, born Septr. 23, 1861. Sponsors Mr. & Mrs. J. B. White, & Miss Anna White

William Capers, born Augt. 2, 1863. Sponsors Dr. Prior & the Parents.

The above record was furnished to Revd. A. Glennie by Mrs. R. G. White.

Also the following children were baptized by Revd. Robt. T. Howard on Feby. 22, 1865--children of W. H. & A. Dorrill:

John White Tuttle, born Septr. 17, 1853. Sponsors S. S. Fraser, & Mrs. McCusker
Moses Leonard, born Jan. 31, 1855. Sponsors the Parents.
Susan Rebecca, born Feby 28, 1857. Spons. Dr. & Mrs. R. G. White
Mary Bush, born March 27 ,1859. Spons. Mr & Mrs. G. F. S. Wright.
Wm. Henry, born May 20, 1863, Spons. Arch. Shaw & Emma Richardson.

Also, by Revd. Richard S. Trapier, on July 29, 1865.
Byrd, born July 7, 1865. Sponsors, the Father & Mrs. McCusker.

This record of the baptism of these six children was copied by Revd. A. Glennie from the Family Bible of Wm. H. Dorrill.

Also, the following baptism by Revd. Robt. R. Howard:
Katharine Ward, born Decr. 14, 1864. Sponsors Margaret B. Ward, Alice Flagg, Martha A. Pyatt, Arthur B. Flagg.
The said child being the daughter of Joseph B. & Joanna Pyatt. This record was furnished to Revd. A. Glennie by Mrs. Jos. B. Pyatt.

Names	Parents Names	When born
Joseph North	Joseph Blyth & Mary N. Allston	Apr. 28, 1866
Lucien Green (col)	Ella Johnson	Aug. 16, 1865
Paul Huot	Paul & Hannah E. Tamplet	Dec. 31, 1863
Lucy Louiza	La Motte	Adult 1787
Anna Ramelle	Alexr. Glennie & Anna Glenn Heriot	Sept. 12, 1866
George Tracey	Charles S. & Caroline Stockman	Apr. 22, 1865
William Starr	"	July 2, 1866
Emma Septima	S. Ewbank & Emilie A. Lucas	Jan. 23, 1867
David Christopher	David & Ellen Huger (col)	1860
David Huger	Samuel & Clarissa Moultrie (col)	Jan. 1867
Emma Heriot	James R. & Mary E. Sparkman	Feb. 11, 1867
Martha	James & Judy Ann Magill (col)	Apr. 1867
Richard	Richard & Elizabeth Dozier	Nov. 5, 1863
Maria Matilda	George Nelson & Martha Ann Warr	March 14, 1861
George Nelson	Warr - an adult	Dec. 31, 1826
Sarah Rowe	Carr - an adult	
Sophronia Ann	Manly Theodore & Annie Caroline Sanders	Oct. 23, 1858
William Theodore	"	Feb. 8, 1860
John Evander	"	Apr. 23, 1863
Ellen Victoria	"	Nov. 3, 1866
Martha Ford	Paul & Martha Selina Fitzsimons	Sept. 6, 1867
James	Andrew & Matilda Waldo (col)	July 26, 1863
Andrew Joseph	March & Minda Simmons "	July 2, 1867
William	William & Martha Trust	1860
Maham Ward	Joseph B. & Joanna Pyatt	Nov. 10, 1867
Benjamin	Benjamin & Fannie Richardson (col)	May 4, 1867
Robert Withers	Robert Withers & Eliza Catherine Vaux	Feb. 4, 1868
Thomas Pierce	Thomas Pierce & Maria Laval Bayley	Aug. 18, 1867
David	David & Georgeana H. Risley	Nov. 18, 1867
Cain	George & Harriet Huggins (col)	1857
John Charles	Paul & Hannah E. Tamplet	Dec. 9, 1867
Francis Marion	William & Hannah Burgess	May 19, 1863
Daniel Thomas	"	Jan. 24, 1865
John Daniel	Agnes Carlyle Stalvey	Jan. 23, 1866
Henry Joseph	William & Sally Parker (col)	March 1867
Joseph Laurence	Prince & Celia Lowry (col)	July 2, 1868
Henrietta Porcher	Blair & Henrietta Porcher Anderson	Sept. 27, 1868
Eliza	Samuel E. & Maria Stalvey	June 22, 1864
Malachi	"	March 26, 1867
Oliver Arnold	Richard O. & Margaret L. Bush	Dec. 25, 1868
Ralph Izzard	Ralph Izzard & Virginia Middleton	Jan. 20, 1869
Benjamin Wilson	C. Irvine & A. Oriana Walker	Aug. 24, 1868
Alexander Glennie	Alexr. Glennie & Anna Glen Heriot	Dec. 26, 1868
George Gaillard	George Gaillard & Elizabeth Chisolm Ford	Nov. 6, 1868
Mary	Alexander & Mary E. Y. Glennie	Apr. 26, 1869
Margaret Jane Bentley	Benjamin P. & Angelica E. Fraser	Aug. 24, 1868
Harriet Arabella	Charles S. & Carolina Stockman	Nov. 9, 1868
Charles Williams	Thomas Pierce & Maria Laval Bayley	Oct. 27, 1868

When Baptized	Sponsors	Place of Baptism
May 27, 1866	Gen. Connor, Arnoldus Vanderhorst, Mrs. P. C. J. Weston	Church
June 17, 1866	David & Rachel Huger (col)	"
June 26, 1866	The Parents	Pawley's Island
July 2, 1866	Witnesses: Mrs. Morgan, Miss C. La Motte	Private
Dec. 21, 1866	Dr. Alex. M. Forster, Mrs. B. H. Wilson, Mrs. J. Coachman	Church
Jan. 27, 1867	Charles S. Stockman, David Risley, Miss Risley	Church
"	" , Mrs. Risley	Do
March 10, 1867	The Father, Mrs. Henning, Anna M. Lucas	Private
Apr. 14, 1867	Samuel & Clarissa Moultrie (col)	Church
"	David & Rachel Huger (col)	"
May 21, 1867	Benjn Allston, M. Emma Heriot, Mrs. Julia Paine	Plantersville
	Frank, M. Emma Heriot, the Mother	"
June 9, 1867	The Father, John Dozier, Miss Lee	Private
" 22, 1867	The Parents: received into the Church June 26, 1869	" very ill
Aug. 4, 1867	Witness: Mrs. Warr	" very ill
" 9, 1867	Witness: Mrs. Davis	" very ill
" 23, 1867	The Parents	Church
"	"	"
"	"	"
"	"	"
Nov. 8, 1867	Christopher F. Vaux, Ann E. Ford, Catharine A. Ford	"
" 24, 1867	Andrew Waldo	"
" " 1867	Andrew Waldo, Yorick Wilson, Rachel Huger	"
" 29, 1867		Private, ill
Dec. 8, 1867	Alexr Glennie, John F. Pyatt, Ann A. Ward	Church
March 1, 1868	Andrew Waldo, Ellen Richardson	"
March 22, 1868	The Father, Paul Fitzsimons, Mrs. Fitzsimons Sr.	"
" 29, 1868	The Father, A. J. Shaw, Susan C. Brown	"
April 5, 1868	Joseph H. Risley, Reese S. Peters, Mrs. B. C. Hirst	"
May 7, 1868		Private, very ill
" 10, 1868	The Parents	Church
Aug. 12, 1868		in Private
"		"
"		"
Oct. 23, 1868	The Mother, Ellen Richardson	Church
Nov. 10, 1868	The Parents	All Saints Ch.
Dec. 6, 1868	Blair Anderson, Mrs. Ellen Heriot, Eliza H. Heriot	Church
Dec. 11, 1868		in Private
Dec. 11, 1868		
March 24, 1869	The Parents & Mrs. Mary A. Jacobs	Church
March 28, 1869	The Father, Revd. Grimke Drayton, Mrs. J. R. Pringle	"
Apr. 18, 1869	Genl. A. M. Manigault, J. A. Shaw, Donella McKay	"
Apr. 23, 1869	Alexr. Glennie, Stephen Coachman, Mary Forster, Mrs. Edwin Heriot	"
May 9, 1869 Whit Sunday	Stephen Elliot Barnwell, Thos Ford, Anna Lucas	"
May 10, 1869	Revd. W. A. Fiske, Mrs. J. H. Read, Mrs. J. H. Willard, Sarah A. Trapier	"
May 17, 1869	Revd. Lucien C. Lance, Mrs. Jane R. Fishburne, Madelin M. Farquharson	Prince Fredks Chapel
May 21, 1869	Richard T. Stockman, Mrs. John J. Baker, Miss E. M. Hayward	Church
June 2, 1869	The Father, Dr. A. M. Forster, Anna Lucas	"

Names	Parents Names	When born
Annie Eugenia	George Nelson & Martha Ann Warr (Adult)	Oct. 7, 1854
George Alexander	"	Sept. 21, 1856
Charles Pinckney	"	Jan. 11, 1859
Robert Nelson	"	Aug. 11, 1863
Mary Hannah	"	Aug. 25, 1866
Julia Ann	Sellard-- wife of T. Thorsen (Adult)	Mar. 16, 1849
Eugenia Stoney	Paul & Martha Selina Fitzsimons	May 25, 1809
Edgar Stoney	Robert W. & Eliza Catherine Vaux	Sept. 30, 1869
Benjamin	March & Minda Simmons (col)	Sept. 23, 1869
Lucretia Elizabeth	Wm. Henry & Hortensia Elizabeth Ann Jones (col)	Jan. 12, 1870
Margaret	Divine-- An Adult	
Alfred Hatch	Adult: Joseph M. & Eveline H. Brown	Aug. 6, 1854
William Julius	T. & Julia Ann Thorsen	Sept. 27, 1869
Mary Louise	Manly Theodore & Annie Caroline Sanders	July 20, 1869
Eliza Stark	William & Martha Emma Sparkman	June 17, 1870
Robert Smith	Thomas Pierce & Maria Laval Bailey	June 4, 1870
Lena Elizabeth	Henry & Caroline Ann Swan	Aug. 22, 1870
Willm Augustus	"	May 31, 1868
Eleanor Jane	Riley: Adult	Dec. 15, 1847
James Franklin	Peter & Elizabeth Ann Ehney	Sept. 19, 1870
Eunice Melville	Richard O. & Margaret L. Bush	Oct. 29, 1870
Alexander Glennie	George Nelson & Martha Ann Warr	March 6, 1870
Mary Taylor	Arthur Middleton & Emma Izard Parker	Nov. 29, 1870
Wm. Henry	Lockhart: Adult	March 1, 1848
James Henning	Simons Ewbank & Emily Anna Lucas	Oct. 18, 1870
Cornelius Irvine	C. Irvine & A. Orianna Walker	Dec. 3, 1870
Helen Fredrine	A. Glennie & Anna Glenn Heriot	March 4, 1871
Laura	Centy & Grace Donelly (col)	June 15, 1865
Keturah Gavit	Samuel R. & Emma Matilda Carr	
Andrew Beirne	Thomas Alston & Mary Beirne Middleton	Apr. 30, 1867
John Izard	"	Jan. 7, 1869
Thomas Alston	"	May 22, 1870
Mary Elizabeth	Stephen & Sarah Laura Rembert	Jan. 1, 1868
Frances Isabella	Joseph E. & Margaret A. Collins	Nov. 1868
Alford	Dedric & Kezine Semke	June 11, 1868
Dedric	"	"
Mary Elizabeth	James Ervin & Willie Mariam Welsh	Jan. 24, 1869
Reese Peters	David & Georgie H. Risley	Feb. 18, 1871
Catherine Mansfield	Peter James & Elizabeth Stalvey	May 19, 1866
William Joseph	"	Jan. 5, 1868
George Allen)	Georgeana Hughes (col)	Sept. 10, 1870
Augustus Wall)		
Josephine	Ross & Rhoda Johnson (col)	Sept. 2, 1867
Mary Ely	Robert Withers & Eliza C. Vaux	June 23, 1871
John Harleston	John Harleston & Ann Elizabeth Read	Sept. 21, 1871
Elizabeth Heyward	Edward S. & M. H. Horry	Oct. 8, 1870
Alfred Rasul	Paul T. & G. H. Horry	July 13, 1870
Charlotte Risley	Charles S. & Caroline Stockman	Nov. 4, 1871
James Sparkman	Robert Stark & Martha Helen Heriot	Feb. 9, 1872
George Albert	Richard O. & Margaret L. Bush	Jan. 25, 1872
Andrew Jackson	Samuel & Grace Small (col)	Apr. 5, 1872
Ralph Stead	Ralph M. & E. Jane Izard	Jan. 9, 1872
Mary Laval	Thomas P. & Maria L. Bailey	Nov. 22, 1871
Chas. Edw. Belin	Arthur B. & Georgiana Flagg	July 22, 1871

When Baptized	Sponsors	Place of Baptism
June 25, 1869	The Parents	[Church]
"	"	"
"	"	"
"	"	"
"	"	"
Oct. 2, 1869		Private, very ill
Oct. 31, 1869	Mr. Matheson, Mrs. Eugenia Matheson, Annie Stoney	Church
Nov. 21, 1869	Edgar George Stoney, Ann Elizabeth Stoney	"
Jan. 7, 1870	Andrew Waldo, Marianne Scriven	Church
" 26, 1870		Private, very ill
Apr. 1, 1870	Witness: Mrs. Emma A. Henning	Church
Apr. 29, 1870	Witnesses: Alex M. Forster, Mrs. E. H. Brown	Church
May 13, 1870		Private, sick
June 2, 1870	The Parents, Mrs. Benj. H. Wilson	Church
Aug, 28, 1870	James R. Sparkman Jr., Eliza S. Heriot, Mary Caldwell	Plantersville
Sept. 18, 1870	The Parents, Genl. A. M. Manigault, Mrs. S. L. Lawton	Church
Oct. 14, 1870	The Parents	"
in 1868	" " baptized in private & received into the church Oct 14, 1870	
Oct. 17, 1870		Private, very ill
Jan. 13, 1871	Benjamin A. & Martha Coxe	Church
March 8, 1871	The Parents, Mrs. Jacobs	"
March 15, 1871	The Parents	"
March 19, 1871	Ralph Izard Middleton Jr., Mrs. R. Ion Lowndes, Mrs. Benj. Huger	"
April 2, 1871		Private, very ill
April 9, 1871	The Parents	Church
April 29, 1871	Benj. H. Wilson, Robt. E. Fraser, Miss Legare	"
"	W. W. Shackelford, Mrs. Shackelford, Eliza S. Heriot	"
June 19, 1871		Private, very ill
July 7, 1871	Mrs. Emma M. Carr	Church
July 9, 1871	J. J. Pringle, Garnett Andrews, Rose Andrews	Plantersville
"	J. I. Middleton Sr., Peter Minor, Lucy Minor	"
"	T. A. Middleton, Carter Minor, Mary B. Middleton	"
July 14, 1871	Mrs. S. L. Rembert	Church
Aug, 5, 1871		Private, very ill
Aug. 16, 1871		"
"		"
"		"
Sept. 1, 1871	J. R. Sank, Judge Dickey, Mrs. C. R. Stockman	Church
Sept. 4, 1871		Private, sick
"		"
Sept. 7, 1871		", very ill
Oct. 1, 1871	York Price, Minda Simmons & the Mother	Church
Nov. 13, 1871	J. Harleston & Ann E. Read, Mrs. C. A. Vaux	The Parsonage
"	The Father, Robt. W. Vaux, Mrs. J. H. Read Senr	"
Dec. 17, 1871	Mr. & Mrs. A. W. Cordes, M. Deas	N. Santee:Church
"	P. T. Horry, Josephine A. Deas	"
Feb. 21, 1872	Revd. Dr. Castle, Mrs. Castle, Mrs. Brown	Church
Apr. 21, 1872	B. Huger Ward, Jane M. Ward	"
Apr. 26, 1872	The Parents	"
Apr. 27, 1872		Private, ill
Apr. 28, 1872	John Julius Pringle, J. Harleston Read, Josephine Izard	Church
Apr. 28, 1872	The Parents, A. McP. Hamby, Hess B. Williams, Olivia V. Williams	Church
Apr. 28, 1872	Bentley Weston, B. Huger Ward, Anna A. Ward, Georg'a Flagg Jr.	Church

Names	Parents Names	When born
Joanna	Renty & Josephine Tucker (col)	Sept. 29, 1871
Wilson	March & Minda Simmons (col)	Dec. 17, 1871
Eliza Ellison	S. Sidney & Sarah Fraser	Apr. 29, 1871
Mary Thomasine	Thomas & Ann Elizabeth Ford	March 12, 1872
Georgia Chisolm	Blair & Henrietta P. Anderson	March 9, 1871
Johanna Amelia	J. Lewis & Sarah Haenel	March 15, 1872
John Lemuel	Lemuel & Frances Elizabeth Springs	Dec. 15, 1859
Ellen Bailey	Wm. H. & Alafair Dorrell	March 21, 1872
Maria Rees	Alexr Glennie & Anna Glen Heriot	Oct. 10, 1872
William	Richard I'on & Alice Izzard Lowndes	Aug. 10, 1872
Francis	Arthur Middleton & Emma Izzard Parker	Sept. 21, 1872
Henry Detynes	James Hamilton & Maria Elizabeth Vernon	July 4, 1868
Mary Frances	"	Oct. 28, 1869
Lawrence Lee	"	Nov. 24, 1871
Catherine Dana	William C. & Marianne Williams	May 15, 1861
Gabriel Ross	Ross & Rhoda Johnson (col)	Aug. 5, 1872
George Ezra	David & Georgie H. Risley	Dec. 21, 1872
John Harleston	John Harleston & Ann Elizabeth Read	May 4, 1873
Susan Elizabeth	Peter & Elizabeth Ann Ehney	June 3, 1873
Cleland Kinloch	Byrd: An Adult	Nov. 20, 1823
Hugh Wilson	S. Sidney & Sarah Fraser	June 30, 1872
Julia Wilson	C. Irvine & A. Orianna Walker	March 2, 1873
Irene Simons	Frederick S. & Irene Magdalen Barth	July 2, 1857
Catherine Sarah	"	Oct. 28, 1860
Walter Blake	Ralph M. & E. Jane Izard	May 16, 1873
William Henning	Frederick & Laura Young	Jan. 26, 1873
John Louis	J. Louis & Sarah Haenel	Jan. 9, 1874
Corinne Williams	Blair & Henrietta Porcher Anderson	March 19, 1873
James Rees Ford	Robt. Stark & Martha Helen Heriot	Nov. 24, 1873
Paul FitzSimons	Robert W. & Eliza C. Vaux	Nov. 24, 1873
Sarah Ann	Blackwell: an Adult	March 31, 1839
Annie Maria	Collins: an Adult	Aug. 1845
Mary Etta	William & Mary Ann Jacobs	Feb. 12, 1862
Willm. Jeannerette	William O. & Ida C. Bourke	Aug. 9, 1873
Hester Ann Wilson	March & Minda Simmons (col)	Apr. 7, 1874
Anne Stoney	J. Harleston & Anne E. Read	May 18, 1874
Louis Frederick	Hippolyte & Sybil Capel	Jan. 6, 1874
John Potts	Thomas & Anne Elizabeth Ford	May 9, 1874
John William	Alexr Glennie & Anna Glenn Heriot	June 7, 1874
Mary Allen	Hasford & Eliza H. Walker	July 29, 1874
Alethea	Simons Ewbank & Emily Anna Lucas	Nov. 4, 1874
Mary Margaret	Richard O & Margaret L. Bush	Sept. 2, 1874
Robert Ellison	R. Lovat & Catherine V. Fraser	Jan. 18, 1875
Allard Belin	Thomas P. & Maria L. Bailey	Jan. 20, 1875
Samuel Sidney	S. Sidney & Sarah Fraser	Feb. 22, 1874
Harleston Read	Ralph M. & E. Jane Izard, by Rev. L. C. Lance	Oct. 27, 1874
Laura Susan	Alexius M. & Mary P. Forster	May 16, 1875
Warren	Warren & Hess H. Atkinson	Apr. 10, 1875
Clarence Eugene	Clarence R. & Ella Eugenia Anderson	June 13, 1875

When Baptized	Sponsors	Place of Baptism
Apr. 28, 1872	Ross & Rhoda Johnson	[Church]
Apr. 28, 1872	Yorick Wilson, Sarah Wilson	"
May 8, 1872	The Mother, Mrs. J. H. Wilson, Robt. E. Fraser	"
May 19, 1872	The Father, Mrs. M. W. Ford, Mrs. M. S. FitzSimons	"
May 26, 1872	The Parents, Mrs. David Risley, Sallie E. Anderson	"
May 26, 1872		Private
May 31, 1872	The Mother	Church
June 6, 1872	Dr. T. P. Bailey, Mrs. Rumley, Mrs. McCusker	"
Dec. 5, 1872	Robt. Stark Heriot, A. Elizabeth Sparkman, Frances Forster	Private
	Received into the Church Nov. 5, 1873	
Jan. 19, 1873	Robt. T. Smith, Ar. Delancey Middleton, Emily R. Lowndes	Church
Jan. 19, 1873	Francis S. Parker, James R. Parker, Mrs. Julia R. Burgess	"
Feb. 18, 1873		in private
Feb. 18, 1873		"
Feb. 18, 1873		"
Apr. 28, 1873		"
May 25, 1873	Andrew Waldo, Pompey Small, Louisa Johnson	Church
June 16, 1873	Robert W. & Mrs. Vaux, Benj. H. Read	The Parsonage
June 22, 1873		in private
July 16, 1873	Witneses. Mrs. McCusker, Mrs. Dorrell	in private: ill
July 29, 1873	Recd into the Church Apr. 21, '75, Hugh Wilson, S. S. Fraser, E. C. Goodwin	"
Sept. 20, 1873	Recd. into the church Oct. 27. Benj. H. & Mrs. Wilson, Julia M. Verdier	"
Sept. 28, 1873	Mrs. Martha J. Heston, Mrs. Mary A. Jacobs	Church
Sept. 28, 1873	"	"
Dec. 16, 1873	James R. Parker, Wm. B. Read, Eleanor W. Read	"
Feb. 8, 1874		in private
Feb. 8, 1874		"
Feb. 15, 1874	Dr. Hasford Walker, Mrs. Fromberger, Mrs. B. Anderson	Church
Feb. 22, 1874	Dr. A. M. Forster, Wm. R. Ford, M. Clara Ford	"
March 15, 1874	L. P. Miller, Mrs. Martha S. FitzSimons	in private
Apr. 7, 1874	Witness: Mrs. Mary A. Jacobs	Church
Apr. 7, 1874	Witness: Alexr Glennie	"
Apr. 7, 1874	Mrs. Martha J. Heston	"
May 3, 1874	Dr. Richard G. White, Wm. O. Bourke, Catherine V. White	Church
May 31, 1874	Sharper Rice, Hannah Harrel	"
Aug. 2, 1874	Dr. John F. Ely, Mrs. Wm. Eve, Ella W. Read	"
Sept. 10, 1874		in private
Oct. 16, 1874	J. Rees Ford, G. Gaillard Ford, Eliza H. Ford	Church
Nov. 4, 1874	Francis G. Coachman, Charles W. Forster, Mrs. F. G. Coachman	"
Nov. 25, 1874	The Father, Mrs. Henrietta P. Anderson, Julia Verdier	"
Feb. 2, 1875		in private, ill
Feb. 24, 1875	The Parents, Mrs. Barnes, Mrs. Jacobs	Church
March 28, 1875	Robt. E. Fraser, Dr. & Mrs. R. G. White	"
Apr. 11, 1875	R. T. Middleton, T. P. Bailey, Mrs. A. E. Warley	"
Apr. 21, 1875	C. Matthews, G. Gaillard Ford, M. Matthews	"
May 2, 1875	Rev. L. C. Lance, Pinckney Izard, Mrs. Julius Pringle	Prince Frederick's
June 16, 1875	Charles W. Forster, Mary W. Forster, Ann E. Pinckney	Church
July 25, 1875	Samuel. T. Atkinson, Warren Atkinson, Mrs. Prior	Church
Aug. 18, 1875	The Father, George C. Wharton, Libertie C. Wharton	"

Names	Parents Names	When born
Mary Ann	Detyens: an Adult	Jan. 28, 1850
Mary Ella	James H. & Mary Ann Detyens	Oct. 23, 1872
Edgar Stoney	J. Harleston & Anne C. Read	July 11, 1875
Claudia Allan	Daniel & Susan Pinckney Tucker	March 5, 1874
Elizabeth Weston	"	March 14, 1875
John	Haenel. Adult	Aug. 24, 1858
Joshua John	B. Huger & Jane M. Ward	Apr. 19, 1875
Alexius Mador Forster	Robt. Stark & Martha Helen Heriot	Jan. 18, 1876
Henrietta White	William O. & Ida C. Bourke	Apr. 17, 1875
George Frederick	Frederick & Laura Young	Jan. 27, 1876
James Hamilton	James Hamilton & Maria Elizabeth Vernon	March 29, 1874
Maria Annette	"	Feb. 25, 1876
Sarah Eliza	James Henning & Mary Ann Detyens	Mar. 21, 1876
John Stoney	Robert W. & Eliza C. Vaux	Mar. 9, 1876
Ann Elizabeth	Thomas & Ann E. Ford	Mar. 14, 1876
Florence Lester	Richard O. & Margaret L. Bush	Apr. 10, 1876
Zechariah	Renty & Diana Tucker (col)	Apr. 30, 1875
Edwin Cuttino	Wm. Gaillard & Mary Blake Dozier	Sept. 27, 1865
Mortimer Roberts	"	Mar. 27, 1867
Edwin Nathaniel	Edward M. & Amelia C. Tilton	Mar. 21, 1870
William Walter	Hasford & Eliza P. Walker	May 20, 1876
Edward	March & Minda Simmons (col)	Apr. 6, 1876
James Detyens	Peter & Elizabeth Ann Ehney	Sept. 15, 1875
Elizabeth Burgess	William & Martha Emma Sparkman	Sept. 17, 1876
Mary Dozier	Richard Dozier & Mary Elizabeth Lee	Aug. 11, 1876
John Labouladrie	John Labouladrie & Ida DeTreville	July 10, 1876
David	Thomas P. & Maria L. Bailey	Dec. 4, 1876
William Bond	J. Harleston & Anne E. Read	Apr. 2, 1877
Samuel	Robt. Lovatt & Catherine Vaux Fraser	May 17, 1877
Arthur Middleton	Arthur M. & Emma Parker	Aug. 13, 1877
Georgeana Lavinia	John & Flora Higgins (col)	Aug. 28, 1872
Elisa Hasford	Hasford & Eliza H. Walker	Aug. 20, 1877
Ormbay Pinckney	William O. & Ida C. Bourke	Apr. 6, 1878
Mary Catherine	Thomas M. & Mary L. Merriman	Aug. 1, 1876
Lilian Maud	"	May 1, 1878
Annie Estella	Fritz & Laura Young	Apr. 27, 1878
Sarah Ann	Pickens B. & Eugenia A. Holsenback	Sept. 25, 1874
Julia Eliza	"	Nov. 21, 1876
Theodore Ardolph	Peter & Elizabeth Ann Ehney	Jan. 29, 1878
James Mazyck	March & Minda Simmons (col)	June 5, 1878
Andrew	Andrew Jackson & Pamelia Ann Smith	Sept. 8, 1878
James Frederick	James Henning & Mary Ann Detyens	Aug. 11, 1878
LeGrand Guerry	Le Grand Guerry & Catherine Turpin Walker	Dec. 4, 1875
Virginia Caroline Thomas	Do	June 8, 1878
James Hamilton	S. Sidney & Sarah Fraser	July 1, 1876
Florence	Robt Lovat & Catherine V. Fraser	July 16, 1878

When Baptized	Sponsors	Place of Baptism
Sept. 1, 1875	Witnesses: Mrs. Martha Coxe, Mrs. Sarah A. Blackwell	Church
Sept. 1, 1875	Sprs. Mrs. Martha Coxe, Mrs. Sarah A. Blackwell	"
Nov. 6, 1875	Edgar Stoney, M. Lance Read, Flora Matheson	Plantersville
Nov. 6, 1875	Paul W. Fraser, Mary A. Tucker, M. Selina Tucker	"
"	Francis & Mrs. Weston, Mrs. John Tucker	"
Dec. 8, 1875	Witnesses: Dr. T. P. Bailey, Mrs. B. H. Wilson	Church
Dec. 19, 1875	J. H. Sparkman Junr, George Sparkman, Margaret B. Ward	Prince Fredericks
Apr. 5, 1876	Dr. T. P. Bailey, Benj. A. Munnerlyn, Mrs. E. Chisolm	Ford Church
Apr. 18, 1876	Edw. N. Jeannerette, Mrs. S. E. White, Mrs. J. McKinley	"
May 17, 1876	Dr. T. P. Bailey, Mr. & Mrs. Bleckwehl	"
May 24, 1876	James H. Detynes, Anna E. Detyens	"
May 24, 1876	James H. & Mary A. Detyens	"
May 24, 1876	Mrs. McCusker, Anne E. Detyens	"
June 11, 1876	Wm. E. Stoney, John S. Ely, Mrs. Susan H. Belt	Plantersville
June 11, 1876	Revd. A. T. & Mrs. Porter, Catherine A. Ford	"
June 21, 1876	The Parents, Susan R. Dorrill	Church
July 12, 1876		Private
July 12, 1876	Warren & Ar. O. & A. Eliza Atkinson, Mrs. Atkinson Sr.	Church
July 12, 1876	" " & Emily B. Atkinson	"
July 12, 1876	The Parents & Mrs. McCusker	"
July 12, 1876	W. W. Walker, Judge A. J. Shaw, M. Nannette Shaw	"
July 12, 1876	The Parents	"
July 14, 1876		Private
Dec. 15, 1876	George E. T. Sparkman, Miss A. Elizth & Pamela M. Sparkman	Peedee
Dec. 27, 1876	Dr. A. M. Forster, Mrs. R. Dozier, Mrs. R. D. Lee, Elizabeth LaBruce	in Private
Feb. 7, 1877	Dr. A. M. Forster, Ar. M. Parker, Cornelia DeTreville	Church
Apr. 22, 1877	The Father, L. G. Harmon, Mrs. David Bailey	Church
May 29, 1877	The Father, Wm. Bond Read, Mrs. R. W. Vaux Senr	Church
Sept. 16, 1877	Robt. E. Fraser, S. Sidney Fraser, Florence A. Tamplet	"
Oct. 28, 1877	A. Delaney Middleton, Rutledge Parker, Lilah Newton	
Nov. 10, 1877		private, ill
Jan. 23, 1878	The Father, Mary Shaw, Virginia Thomas	Church
June 5, 1878	G. Guyton, Wm. Pinckney, Mrs. Mary L. Merriman	"
June 5, 1878	James C. Congdon, Mrs. M. A. Logan, Mrs. A. C. Tilton	"
June 5, 1878	Charles M. Tilton, Mrs. Ida C. Bourke, Lilly A. Tilton	"
July 24, 1878	The Parents	"
Aug. 7, 1878	Dr. A. M. Forster, Rosa Richter	"
Aug, 7, 1878	Ardolph Bleckwehl & Mrs. Bleckwehl	"
Aug. 7, 1878	"	"
Aug. 18, 1878	John James Hughes, Penelope Gordon	"
Sept. 14, 1878		private, ill
Oct. 23, 1878	The Parents	private
Nov. 6, 1878		private, ill
Nov. 13, 1878	W. W. Walker, Virginia C. Thomas, Miss Gibson	Church
Nov. 28, 1878	James H. Wilson, G. Fraser Wilson, Mrs. E. R. Wilson	"
Dec. 8, 1878	Dr. T. P. Bailey, Mrs. R. G. White, Minnie Tamplet	"

Names	Parents Names	When born
Albert Isaiah	Albert & Anna Eliza Hickman	Jan. 2, 1879
Eliza Espy	Espy & Ann Eliza Sessions	March 23, 1878
Alafair Elizabeth	Moses L. & Elizabeth B. Dorrill	Oct. 20, 1878
Wm. Henry	Wm. Ashley & Rebecca Croft	Aug. 30, 1877
Katherine Elizabeth Ferguson	Henry & Gorgeana Izard (col)	July 23, 1878
Elizabeth Dozier	Richard Dozier & Mary Elizabeth Lee	Sept. 1, 1878
Howard Sank	David & Georgeana H. Risley	Oct. 30, 1878
Florence Elizabeth	James & Lydia Ann Phillips	June 29, 1877
James Stephen	"	Oct. 5, 1878
Anna Glenn	A. Glennie & Anna Glenn Heriot	Oct. 25, 1878
Ralph Izard Middleton	Arthur M. & Emma T. Parker	Aug. 19, 1879
Anna Tilton	William O. & Ida C. Bourke	Sept. 17, 1879
Hasford	Hasford & Eliza H. Walker	Sept. 25, 1879
John Emilius	Rutledge & Charlotte Parker	Oct. 6, 1879
Elizabeth FitzSimons	J. Harleston & Anne E. Read	Dec. 20, 1879
Emma Mercedes	J. Louis & Sarah Haenel	Feb. 12, 1879
Robert Morris	Nathaniel B. & Lillie A. Tilton	Dec. 17, 1879
Joseph Church Wilson	Washington & Sybil Robinson (col)	Aug. 30, 1879
John Nicholas	Nicholas & Concklin	Oct. 23, 1856
Adrianna (adult)	Mrs. George R. Congdon By the Bishop	Sept. 8 /42
Arthur Dorrill	Louisa A. & Susan R. Butts (by B. Allston)	Sept. 24 /80
Maria Williams	Dr. T. P. & Maria L. W. Bailey (by B. Allston)	Feb. 14/ 81
Laval Williams	" "	Feb. 14/ /81
William Pryor	George R. & A. S. Congdon "	July 12 /72
Charles Seavey	"	Apr. 26 /74
Georgia Alberta	"	Sept. 29 /77
Sarah Lourette	Fritz Young & Laura Young	Feb. 6 /81
Mary Harriet Glennie	March & Minda Simmons (col)	Dec. 24 /80
Caroline Ford	A. Glennie Heriot & Ann G. Heriot	Apr. 25 /81
Anna Huger	Rutledge & Charlotte Parker	March 26 /81
Ansley Jefferson	wife of Thos Jefferson (col)	----
Sarah Freeborn	Allen P. & Alice Hazzard (by J. W. Keeble)	Aug. 2, 1881
Julia Caroline	Thos Mador & Julia C. Gilmore "	Oct. 1881
Mary Eva	LeGrand G. & K. T. Walker "	Aug. 7, 1881
Alice Forster	Frank F. & Alice Gilmore "	Jan. 15, 1882
Eleanor May	D. H. & E. E. Smith (Mrs. Dr. Forster)	
Esther Holbrook	Miss Fannie Forster	
James Rose	James Rose and Penelope Bentley Parker	Jan. 15, 82
	Rutledge Parker Alston Pyatt, Martha Alston Pyatt	

When Baptized	Sponsors	Place of Baptism
Jan. 14, 1879		private
Feb. 19, 1879	The Father, Mrs. W. Atkinson, Mrs. R. L. Private	"
March 26, 1879	Wm. H. Dorrill, Mrs. Ora D. Porter, Mary B. Dorrill	Church
March 26, 1879	Wm. D. Dorrill, Mrs. W. H. Dorrill, W. Ashley Croft	"
Apr. 13, 1879	Henry Vereen, Amy Allston, Sarah Keith	"
May 4, 1879	Richard & Mrs. Dozier, M. Nannette Shaw	private
June 15, 1879	Mr. & Mrs. J. R. Sank	Church
July 14, 1879		private, ill
July 14, 1879		
July 16, 1879	Revd. & Mrs. A. Glennie, Mrs. Rutledge Parker, Margt Ford	Church
Oct. 26, 1879	H. D. Lesesne, Danl Parker Martha Pyatt M. B. Dehon	"
Nov. 8, 1879		private, ill
Dec. 24, 1879	R. M. Cooper, Legrand G. Walker, Mrs. H. F. Heriot	private
March 3, 1880	Francis S. Parker, Edwd H. Prioleau, Marianna Prioleau	Church
March 23, 1880	Middleton Read, Mrs. R. M. Izard, Kate LaBruce	"
March 28, 1880	Mr. & Mrs. Frederick Young	"
Apr. 13, 1880	N. O. Tilton, Thos. M. Merriman, Mrs. E. M. Tilton	"
May 5, 1880	John S. Wilson, Joseph H. Tunno, Mary E. Douglas	"
March 16, 1881	Mrs. Concklin	Church
Apr. 8, 1881	Mrs. Alex. Glennie	Church
Apr. 10, 1881	Oliver J. Butts, Wm. H. Dorrill, Mary A. Butts	"
Apr. 10, 1881	Mary T. Lawton, Alice B. Flagg & Louis L. Williams	"
Apr. 10, 1881	Sally B. Wilson, Louis L. Williams & the Father	"
Apr. 10, 1881	Dr. T. P. Bailey & the Mother	"
Apr. 10, 1881	"	
Apr. 10, 1881	Mrs. Alex. Glennie, the Mother & Dr. T. P. Bailey	
June 26, 1881	The Parents	Church
June 26, 1881	Mary Glennie, Judy Ann Magill, Stephney Moultrie (col)	"
July 11, 1881	M. Eliza Heriot, Ella Ford, M. Walter Heriot & O. M. Read	At home
July 24, 1881	Emily A. Read, Ellen A. Parker, & Rutledge Parker	Church
Oct. 16, 1881	Renty Tucker, Minda Simmons & Tom Jefferson	Church
Dec. 18, 1881	Allen P. & Alice Hazzard	At Home
Jan. 1, 1882	Rutledge Parker, Frank F. Gilmore, Miss Alice F. Gilmore	Church
March 1, 1882	Jas. H. Detyens, Miss Minnie Tamplet	Church
-----	Mr. LeGrand Walker, Mrs. K. T. Walker	Church
March 19, 1882	Ralf I. Middleton, Mary W. Forster, Julia C. Gilmore	Church

[N. B. For the first twenty entries below, the surname is listed with the names of most of the baptized but not repeated after the names of the parents.]

Names	Parents Names	When born
Sarah Freeborn Hazard	Allen P. & Alice	Aug. 2, 81
Julia Caroline Gilmore	Thos Mador and Julia C.	Oct 81
Mary Eva Walker	LaGrand G. & Kate T.	Aug. 7, 81
Alice Forster Gilmore	Frank and Alice	Jan. 15, 82
Eleanor May	D. H. & E. E. Smith	------
Esther Holbrook		
James Rose Parker	James Rose, Penelope B.	15 Jan. 82
Mary Ann E. Conklin	John N. & Hester	11 Feb 82
Edith Belle Geogherty	Thomas and Rebecca	Aug 21 /81
Sam'l Morse Risley	David & Georgianna	-----
Clara O.) Elliott	Zacheriah and Elizabeth R.	Apr. 14, 64
Mary Lou)		
Jno Wilburn Butts	Lewis and Susan	June 17, 82
Annetta Detyens	James H., Mary A.	March 24, 82
Wm. James Avant	Wm. G. & Georgana J. (col)	March 82
Jessie Jenivive Viola Burke	Wm. O. & Ida C.	Dec. 4, 80
Marianne Meade Parker	Rutledge & Charlotte	June 30, 82
Faironda Fairfax Forster	Chas. W. & Faironda Cary	Apr. 16, 1882
William Trim	E. N. & S. E. Jennerett	Oct. 24 /82

Names	Parents Names	When born
Anna Margaret Durward	Peter R. & Anna E. Ehney	Dec. 3d /80
Walter Samuel	George C. & Julia J. Anderson	Apr. 29 /73
Isabella	"	Apr. 12 /76
Julia Jessie	Wife of George C. Anderson	Aged 35 years
Julia Caroline	David H. & E. E. Smith	
Samuel Robinson Carr (Adult)		New Port Jan. 23 /18
Louise	Thos M. & Mary L. Meriman	Apr. 21 /83
Fritz	Fritz & Laura Young	March 24 /83
Ethel	Le Grand G. & Katherine T. Walker	July 10 /83
Edward Laval	T. P. & Maria L. W. Bailey	Sept. 14/ 83
Anna Alafair	L. A. & Susan R. Butts	Feb. 28 /84
Agnes Jane	Stephen & Leize Rouquie	Apr. 4 /84
Mabel Estella	Edwin & Harper	Oct. 2 /78
Frederick William	"	Nov. 6 /79
Mattie Belle	"	Apr. 1 /81
James Edwin	"	Dec. 22 /82
Walter Rowland	Walter & J. Minnie Hazard	Sept. 21, /84
John Albert	J. L. & Sarah A. E. Haenel	Feb. 20 /84
Zacheus Farrow, Adult		Dec. 13, 1801
John Potter		
Susan Coleman Wicker. Adult		Feb. 17 /62
Liddy	A. Jackson & Amelia A. Smith	Oct. 29 /82
Martin VanBuren	Richard R. & Sarah E. Canies	Aug. 29 /67
George Alexander	March & Minda Simons (col)	July 25 /84

When Baptized	Sponsors	Place of Baptism
Dec. 18, 81	Allen P. and Alice Hazard	At Home
Jan. 1, 1882	Rutledge Parker, Frank Gilmore, Miss Alice Gilmore	Church
March 1, 1882	James H. Detyns, Miss Minnie Tamplet	Church
March 19, 1882	Ralph I. Middleton, Mary W. Forster, Miss Julia C. Gilmore	Church
March 30, 1882	Mrs. E. W. Forster, Miss Fannie Forster	Church
Apr. 9, 1882	Rutledge Parker, Allston Pyatt, Miss Mattie A. Pyatt	Church
Easter day	A. Pyatt	Church
May 21, 1882	Parents and Grandmother	Church
May 31, 1882	James M. Ward, Minnie Ward	At Mr. Wards
		Church
	Le Grand Walker, Mrs. S. White	Church
July 19, 1882	Jno. W. Dorrill, Dr. George Sparkman, Mrs. Elsie Johnson	Mr. Dorrill's
July 26, 1882	James H. and Mary A. Detyens	at Home
Aug. 6, 1882	Renty Tucker and Parents of Child	at R. Tucker's
Aug. 30, 1882	Jessie Pinkney, Jennie McKinstry	At Home
Nov. 11, 1882	Rutledge Parker, Miss E. W. Duncan, Mrs. James A. LaFitte	Church
Dec. 4, 1882	W. H. Barton, Emily M. R. Payne Mrs. Dr. Forster	Rectory
Dec. 18, 1882	Dr. T. P. Bailey, Mrs. W. O. Bourke, & E. N. Jennerett by Rev. J. W. Keeble	

By Rev. B. A. Allston, Rector

Apr. 4, 1883	Mr. & Mrs. Lloyd & Mrs. B. Allston	Church
Apr. 4, 1883	Mr. & Mrs. Lloyd & Emma Anderson	Church
Apr. 4, 1883	"	Church
Apr. 8, 1883	Mrs. W. C. Lloyd (witness)	"
Apr. 11, 1883	Mother & Mrs. Lloyd (Witnesses)	
June 4, 1883	Le. G. G. Walker, Mrs. S. E. White (witnesses)	At Home (sick)
June 30, 1883	Mary E. Wallace & Rebecca A. Tilton	Church
Sept. 23, 1883	George H. & Fredrica Brahmer	Church
Oct. 21, 1883	Mrs. Margaret Rouquie & Parents	Church
March 16, 1884	Mrs. Anthony Atkinson & Dr. Allard B. Flagg & Father (proxies)	Church
April 3, 1884	Mrs. Molly Wilburn, Mrs. Leela Dorrill & Gen. H. Heth	at home in country
June 1, 1884	Benj. A. Munnerly & Mrs. B. A. Munnerlyn	At home
June 25, 1884	Mrs. Sarah A. Davidson & Leonora A. Elliot	at home (mission)
June 25, 1884	"	Mission Station
June 25, 1884	"	"
June 25, 1884	"	"
Nov. 27, 1884	Parents & Melancthon W. Jacobus	Church
Jan. 6, 1885	Albert Majewski, Jno Voss & Mother	"
Feb. 2, 1885	James Divine (witness)	Church
Feb. 3, 1885	Andrew & Wm. H. Johnstone & Alice L. Bayles	"
Feb. 19, 1885	Mrs. R. O.Bush & Rector	(ill in bed) private house
March 7, 1885	Mrs. L. G. Allston & Victoria Smith	at home (sick)
Apr. 3, 1885		Sick in bed
May 8, 1885	Mrs. Rose Murrell & Mother	Church

Names	Parents Names	When born
Robert James Donaldson	Richard R. & Sarah E. Canies	Oct 17 /79
Helena Rebecca	Fritz & Laura Young	Apr. 3 /85
Andrew Jackson Smith	(adult)	Sept. 27, 1827
Allen Hamby	Dr. T. P. & Maria L. W. Bailey	Jan. 12 /85
Ida	Andrew Jackson & Amelia Smith	May 20 /75
Victoria	"	July 12 /70
Horace	"	Oct. 3 /72
Anna Wiggins		Oct. 6 /64
Kate Louise	Mr. & Mrs. LeGrand G. Walker	March 3 /85
Georgie Auril	C. R. & Ella E. Anderson	Feb. 13 /86

BAPTISMS BY BISHOP W. B. W. HOWE

Nigel Wharton	C. R. & Ella E. Anderson	June 27 /78
Norma Eugenia	"	Feb. 9 /80
Benjn. Ingell	Allen P. & Alice B. Hazard	Nov. 23 /85

BAPTISMS BY REV. BENJN. ALLSTON

Oliver J.	Oliver J. Butts Jn'r	Jan. 18, 1887
Sarah Elizabeth	Richard R. & Sarah E. Caines	June 29, 1865
Joseph Jenkins Hucks	"	March 9 /76
Hasford Walker	James H. & Mary A. Detyens	Aug. 16 /86
Anna Eliza	"	May 8 /84
Jennie Louise	Louis A. & Susan R. Butts	March 5 /86
LeGrand Guerry	LeG. G. & Katherine T. Walker	Dec. 2 /86
Elizabeth Warham	C. W. & F. C. Forster	Dec. 23, 1886
Paula Elizabeth	Walter & Jessie Minnie Hazard	Feb. 8, 1887

Date	Name & Place	Sponsors
Sept. 22, 1887	Percival Elma in private	S. M. Ward, Allard B. Flagg, Alice B. Flagg
Nov. 23, 1887	Oliver Perry Private, In extremis	
Jan. 26, 1888	Julian Dunbar Church	Walter Hazard, R. F. Dunbar, V. Douglass McQueen
Jan. 26, 1888	George Sparkman Church	B. H. Ward, R. S. Sparkman, Hattie B. Sparkman
March 3, 1888	Mary Bailey in private quite sick	Wm. H. Dorrill, Mary B. Wilburn, Sarah M. Taylor
March 11, 1888	Alice Elizabeth Church	Richard Dozier Jr., E. K. Dozier, Jr.
March 11, 1888	Robert Allston Church	Harriet H. Dozier
March 11, 1888	Harriet Gibbes Church	"
March 11, 1888	Kate Hampton Church	"
March 11, 1888	Lena May Church	Adult
March 11, 1888	Ruth Amelia Church	"
March 11, 1888	Hattie Wilbour Church	"
March 18, 1888	Allen Presbrey Church	Allen P. Hazard, Walter Hazard, Sarah F. Hazard

When Baptized	Sponsors	Place of Baptism
May 26, 1885	The Mother (Mrs. Caines)	Sick in bed
Oct. 18, 1885	Father & Mother	Church
Oct, 21, 1885	Witness: LeG. G. Walker	Sick in bed
Nov. 1, 1885	The Father, Rutledge Parker & Adrianna Congdon	Church
Dec. 27, 1885	Witnesses: Mrs. B. A. Munnerlyn & Mrs. R. O. Bourke	Church
Dec. 27, 1885	Witnesses: Mrs. B. A. Munnerlyn & Mrs. R. O. Bourke	"
Jan. 1, 1886	Mrs. B. Allston & Mr. & Mrs. LeG. Walker	"
Jan. 1, 1886	"	"
Jan. 1, 1886	Sponsors: Mrs. B. Allston & Parents	"
March 28, 1886	Mr. George Risley, Miss Aurelier Teasdale, D. Risley Jr.	At home
March 28, 1886	J. H. Wharton, Mrs. F. Fuller, Mrs. Merriman	Church
March 28, 1886	Mrs. E. J. Wilson, Miss A. Teasdale	"
March 28, 1886	B. I. Hazard Senr & Parents	At home
May 27, 1886	Witnesses: Mrs. Siau, T. W. Brightman	
June 14, 1886	Miss S. B. Wilson, Witness, & parent	At Home
June 14, 1886	" , Sponsor & Parent	"
Nov. 22, 1886	The Parents	at Home
Nov. 22, 1886		"
Nov. 22, 1886	Bird Dorrill, Mrs. Florence Rogerson, & Miss Susie Butts	"
Feb. 11, 1887	J. B. Steele, The Father & Mrs. C. V. Fraser by Rev. B. Allston at home	
Apr. 24, 1887	Mrs. M. T. Barton, Miss Minna Scott & J. D. Letcher	At church by Bishop Howe
Apr. 24, 1887	Parents and Florence A. Tamplet	At church by Bishop Howe

REV. STEWART MCQUEEN

Birth	Parents	Clergyman
June 24, 1887	S. M. & K. LeB. Ward B. I. Hazard S. F. Hazard	
Oct. 24, 1887	S. & V. D. McQueen	Rev. John Kershaw
Oct. 25, 1887	B. H. & J. McC. Ward	
Dec. 6, 1887	Louis A. Butts, Susan R. Butts	
July 2, 1873	John F. & R. H. Dozier	
Jan. 9, 1876	"	
May 21, 1880	"	
Jan. 10, 1883	"	
Nov. 26, 1869	B. I. & S. F. Hazard	
Apr. 28, 1872	"	
Oct. 23, 1874	"	
Dec. 2, 1887	A. P. & Alice B. Hazard	

Date	Name & Place		Sponsors
July 1, 1888	Julia Isabella	Church	James Y. & Julia Young
Oct. 14, 1888	Emily Fairfax	Church	Jno D. Letcher, prox. Sarah P. Gibbs, prox. Katie LaB. Ward
Dec. 30, 1888	LaGrande	Church	The Parents [Walker]
Apr. 21, 1889	Minnie Tamplet	Church	The Father, Sarah F. Hazard & Florence A. Tamplet
Mar. 10, 1889	Lucile Gould	Church	Allen P., Alice B. & Emily C. Hazard
May 26, 1889	Henry Donald	Church	T. M. (prox) & Mary L. Merriman
June 10, 1889	Herbert Lee	Church	G. E. T. Sparkman, David T. Smith, Ellen C. Anderson
July 9, 1889	John Saville	Church	Joseph B. Pyatt, Wm. Percy Smith, Elinor E. Smith
July 16, 1889	Joseph Morgan	At Home	The Parents
Sept. 22	Olive Caroline	Church	George A. & Eunice M. & Margaret L. Bush
Nov. 13	Herbert Lee Smith		Adult
Nov. 13	Wm Percy Smith		Adult
Nov. 18	Mary		Charlotte D. Rush, Elizabeth K. Dozier, T. P. Bailey, M. D.
Dec. 11, 1889	Nicholas		The Father & Fanny E. Springs
Jan 15, 1890	Bertha Marie	At Home	In Extremis
Jan. 20	William Harlee	At Home	The Father, Stephen F. Coachman, Mary Walter Heriot
Feb. 16, 1890	Hattie Leola (col)	At Home	Mary DesVerney, Peg Johnson, Stephen F. Tunno
Apr. 24	Katherine LaBruce	At Church	The Father, M. J. B. Fraser, Alice B. Hazard
May 22	Rosalie Sanders	At Home	Rosalie S. Sanders & Parents
June 3	Oswald Richard Krengel		Infant (in extremis)
June 22	Wm. Buck Wright		Infant (in extremis)
Sept. 23	James Logan	At Church	Amelia C. Tilton & Parents
Sept. 23	Robert Edwin	"	Jane A. Tilton & Parents
Sept. 23	George Congdon	"	Ella F. Tilton & Parents
Feb. 1, 1891	Frank Arthur	At Church	Walter, & A. P. & Sarah F. Hazard
Feb. 1, 1891	Jonathan Ingell	"	B. I. & Ruth A. Hazard & The Father
Feb. 1, 1891	Jonathan Ingell Hazard (adult)	At Church	
March 6	Fannie Joseph	at Home	Jonathan I. & Fannie Hazard
March 6	Luda Buck	at home	"
March 6	Paul Eve	"	G. E. T. & Julia Sparkman
March 16	Harriet Eleanor Pyatt	infant	in extremis
March 22	William Hasford	At church	Reid Whitford & Parents
April 12	Emma A. Twiggs (adult)	in Church	
April 12	Lucinda B. Gilbert (adult)	in Church	
June 7	Karl Benjamin	in Church	John H. Gould (prox), The Parents
Oct. 11	Julius Stewart	at Home	The Parents
Oct. 11	William Benjamin	"	The Parents
Jan. 17, 1892	Frederick Ford (at Dr. Bailey's)		Louise S. Jervey Edward H. Williams, Maria F. Jervey
May 15, 1892	Allen Rutledge	Church	Rev. Stewart McQueen, Arthur B. Flagg, Martha LaV. Flagg
May 15	William Henry	Church	S. M. Ward, W. Percy Smith, Elizabeth G. Matthews
May 26	Alberta	Church	George R. Congdon Jr., Fannie B. Sewell (by proxy), George A. Congdon

Birth	Parents	Clergyman
Dec. 7, 1887	Fritz & Lauretta J. J. A. Young	
May 8, 1888	C. W. & F. C. Forster	Stewart M. McQueen
Apr. 17, 1888	LeG. G. & Katherine T. Walker	"
Dec. 22, 1888	Walter & Jessie M. Hazard	"
Nov. 8, 1888	B. I. Jr. & Emily C. Hazard	"
March 30, 1889	Henry D. & Mary E. Potter	"
Apr. 29, 1889	Herbert L. & Rebecca W. Smith	"
Oct. 6, 1888	John S. & Elinor May Pyatt	"
June 13, 1889	James H. & Mary E. Detyns	"
June 20, 1889	Oliver A. & Inez Mary Bush	"
Oct. 2, 1889	Stewart & V. D. McQueen	Bp. Howe
	—	
Feb. 8, 1884	John N. & Hester H. Concklin	Stewart M. McQueen
Dec. 28, 1889	Henry C. A. & Marion Metzger	"
Dec. 24, 1889	Francis G. & Martha S. Coachman	"
Oct. 28, 1888	Benj. J. & Priscilla Tamplet	"
Dec. 1889	S. M. & K. LaB. Ward	"
Dec. 14, 1888	Wm. B. & Fannie M. McClellan	Stewart M. McQueen
Dec. 23, 1885	Thomas M. & Mary Louise Merriman	"
Dec. 7, 1887	"	"
July 23, 1890	"	"
Sept. 14, 1890	Allen P. & Alice B. Hazard	"
Nov. 20, 1890	Jonathan I. & Fanny Hazard	"
Aug. 19, 1886	Joseph A. & Margaret Twiggs	"
Dec. 27, 1885	Paul E. & Emma A. Twiggs	"
Dec. 17, 1887	"	"
	John S. & Elinor May Pyatt	"
Nov. 16, 1890	LeG. G. & Kate T. Walker	"
Apr. 6, 1891	B. I. (Jr.) & Emily C. Hazard	"
Sept. 12, 1891	John A. & Martha S. McInnes	"
Feb. 22, 1891	William B. & Fanny M. McClellan	"
Sept. 17, 1890	Louis Laval & Ella Hume Williams	"
Oct. 8, 1891	S. Mortimer & Kate LaB. Ward	"
Sept. 16, 1891	Herbert L. & Rebecca W. Smith	"
June 6, 1891	Wm. B. & Mary Alston Wright	"

Date and Place	Names	Birth Place
Christmas 1892 at 11 A M the Church	Ruth Hattie Howard	Georgetown, SC Sept. 20, 1892
In the Church, March 8, 1893, 12:15 AM in Lent	Pearl Merriman	Georgetown, SC Sept. 10, 1892
In the Church, Friday AM, March 17, 1893	James Albert Conckling	Georgetown, SC Born 1892
In the Church, Mar. 22, 1893, Wed. in Lent	May Allston Pyatt	Born July 26, 1892 Georgetown, SC
In the Church, Friday, April 21, 1893, 2d week after Easter	Charles Leroy Young	Georgetown, SC June 1, 1892
In the Church, Monday after 4th Easter Sunday, May 1, 1893	Lily Beaumont Hazzard	Asheville, NC Oct. 13, 1892
Saturday, Dec. 9th 1893., Georgetown His Home died '93	George Reynolds Congdon	Born May 1839 Georgetown, SC
Friday, Dec. 22d, 1893, Mr. Lucas house died '93	Anna Maria Lucas	Whites Bridge, July 25, 1893 Georgetown, SC
At Mrs. Tucker's Feb. 26, 1894	Charles Delamer Rosa	Georgetown SC, Mrs. Tucker's Jan. 12, 1894
The Church, June 1, 1894	Joshua Ward	Georgetown, SC Jan. 22, 1894
Walker home July 16, 1894	Mary Walker died 94	July 15, 1894 Georgetown, SC
Dec. 28, 1894 Holy Innocent	Lula Mary Doar	Sept 24, 1894 near Georgetown
In Church, Jan. 18, 1895, Friday after 1st Sunday after Epiphany	Charlotte Josephine Pyatt	Georgetown, SC
Church, Conversion of St. Paul, Jan. 25, 1895 died May 3, 1896	Desdemona Merriman	Georgetown, SC
May 9th 1895 Mr. Hazard's house died July '95	Hattie Gwendolyn Hazard	Georgetown, SC Oct. 11, 894
Mr. Emerson's house March 31, 1895, 5th Sunday in Lent	William Clarkson Johnstone	Georgetown, SC March 7, 1895
South Island at Mr. Rosa's house or the little Chapel, July 30, 1895	Charles Weston Rosa	Santee Apr. 22, 1895
Monday, Aug. 12, 1895, Mr. Young's house	Milly Hilton Young	Georgetown, SC Apr. 25, 1895

Parents	& Sponsors	Signature
Jonathan Ingell Hazard Fannie Wright Hazard	Ruth A. Hazard, Mary Allston Wright, William B. Wright, Aunts & uncle of the child	Jno. B. Williams, Rector
Thos. M. Merriman & Mary Louise Merriman	Congregation, Mrs. Congdon, Mrs. Smith	"
John N. Conckling Hester A. Conckling (dead)	Mrs. Ward, Mrs. Conckling, Grandmother	"
Jno. S. Pyatt & Eleanor Smith Pyatt	Herbert L. Smith & Julia C. Smith Mrs. Harleston Read	"
Fritz Young & Laura B. Young	Annie Young, present, sister	"
Elliott W. Hazzard & D. B. Hazzard	Emily T. Hazzard, S. B. Hazzard & Harry A. G. Abbe	"
	Mrs. Congdon, Bertha and Willie were the only persons present	"
E. M. Lucas Mrs. E. M. Lucas		"
Chas. Weston Rosa & Eliza Sparkman Rosa	Franz D. Rosa, W. Ervin Sparkman Sarah Allen Tucker	"
S. M. Ward & K. LaB. Ward	Parents & Sponsors	"
LeGrand Walker & Kate T. Walker		Baptized by Mr. Walker Jno. B. W.
Marion Elias Doar Mary Eleanor Doar		Jno. B. Williams
Jno. Saville Pyatt & Eleanor May Pyatt	Victoria S. Nowell Rebecca Green Smith	"
Thos. M. Merriman & M. L. Merriman	Mrs. Gilbert and Lester Johnson	Jno. B. Williams
A. P. Hazard A. B. Hazard		"
William Henry Johnstone & Elise Moore Johnston	Mrs. H. Johnstone, Henry Schultz Burdon, Mary Johnstone Penniman	"
Charles Weston & Eliza Stark Rosa	Mrs. J. W. LaBruce, E. B. Sparkman, C. W. Rosa	"
Fritz Young & L. J.Young	Private	"

PRINCE GEORGE WINYAH RECORDS 1815-1916

Date and Place	Names	Birth Place
Church at 4 PM Nov. 29, 1895	Catherine Mary Whitton	Camfimas, Les Pattlo, Brazil Jan. 16, 1888
Easter Tuesday, Apr. 7, 1897, The Church at 12 AM	Ellen Grier Smith •	Georgetown, SC Dec. 17, 1895
Sunday, 6 PM, 5th Sun. after Easter, May 10, 1896, Episcopal Church	Allan McPherson Hamby	Georgetown, SC Nov. 21, 1895
Aug, 2, 1896, 6 PM 9 after Trinity, at Mr. Detyens House	Julian Henning Detyens	July 22, 1896 at home in the country
Dec. 29, 1896 House out of town	Elias Marion Doar	July 12, 1896 in Country, near town
Dec. 30, 1896 At Home	Edward Nowell Pyatt	Whites Bridge, SC May 6, 1896
March 19, 1897, Home in the Country, 6 miles on Black River	Isabel Elliott Hazard	July 27, 1896 Asheville, NC
Wed. March 24, 1897 Church	Charles William Bailey	Georgetown, SC Dec. 17, 1896
Easter, April 18, 1897, The Church	Frances Conyers Smith	Sept. 25, 1896 Sumter, SC
Easter at the Church, 18 Apr. 1897	Mary Alston Wright	Memphis, Tenn. Sept. 16, 1895
Church, Sept. 3, 1897, 6 PM Friday	Grace Elizabeth Hawkins	July 4, 1897 Georgetown, SC
The Church, Jan. 28, 1898, after 3d Epiphany	Alva Waldo Young	Jan. 5, 1897 Georgetown, SC
4th Sunday after Easter, 1 PM Church, May 8, 1898	Alice LaBruce Ward	Nov. 27, 1897 Georgetown, SC
Trinity Sunday, 1898, June 5th 6 PM Home	Mary Elizabeth Hamby	Georgetown, SC Apr. 26, 1898
Church, Sept. 27, 1898	Maria Laval Williams Bailey	Georgetown, SC 1898

Parents	& Sponsors	Signature
T. C. Whitton & Mary Hamworth Whitton		Jno. B. Williams
Herbert L. Smith and Ellen Grier Smith	Mrs. Jno. Pyatt and Hess Smith, sponsors	John Bryan Williams
Allen McP. Hamby & Mary Sparkman Hamby	Emma H. Sparkman, Rob. S. Sparkman Thos. B. Hamby	"
James H. Detyens, & Margaret Selby Detyens	Mrs. Selby, the grandmother was present	"
Elias Marion Doar Mary Eleanor Doar		"
John S. Pyatt Eleanor May Pyatt	Miss Esther H. Smith (Aunt) S. M. Ward	"
Mrs. Liby Johnstone Hazard	Mr & Mrs. Gardner Penniman, uncle & aunt Dr. Westry and Mrs. Alice Battle, Asheville	
Charles Williams Bailey and Dalton Whitford Bailey	Reid Whitford, Thos. P. Bailey, Jr. Mrs. T. P. Bailey	Bishop Capers
Mrs. W. Percy Smith and Mary Bossard	Mrs. Freeman, Mrs. John S. Pyatt, H. L. Smith	Jno. B. Williams
W. B. Wright and M. A. Congdon Wright	Mrs. A. S. Congdon, Mrs. Jno. S. Bull, Geo. N. Congdon, Jr.	John Bryan Williams
J. W. Hawkins & Kate Hawkins	Mrs. Grace Waddell & Eliza Waddell Gilbert Johnson Wilmington, NC	"
Fritz and Laura Young		"
S. M. Ward & Kate LaBruce Ward	Anna P. Waring, M. Hannahan Sponsors: Emily Fraser	"
Allen McPherson Hamby & Mary Eliza Tucker Sparkman Hamby		"
Charles Williams Bailey & Joanes[?] Dalton Whitford Bailey	David Bailey, Olivia Williams & Mary Laval Bailey	Rev. L. F. Guerry

BY REV. GEO. H. JOHNSTON, D. D., RECTOR

Names	Parents Names	When born
Peter Kieffer	Robert W. and Dorothy Vaux	Nov. 3, 1897
David Thomas	Adult	
Clara Bates	Herman and Georgia Bryan	Jan. 16, 1889
Laura Lane	"	June 14, 1892
Hugh Lawson	Hugh Lawson & Etta White Oliver	Mar. 12, 1899
Charles Douglas	Albert Adams & Maura Morris Springs	Nov. 24, 1898
Henry Smith	John Saville & Eleanor May Pyatt	Oct. 1, 1898
William Sparkman	James M. & Christena C. Nettles	July 15, 1899
Elizabeth Edmonston	" twins	July 25, 1899
Alice Marie	Edward C. & Alice Elizabeth Haselden	Dec. 29, 1899
Henry Mortimer	John & Pauline T. LaBruce	Dec. 8, 1899
Edie Francis	Nelson and Mary Frances Cooper	Aug. 6, 1900
Eleanor Clyde	E. Marion & Mary Eleanor Doar	Sept. 28, 1900
Julia Bossard	John S. & Elinor May Pyatt	Feb. 27, 1900
Bertha Lauretta)	Elhanan Victor & Anna E. Emerson	Aug. 23, 1899
-------)	Adult Elhanah Victor Emerson	Mar. 23, 1871
Hugh Lawson Oliver		
Leone Colclough Bacon	David Thos. & Chevine C. Smith	Feb. 16, 1900
Gilbert Lester	John Benjamin & Georgia Skinner	Mar. 19, 1898
Benjamin	William Wilson & Lucy M. Munnerlyn	Sept. 16, 1901
Buford Colclough	David Thomas & Leonie Colclough Smith	Sept. 7, 1901
Margaret Elizabeth	Albert Adams & Maude M. Springs	July 10, 1901
Elizabeth	LeGrand G. & Julia Tull Walker	June 4, 1902
Edwin Rowlinski	Edwin Theodore Siau and Gertrude	May 2, 1896
Theodore	"	Oct. 26, 1902
William Chisolm	Elliot M. and Henrietta Lucas	Sept. 27, 1887
Eloise Perry	Schuyler and Adelaide Perry Hazard	Feb. 24, 1900
Thomas		
Shepherd		
Daggett		
Katherine Parkhill	Hugh W. & Katherine Parkhill Fraser	Jan. 14, 1902
Virginia Bernice	Edward and Alice E. D. Haselden	Sept. 19, 1902
John Percival	John & Pauline T. LaBruce	Nov. 3, 1902
Harry Lum	Henry and Rosa Lum	Mar. 3, 1903
Louise)	Arthur O. & Mary Katharine Johnson	Sept. 14, 1901
Pauline)	"	
Kathryn)	"	Nov. 20. 1902
Florence)		
Marjorie Lilian	Abram J. & Lilly A. Slocum	Feb. 13, 1901
Myrtle Josephine (Adult)	Frederick Wm. & Sousan Young	Nov. 17, 1888
Frederick Tulis	Nelson & Mary F. Cooper	Dec. 2, 1903
Henrietta Hunt	Hugh L. & Etta W. Oliver	Nov. 13, 1901
LeRoy Henning	E. Marion & Mary E. Doar	Dec. 15, 1902
Jessie Theodosia Butler	Adult, wife of Isaac Butler	July 7, 1863
LeRoy Henry	"	Apr. 20, 1888
Jessie Theodosia	"	Mar. 21, 1890
Hugh Wilson	Hugh Wilson & Katharine Parkhill Fraser	Feb. 4, 1904
Ruth De Wolfe	Allen McPherson & Mary Eliza Hamby	Sept. 23, 1903
Walter Baer, Jr.	Walter Baer Johnston & Mary his wife	
John Tull	La Grand G. & Julia Tull Walker	June 17, 1904

When Baptized	Sponsors	Place
Mar. 14, 1899	Mary E. V. Whitford, Edgar S. Vaux	Church
Mar. 19, 1899	Mrs. Eleanor M. Smith (mother)	Church
Apr. 2, 1899	Mrs. E. V. White	Church
Apr. 2, 1899	"	"
May 28, 1899	James Harrison Oliver and Ormsby Pickney Bourke	Church
June 4, 1899	Mr. H. B. Jerrett, N. C., Mr. P. R. Lachicotte, Miss L. D. Morris, N. C.	Church
Oct. 18, 1899	J. Boykin Hayward and Edward P. Guerard	Church
Sept. 28, 1899	Mr. Waring & Dr. W. E. Sparkman By Rev. F. Guerry, Private	
Nov. 6, 1899		Private
Apr. 8, 1900	Grand Parents	Private
May 27, 1900	Rev. L. F. Guerry & H. M. Manigault	By Rev. Guerry, Private
Mar. 7, 1901	Mr. and [Mrs.] Foxworth	Private
Mar. 12, 1901	Grand Mother & Aunt	Private
Apr. 7, 1901	Cath. Ward Pyatt & Lena Colclough Smith	Church
Apr. 18, 1901	The Parents	by Rev. L. F. Guerry
Apr. 18, 1901		Private
Apr. 18, 1901	(Adult) Wife & Mrs. O. P. Bourke	Church
June 16, 1901	Leonie Colclough Smith & Emma B. Colclough	Private
Dec. 13, 1901	Gilbert & Ella Johnson	Private
Dec. 22, 1901	Benj. A. & Jennie Munnerlyn	Church
Mar. 30, 1902	Wm. Percival & Esther Smith	Private
June 15, 1902	Jno. I. & Mrs. Hazard, Mrs. W. E. Sparkman	Private, ill
Oct. 12, 1902	LeGrand G. Walker, Julia Tull Walker,, Miss Lizzie S. Tull	Church
Oct. 27, 1902	Parents and Mrs. Rowlinski	Private
Oct. 26, 1902	Dr. Black and Mrs. Rowlinski	Private
Nov. 11, 1902	Parents	Private
Apr. 5, 1903	Mrs. Sarah F. Hazard & Parents	Church
Apr. 19, 1903		Church
	S. S. Fraser Sr., Mrs. R. C. Parkhill at Monticello Fla.	
Apr. 26, 1903	Grand Parents	Private
May 25, 1903	Dr. Wm. E. Sparkman and Mr. G. LaBruce Ward	Private
Aug. 9, 1903	Miss Anna M. Johnston, Walter Hazard and Mrs. J. Harleston Reed	Church
Mar. 30, 1904	Thos M. Merriman & Wife, Grand Parents	Church
Mar. 30, 1904	"	"
Feb. 28, 1904	The Sunday School	"
Mar. 27, 1904	Mrs. Gilbert Johnson & Mrs. T. P. Bailey	"
Feb. 25, 1904	Parents	Private
Feb. 7, 1904	Dr. C. W. Hunt & Wife & Miss Georgia A. Congdon	Church
Nov. 27, 1903	J. Walter Doar & Wife	Private
June 19, 1904	S. M. & Mrs. Ward, Mrs. Sara White Mrs. Katherine Fraser, Mrs. Reid Whitford	Church
June 19, 1904	"	"
June 19, 1904	"	"
June 26, 1904	James Hamilton Fraser and Miss Genevieve Parry Parkhill	Church
July 3, 1904	Ruth A. Hazard, Geo. Eugene Tucker	Church
Sept. 18, 1904	Geo. H. Johnston, Jr., & Elizabeth his wife	Private
Sept. 25, 1904	John Tull, M. D., & the Parents	Private

Names	Parents Names	When born
Mabel Farr	Edgar L. Lloyd & Maud Storrs Lloyd	Nov. 15, 1903
Leroy	Henry J. & Lula L. Thieker	July 26, 1904
Wm. Walter	John Walter & Elizabeth Doar	Apr. 14, 1903
Eugene W.	E. V. Weeks	June 19, 1872
Mary Congdon	John Edwards & Ruby May Taylor	June 25, 1904
Caroline Davies	Edwin N. & Ellen R. Wise	Nov. 26, 1904
Wm. Wilson	Wm. Wilson & Lucy Munnerlyn	Aug. 7, 1905
Mary Laval	J. F. & Mary McClure	Oct. 18, 1905
Edward Olin)	James Edward & Annie Gardner Ed Olin	9/ 26/ 04
Mary Cath.)		
Lily Ellison	Hugh W. & Kate Parkhill Fraser	Mar. 6, 1906
Lucy Tucker	John & Pauline T. LaBruce	Aug. 7, 1905
Theo. LaFayette	Theophilus L. & Mary P. Hyman	Nov. 7, 1905
Mabel Taylor	Samuel Sydney & Mabel Fraser	Apr. 4, 1906
Harry Stuckler	Harry S. & Bulah Shade	Aug. 15, 1906
Anna Catharine	Geo. H. & Elizabeth Johnston (Jr)	Dec. 4, 1905
Earnest Humes	Earnest Humes & Mildred Duvall	May 8, 1906
Eliz. Cheadell	Porter & Louise Nierusee	Oct. 7, 1906
Herman Douglas	Gustav Adolph & Kate Dozier Lohse	Apr. 6, 1905
John James	James Edward & Mary Anna Gardner	Jan. 14, 1907
Wm. H. Hollemen	Adult	
Virginia Doar	J. Walter Doar & Elizabeth B. Doar	Jan. 15, 1906
Virginia Bourke	Hugh L. & Etta White Oliver	July 30, 1904
Sarah McQuade	Robert M. Fruticher & Florence Fruticher	Nov. 10, 1907
Miriam Leota	Clement F. & Claudia H. Kent, child by adoption	Dec. 15, 1907
Marion Pearl	Arthur O. & Kate Johnson	Oct. 24, 1906
Jane Oliver	"	Apr. 5, 1908
Richard Parkhill	Hugh Wilson & Katharine Fraser	Aug. 13, 1908
Kath. Dozier	Gustav & Katharine Lohse	Nov. 11, 1908
Margaret Steadman	Robt. W. & Florence Hodges	July 20, 1909
Thos. Marion	Thomas Marion & Mary Gordon Merriman	May 8, 1908
Mary Gordon	Sponsors: Mr. A. O. Johnson & Dr. W. Gaillard	
Bapt. Jan. 25, 1910		Oct. 11, 1909
Samuel Mortimer	Mr. & Mrs. S. Mortimer Ward Jr.	Sept. 18, 1909
Susan Virginia	Mr. and Mrs. S. H. Young	
Hans Edward) Twins	Hans M. Chreshan	May 10, 1909
Edna Maria)	Ida Maria Prochnow	
Karl Edward		Oct. 24, 1910
Anita Frances	Gustavus Adolphus & Alma E. Anderson	Apr. 11, 1910
James Hamilton)	James Hamilton Fraser	Georgetown
Ellen Aldridge)	Harriet Gibson Fraser	
Francis Elliott	Francis Elliott Johnston- Eleanor Nicholson	Apr. 22, 1910
		Georgetown
Alice DeLancey	Arthur Middleton Parker - Julia Sturgon	Jan. 5, 1912
		Wilmington, NC
James Logan	James Logan Merriman	Feb. 11, 1912
	Florence Gordon	Georgetown
Elizabeth Deas	Fred. and M. Lucas Ford	Georgetown
Laura Elizabeth	L. & M. Riggs (one day old)	
Orrin Hickman	Orrin Elwood Anderson -Marie Lucille	Sept. 18, 1912
	(Removed) Wagner	

When Baptized	Sponsors	Place
Oct. 9, 1904	Edgar L. Lloyd & Mrs. L. Wayne Holmes	Church
Dec. 15, 1904	The Parents	Parents
Jan. 8, 1905	Capt. Black and Parents	Private
Dec. 26, 1904	Wife and Sister	Private
Oct. 22, 1905	Mrs. Geo. R. Congdon & Mrs. W. B. Wright	Church
May 7, 1905	Parents	"
Nov. 12, 1905	Mr. J. B. & Mrs. J. B. Hamby & Mr. J. C. Tamplet	"
Feb. 26, 1906	Dr. C. W. Bailey & Wife & Grand-mother Williams	"
Apr. 1, 1905		Private
June 10, 1906	Mrs. Reid Whitford & Walter Hazard	Church
May 4, 1906	Mrs. Thomas Prioleau & Jas. S. Hanahan	Private
May 13, 1906		Church
July 1, 1906	Grand-Parents	Private
Sept. 4, 1906	Chambersburg, Pa.	"
Sept. 16, 1906	Grandmother	Private
Oct. 7, 1906	Howard M. & Elise Duvall	Church
Oct. 15, 1906	Mary Vaux Whitford	Private
Oct. 23, 1906		Church
Jan. 21, 1907	Grandmother	Private
Feb. 13, 1907	Gilbert Johnson & wife	Church
Jan. 19, 1908	Capt. Black	Private
	Mrs. D. T. Pope, Miss Esther H. & W. Percy Smith	Church
June 21, 1908	Mrs. Guilbert Johnson, Anna M. Johnston	Church
June 30, 1908	Foster Parents	Private
Oct. 16, 1908	Janie Varnadoe & John M. Johnson	"
Oct. 16, 1908	Matilda P.Johnson & Logan Merriman	"
Jan. 17, 1909	James H. Fraser & Parents	Church
May 2, 1909	Mrs. E. C. Haselden & G. A. Lohse	"
Apr. 14, 1909	Parents & Margaret Hodges	Private
Jan. 5, 1911	Annie Nicholson. John LaBruce Ward	Church
Nov. 25, 1911	Eugene Gordon Campbell	
Nov. 25, 1911	Parents Employees of Des. Je[?] Temporarily in harbour	Home
Nov. 25, 1911	Rees F. Fraser, John A. Gibson, M. D.	Church
Apr. 15, 1911	Mrs. H. W. Fraser	
	Hugh W. Fraser, Minnie T. Hazard, Winnie T. Bowie	Church
Jan. 31, 1912	Lillian Lee Nicholson. T. Cordes Lucas	Home
Apr. 1, 1912	A. Dehon Trapier, Mary Taylor Parker	Church
	Frank Parker, U. S. A.	
Apr. 16, 1912		Church
Feb. 2, 1913	Dr. Gaillard, Mrs. Helen LaBruce	Church
Apr. 1, 1913	Norma Sharkey. At point of death	Private
Apr. 1, 1913	L. Marvin Overton, Oliver Emmet Hickman	Private
	Mrs. E. B. Anderson	
Apr. 22, 1913	Mrs. Josephine Simmons, Wayne Darlington	Private
June 2, 1913	Albert Rhett Nicholson	
	Isabelle F. Johnstone, Olive Penniman	

Names	Parents Names	When born
Lillian Lee)	Francis Elliott Johnstone	
Albert Nicholson)	Eleanor Nicholson	Apr. 29, 1913
Ruby Violet	Joseph Jenkins Hucks Cains	July 15, 1899
Bertha Ray	Ida McCormick	Nov. 12, 1900
Joseph Jenkins Hucks		Sept. 18, 1908
William Coleman	Henning W. & Annie B. Boney Young	July 5, 1913
George Thomas	George Thomas and Katharine Osborn DeVeaux	Jan. 10, 1912
Morgan Preston Moorer	Morgan Preston Moorer- Mary Eva Walker	
Elwood Talbird Anderson	Orrin Elwood Anderson, Lucile Hucks	Aug. 28, 1913
John Charles Tamplet	John Charles Tamplet - Pauline LaBruce	Nov. 18 1914
Shirley Elizabeth Lohse	Gustav A. - Katherine Dozier Lohse	July 5, 1914

Names	Parents Names	Born
Boyt		
Priscilla Gardner	John Boyt, Blanche Eliason	Wilmington, Del. Jan. 17, 1914
Arthur Middleton	Arthur Middleton Williams, Katharine LaBruce Ward	Sept. 14, 1914
Hucks		
May 9, 1915		
Ora Belle	Herbert Michel & Ora Belle Hucks	Jan. 12, 1915
Duffy	Robert Lee and Mary Biddle Duffy	May 26, 1914
Rosa Biddle		
Gardner		
Dorothy Edna	Edward Gardner, Annie Concklin	June 1913
Helen Vivian		Aug. 2, 1915
Holmes Courtney	Harvey Lafayette Gardner Alice Springs Gardner	Georgetown, S. C. Feb. 16, 1916

PRINCE GEORGE WINYAH RECORDS 1815-1916

When Baptized	Sponsors	Place
Aug. 31, 1913	North Island	Private
Dec. 25, 1913	Mrs. Caddie Fraser, Mr. C. A. Boney Fritz Young	Private
May 26, 1912	Mr. and Mrs. J. V. Croskeys	Church
Jan. 18, 1914	Annie E. Ford, G. T. Ford	
March 25, 1914	Ralph Nesbit, James Rose Parker, Sue Roberson Lee	Church
	Clement F. Kent, Annie Laurie Hucks	Private
Dec. 31, 1914	Walter Hazard, Paul H. Tamplet, Elizabeth C. LaBruce	Private
Nov. 22, 1914	Alice E. Haseldon, Cornelia B. Gardner	Private

When Baptized	Sponsors	Place
May 24, 1914	Mr. & Mrs. J. Frank Eliason, Mrs. John T. Boyt	Church
Dec. 27, 1914	J. LaBruce Ward, Margaret Middleton Williams, Alice LaBruce Ward, W. C. Wilbur	Church
May 9, 1915	George R. Congdon, Ruby Congdon Brooks, Cora Oglesby	Private
July 20, 1915	Very sick child	Private
Jan 30, 1916		Church
Jan 30, 1916		
Apr. 22, 1916	Holmes B. Springs, Douglas Louis Morris, Mrs. Emma S. Lachicotte	Private

CONFIRMATIONS

[Confirmations prior to 1881 are interspersed with the baptisms in the appropriate years. They have been placed together here for convenience.]

Persons confirmed at the visitation of the Right Reverend Bishop Dehon, Sunday November 17 [1816]: Dr. George Ford, Mrs. Sarah Ford, Mr. Samuel Isaac Thurston, Miss Sarah Taylor, Miss Mary Broderick.

Additional names of persons confirmed by the Rt. Rev. Dr. Bowen Friday 8th April 1825 & omitted under the head of baptisms for that year. Rev Mr. Keith, James Keith, Mrs. Potter, Mrs. Briggs, Mrs. Pawls, Mr. Lester, Mr. Henning, Mrs. Porter, Miss Anna Brown, Miss Sarah Brown, Miss Charlotte Toomer, Miss Mary Toomer. Mrs. McKab. 13.

Colored Persons. Abram Wayne, Phillis Brown, Celia Cogdell, Lesett Brown, Mary Ann Brown. -- 5

Names of persons confirmed by the Rt. Revd. Nathaniel Brown on Friday 1st May 1829: Dr. Wm. Prior, Mrs. Martha Prior, Thos. L. Shaw, Mrs. Nannette Shaw, Mrs. Mary Walker, Erasmus B. Rothmahler, Miss Martha Thomas, Miss Eugenia Thomas, Mrs. Sarah B. Carr, Mrs. Mary S. Gallevant, Miss Elizabeth Gallevant, Mrs. Rumney, Mrs. Anna Hall, Miss Sarah Carr, Miss Evelina Allston.

Names of Persons confirmed by the Rt. Revd. Nathaniel Bowen, D. D., Bishop of the diocese on Sunday, 8th April 1832. Mrs. Sands, Miss Laura Smith, Miss Emma Thomas, Miss M. P. Gallivant, Miss Sarah Ann Briggs. 5

Colored Persons: Thomas, Scipio, Beetie, Jean, Frederick, Moll, Jack, Phebe, Annie Charles. 10

Names of Persons confirmed by the Rt. Revd. Nathaniel Bowen, D. D., Bishop of the Diocese on Sunday, 4th May 1834. John Gough North, Mrs. Hannah Ford, Jas. G. Henning, Miss Martha E. Henning, Miss Ann Eliza Shackelford, Miss Sarah Jane Shackelford, Miss Elizabeth Dunbar. 7

Colored Persons: Elias, Sary, Betty, Betsey, Grace. 5

April 13, 1841. Confirmed in private Revd. Messrs Howard & Lance being present, Dr. William Allston, by Rt. Rev. C. E. Gadsden, D. D.

April 18, 1841. Names of Persons confirmed by the Rt. Rev. C. E. Gadsden in Prince George Winyah, Miss Maria Miller, Miss Sarah Smith, Miss Sarah Ford, Miss Sarah E. W. Carr, Miss Mary Lester, Miss Frances Vernon, Miss Sarah Henning, Miss Hannah Porter, Miss S. McCollough, Mrs. Jones, Thomas Henning, Toomer Porter. (No. 12)

April 18, 1841. Colored Persons. Peter Tyall, Ann Allston, Lucy Carr, Harriet Johnson, Simon Carr, Jane Tunno, Jack Pich, Betsy Mitchell (No. 8). Total 20.

Names of persons confirmed by Rt. Rev. C. E. Gadsden, D. D., Bishop of the Diocese, April 6, 1845. Mrs. McWilliams. Persons of color: Harry, Charleston, Binkey.

Confirmed by the Bishop of the Diocese, April 28, 1847. Messrs. J. M. Atkinson & J. J. Dickison, Mrs. Wilmot, Mrs. B. A. Coachman, Miss Atkinson & Miss Ella Christian.

Confirmation April 11th 1849 by B. P. Gadsden. Mr. Benjamin King, Miss Maria F. Ford, Miss Georgiana Ford & Miss Anna Maria Ford.

Confirmed by B. P. Gadsden, March 23, 1851, at the Parish Church. Mrs. Hasford Walker, Mrs. Richard Dozier, Mrs. Peter Goddard, Mrs. Henry Heriot, Miss Sarah E. Prior, Miss Mary B. Atkinson, Mr. B. A. Coachman, Mr. William McNight.

Confirmed by B. P. Davis, Apr. 16, 1854: Mrs. W. W. Shackelford, Mrs. R. O. Bush, Mrs. Merriman, Miss A. E. Atkinson, Miss Virginia Thomas, Mr. Jos Johnso, & Mrs. Paul Tamplet.

Colored persons Silva Carr, Cretia McFall, Ella Carr, Rachael Carr, Lyida Parker, Martha Lewis, Mary Jackson, Hagar Brodut, Lavinia Carr, Catharine Brown, Ambro Vereen, Adam Dunmore, Thos Jefferson, Alonzo Jackson, Ned Green, George Mitchell.
Confirmed by B. P. Davis, April 5, 1855: Mr. Jno. F. Pyatt, Miss Josephine Prior, Miss Ann Elisa Prior, whites. Prince Pyatt, Louisa Car, Judy Waterman & Jane Moultrie, colored.

Mr. Jos. B. Pyatt & his wife were confirmed on Waccamaw Ap. 1 1855 by my consent. They were there on a visit at the time. R. T. H.

Confirmed by B. P. Davis, April 19, 1856: A. T. Atkinson & wife, in private. Mr. A. I. Shaw, April 20, 1856 in Church. Colored: Phillis Pyatt & John Ford.

Confirmed by B. P. Davis, March 18, 1857: Dr. John A Grant, Mrs. Martha Grant, James Rees Ford & Dr. R. G. White.

Confirmed by B. P. Davis March 28, 1858: Mrs. John Tamplet & Miss Orianna Sinclair.

Confirmed by B. P. Davis, Apr. 9, 1859: E. Simmons Lucas Junor, Miss Margaret Ford, Misses Eliza & Alice Ford, & Mrs. Paul Fitssimons. Israel (col) belonging to Mrs. B. Trapier.

Confirmed, March 19, 1861: Mrs. Isabella Cheves, Mrs. E. Leighton, Miss Alicia Middleton, Miss Emily Henning, Miss Anna Parker. Coloured: Tisby Knights, by B. P. Davis.

Confirmed by Bp. Davis on May 2, 1866: R. O. Bush, A. Glenine Heriot, Anna Glen Heriot, Charles W. Forster, Mary W. Forster, Mrs. McCusker, Mrs. Dorrill, Mrs. Eden, Elizabeth M. Smith, Eliza Stoney, Annie Stoney, A. Elizabeth Sparkman, Pamela Sparkman, Martha Pyatt, Eliza Heriot, Anna Ford, Clara Ford, Mrs. Stockman, David Risley, Mrs. Rilsey, Miss Risley. Colored: Marianna Screven, Anne Davis.

Confirmed by Bishop Tho. F. Davis, D. D., May 3, 1868: Benjn H. Wilson, Wm. Prior White, Mrs. R. O. Bush, Agnes R. Haig, Francis Forster, Julia Forster, Mrs. Jacobs, Hesse H. Prior, Anne Ford, white. Minda Simmons, col.

Confirmed by Bp. Thos. F. Davis, D. D., April 10, 1870: James Divine, Mrs. Divine, Mrs. Ellis, Catherine V. White, Hannah E. Harral, Mrs. Springs, Emily R. Parker, Clara Tamplet, Susan R. Dorrel.

Confirmed by Bp. W. B. W. Howe, D. D., February 2, 1873: Jessie Minnie Tamplet, Alice Bonneau Tamplet, Penelope Bentley Pyatt, Mrs. Emma Matilda Carr, Julia Lawrence Waldo, Cornelia Waldo, Rebecca Dennis. February 4 in private, Mrs. Charlotte Trapier. February 18 in private, Mrs. Maria Elizabeth Vernon.

Confirmed by Bishop W. B. W. Howe, April 19, 1874: Warren Atkinson, R. Lovat Fraser, Alice Forster, Catharine A. Ford, Emma Elizabeth Springs, Mrs. Sarah Haenel, Mrs. Sarah A. Blackwell.

Confirmed by Bishop W. B. W. Howe, D. D., Dec. 12, 1875: Emilie Bonneau Atkinson, Mary Julia Atkinson, William Henry Felker, Mrs. Ella Eugenia Anderson, Mrs. Mary Louiza Merriman, Mary Ann Robinson, Eliza Stark Heriot, Florine Sibyl Rembert, Moses L. Dorrill, Ella Atkinson, Hannah Mary White, John Haenel, Mrs. Mary Ann Detyens, Anna Eliza Detyens, Kothena Carolina Ferril, Mary Elizabeth Heriot, Mary Dorrill. Dec. 13, in private: Sarah Lucretia Ferril.

Confirmed by Bishop W. B. W. Howe, D. D., April 1, 1877: Wm. Henry Dorrill, John White Tuttle Dorrill, Francis Forster Gilmore, Madora Isabella Gilmore, Rutledge Parker, Mary Etta Jacobs, Mary Walter Heriot, Little Adelle Tilton.

Confirmed by Bishop W. B. W. Howe, D. D., March 9, 1879: Mrs. Concklin, Mrs. Catherine T. Walker, Elizabeth Fitzsimons, Hester Ellis, Mary Shaw

Confirmations by Rt. Rev. W. B. W. Howe.

Clergyman in Charge: Benj. Allston

April 10, 1881	Mary Alston Congdon	in Church
"	Mary M. Ford	"
"	Mary M. Haig	"
"	Jane Anne Tilton	"
"	Robert E. Fraser	"
"	Wilson Miller	"
"	George LaBruce	"
"	John Nicholas Concklin	"
"	Mrs. Adrianna Congdon	"
April 11, 1881	Mrs. Maria L. W. Bailey	in private

Clergyman in Charge: J. W. Keeble

April 2, 1882	James R. Parker	In Church
	Eleanor May Smith	"
	Esther Holbrook Smith	"
	Mary Eveline Wallace	"
	Annsley Tucker (col)	"

April 15, 1883	Mrs. Ann E. Ehney	In Church
"	Mrs. Julia J. Anderson	"
"	Miss Sallie B. Wilson	
"	Miss Anna J. White	
"	Mrs. Anna Jane Munnerlyn	
"	Miss Julia C. Smith	"
"	Mrs. Rosa Murrel (col)	
"	Miss Clara O. Elliot	

July 27, 1884	Benjamin A. Munnerlyn	"
"	Walter Hazard	
"	John S. Pyatt	
"	Elizabeth M. Rouquie (Mrs.)	"
"	Eugenia A. holsenbach (Mrs.)	"
July 30, 1884	Byrd Dorrill	in private

| Jany /85 | James Divine, restored to com'n | |

| Mar 28 /86 | Laura C. Bowley (Mrs) (col) | In Church |

April 24th, 1887	Mary Elizabeth Detynes, Miss	"

April 8, 1888	Thomas P. Bailey, Jr.	Church
"	Robert S. Bailey	"
"	Mary L. Bailey	"
"	Eunice M. Bush	"
"	Alice E. Dozier	"
"	Eliza E. Fraser	"
"	Benj. I. Hazard, Sr.	"
"	Sarah F. Hazard	"
"	Allen P. Hazard	"
"	Lena M. Hazard	"
"	Ruth A. Hazard	"
"	Hattie W. Hazard	"
"	Emily C. Hazard	"
"	Elliott W. Hazzard	"
"	Anna R. Heriot	"
"	William A. James	"
"	Mary T. Parker	"
"	Mary E. Rembert	"
"	Victoria Smith	"
"	Mary E. Ward	"
"	St. John P. Ellis	In Private

Nov. 17, 1889	Henrietta W. Bourke	In Church
"	Mary M. Bush	"
"	Benj. I. Hazard, Jr.	"
"	Annie J. Munnerlyn	"
"	Emma A. Munnerlyn	"
"	Herbert L. Smith	"
"	Rebecca W. Smith	"
"	Wm. Percy Smith	"
"	Ida L. Smith	"

Clergyman in Charge at time of the above Confirmations: Rev. Stewart McQueen.

April 12, 1891	Julia L. Allston	In Church
"	James H. Detyens	"
"	Lucinda B. Gilbert	"
"	Jonathan I. Hazard	"
"	Fanny Hazard	"
"	Emma A. Twiggs	"
"	William C. White	"

March 7, 1892	J. Harlseton Read	"
	Mary Helen Coachman	"
	Genevieve Maud McKinlay [stricken]	

Rt. Rev. Ellison Capers & Rev. John Bryan Williams

Dec. 10, 1893	George Reynolds Congdon	At Home
	William Prior Congdon	"
	Annie Estelle Young	Church, 11 AM
	Mary Catherine Merriman	"
	Florence Lester Bush	"
	Mary Eva Walker	"

	Virginia Caroline Walker	"
	Fannie Espeth Ferris	"
	Samuel Fraser	"
	Georgie Alberta Congdon	"
	Susan Lowndes Allston	"
	Gilbert Johnson	"
	Elzy Eveline Johnson	"
	Gilbert Lester Johnson	"

Apr. 30, 94 8 PM   David Bailey, 17 age   Church
Howard Sank Risley 15   "
Allen McPherson Hamby 21   "
John David Whitford 19   "
(Harriet Gibbes Dozier 15
(transferred to Trinity Ch Delaware, June 1st 1899
Sarah Freeborn Hazard 13   "
Annetta Detyens 12   "
Maria Williams Bailey   "

Feb 9, '96 11 AM   Mrs. J. H. Detyens 35   "
Dismissed Ap 26, '02
Catherine Ward Pyatt 31   "
Robert Vaux Read 15   "

March 24, 1897   William Wigg Hazzard Holmes   "
Richard Lowndes Allston   "
Bachman Doar   "
Catherine Bryant Hawkins   Gone to N.C.
Elizabeth Blanche Homer   Church
Ethel Walker   "

Apr. 8, '98   Arthur Williams Hamby
Transferred to Trinity, Co., S. C.
Henry Ravenel Lucas
John LaBruce Ward
Catherine Louize Walker
William Buck Sparkman
Dismissed Aprl. 1905 Died 1929

Rector in Charge at time of above confirmations: Jno. B. Williams.

Confirmations by Rt. Rev. Ellison Capers, D. D., Rev. G. H. Johnston, D. D. Rector

Sunday March 19th, 1899
11 AM   Herman Bryan
Reid Whitford Bryan
Thomas M. Merriman
Miss Emma Sparkman Ward
James Ritchie Sparkman
David Thomas Smith

1900, March 15   Mahan Ward Pyatt
Mrs. Laura J. Young
Henry William Young
Fritz Young
Holmes Buck Springs

James Sparkman Tucker
Miss Claudia Allen Tucker
George Eugene Tucker
Bently Douglas Ward
Charles Ellis Morris
Miss Mary Ann Eliza Concklin
Miss Paula Elizabeth Hazard
Rees Ford Fraser
Theodore M. Forgeson

1900 Dec. 2
1st Sunday in Advent

Mrs. Hugh Fraser
C. Harleston Read
Arthur O. Johnson

1901, Apr. 18th

Miss Elizabeth Sherwood Bryan
Minnie Tamplet Hazard
Agnes Jane Rouquie Dismissed to Rocky Mt., N. C.
Lilian Constance Tilton
Eleanor Joseph Petrie. Transferred, Feb. 7th, 1903, to
        St. Peter's, Brooklyn, N. Y.
Kate Hampton Dozier
Katharine Gardner
Sarah Lauretta Young
Lena Rebecca Young
George Reynolds Congdon
Mrs. Rosa Lohr Congdon
Hugh Lawson Oliver
Louis Laval Hamby
Maurice Springs
Robert Merriman
Elhanan Victor Emerson

1901, Apr. 26

Albert Adams Springs
William Freeman Morris
Charles Congdon
Mrs. Charles Congdon
C. Williams Bailey

1902 March 9th

Katharine LaBruce Ward
Julia Isabel Young
Mrs. Johnes Dalton Bailey

1903, Apr. 19th

Thomas Shepherd Daggett
Mrs. Clara Daggett
Miss Edna Daggett
Phillip Heller Arrowsmith
Geo. H. LaBruce
John Saville Pyatt
Miss Emily G. Doty
Herbert Lee Smith
Mrs. Hattie Brantom

May 15, 1904   Miss LeGrand Walker
Sunday AM   Miss Myrtle Josephine Young
                        Miss Lucile G. Hazard
                        Miss Hattie M. Sparkman
                        Nicholas Concklin

Jan. 28, 1906   Miss Mary Pender Hyman
Sunday   Miss Alberta Wright
                        Miss May Pyatt
                        Miss Theodosia Butler
                        Mrs. Julia Butler
                        Mr. Reid Whitford
                        Mr. St. Julian Lachicotte Springs
                        Mr. Johnathan Engell Hazard
                        Mr. Frank Arthur Hazard
                        Mr. Karl Benj. Hazard
                        Mr. Chas. Leroy Young
                        Mr. Geo. Congdon Merriman
                        Mr. Capers Gamewell Barr, Jr. Withdrawn Dec. 1903
                        Mr. Leroy Butler

Feb. 15, 1907   John G. Carraway By Rt. Rev. Bishop Strange, D. D.
Friday 8 PM   Bishop of N. C.
                        Isaac McG. Carraway
                        Miss Janie M. Carraway
                        Miss Elizabeth Carraway
                        William H. Hollemen
                        Mrs. William H. Hollemen
                        Wm. Henry Smith
                        Geo. Reynolds Congdon, Jr.
                        Allen Rutledge Ward
                        James Albert Ward
                        James Albert Concklin
                        Mrs. Herman Bryan

Apr. 29, 1907   Wm. Hasford Walker
Monday, 8 PM   John Johnston Hucks
                        Morgan Preston Moorer, M. D.
                        Miss Mabel Helen Young
                        John Walter Doar, Editor
                        Mrs. John Walter Doar
                        John Herman Carraway

Dec. 15, 1907 Rt. Rev. W. A. Guerry, D. D. Coadjutor

                        Cornelius A. Dorrill
                        John W. Dorrill, Jr.
                        Douglas L. Morris
                        Haskell Carraway
                        Herman Decatur Beckman, M. D.

Jan. 5, '09   Rt. Rev. W. A. Guerry, D. D.
                        Miss Lula Mary Doar
                        Wm. Wigg Hazzard Holmes

Dec. 12, '09   Rt. Rev. W. A. Guerry, D. D.

     Joshua Ward
     Julian Collins
     Delmar Rosa
     Mrs. Florence Marian Fruttiger
     Miss Charlotte Josephine Pyatt

The Fourth Sunday after Ephiphany
Jan. 28, 1912, by the Rt. Rev. Wm. A. Guerry, D. D.

     Helen Smith
     Mary Haselden
     Alice Ward
     Ruth Carraway
     Bertha Emerson
     Ernest Riggs
     Alvah Young
     Bertha Collins
     Peter August Lefoendall
     Lucy Munnerlyn
     Robert Hucks
     Mrs. Fred. Young

Third Sunday in Advent, Dec. 15, 1912. by the Rt. Rev. Wm. A. Guerry, D. D.

     Pack Cains
     Arthur Cains
     Ruth Cains
     Mrs. M. J. Cains
     Clarence P. Webber
     William E. Rosa
     Minnie Backman Doar
     Arthur LaBruce
     Edward N. Pyatt
     Pearl Merriman Adams
     Louis M. Young
     Henry S. Pyatt
     Wentworth F. Ford

The following list for 1914 is from the *Georgetown Times*, Dec. 3, 1914.
On November 29, 1914, the Rt. Rev. William Alexander Guerry, Bishop of the Diocese of South Carolina, confirmed the following persons, presented by Dean Percy Robottom, Rector, in the Church of Prince George, Winyah:

     Mrs. Arthur Parker
     Mrs. Frank Johnstone
     Mrs. Ida Julia Craven
     Helen Snow
     Annie Laurie Hucks
     Florida Kent
     Katherine Fraser
     Mary Perry
     Bernice Haselden
     Margaret Collins
     Francis Earl Davis
     Harold Rose Davis
     Frank Collins
     Lucas Ford
     Dewey Hathcock

Sunday next before Advent, Nov. 21, 1915. Rt. Rev. Wm. A. Guerry, D. D.

        Mariah Nash Hilliard
        Edith Waldo Webber
        [name stricken]
        Henrietta Hunt Oliver
        Eleanor Clyde Doar
        Louise Delemar Rosa
        Benjamin Munnerlyn
        Leroy Henning Doar
        James Richie Rosa
        William Walter Doar
        Virginia Bourke Oliver
        William Richmond Garrison

MARRIAGES

Marriages in 1816 by the Revd. Mr. Lance, Minister of Prince George's Winyaw.

Names of the Parties	Time	Place of Wedding
Octavius Cripps & Esther Allston Deliesseline	April 11	Charleston
John W. Shackelford & Elizabeth S. Tait	April 24	Georgetown
Stephen Ford & Hellin Walter	April 25	Black River, 6 miles from Georgetown
Thomas Loughton Smith Fraser & Isabella Wakefield	May 1	Charleston
John W. Cheesborough & Eliza Stone	Dec. 5	Georgetown

Marriages in 1817:

Marcus & Rose (free people)	April	Georgetown
Dr. Henry Denison & Hannah C. Waldo	May 14	Do
John Lewis & Sarah Williamson (free)	Dec. 25	Do
Guy, Servant of Mrs. S. Smith, & Amey, of Mrs. C. Allston	Dec. 28	Do

Marriages in 1818:

Joseph Sessions & Martha Mary Wilson	August 1	Georgetown
John Gordon & Jane M. Burgis	Nov. 19	Williamsburgh
Joseph W. Allston & Sarah Prior	Dec. 15	Georgetown
Dr. James Doughty & Sarah B. Pawley	Dec. 17	Do
Thomas C. Fay & Mary Broderick	Dec. 31	Do

Marriages in 1819:

Henry A. Middleton & Hariet Kinloch	Jan. 20	Kensington near G.T.
James C. Coggeshell & Margaret Prior	Jan. 28	Georgetown
Charles Munnerlyn & Hannah Shackelford	May 13	Do
John White, Captn. of Schr. Little Emily, & Jane Keyes	Nov. 8	Winyaw Bay
Francis Lance & Elizabeth Ball	Nov. 18	Charleston
James Mazyck & Nancy Mosely (people of color)	Dec. 16	Georgetown
John Porter & Esther Toomer	Dec. 16	Do

Marriages in 1820:

Isaac Carr & Sarah B. Wilson	May 18	Georgetown
John Shackelford & Mary Godfry	Dec. 19	Do in Church
George Baxter & Nancy Johnson (people of Color)	Dec. 21	Do

Marriages in 1821 by Maurice H. Lance, Rectr. Prince George Winyaw

Richard Nites & Susannah Mitchell (people of colour)	March 8th	Georgetown
William Burgis & Maria Peake	May 3d	Do
Nathaniel Roe & Mary Clarke	May 19th	Do
John Moultrie & Catherine Roe (people of colour)		Do
Henry Inglesby & Mary Scriven	May 29th	Black River
George Washington Egleston & Sophia Heriot	Dec 24	Black River

Names of the Parties	Time	Place of Wedding
1822		
William Jones & E. D. Croft	Jan. 24	Geo: Town
Theodore Gourdin, M. D. & Elizabeth F. Allston	March 26	Do
Banister Lester & Margaret McDowall	Apr. 18	Do
Dandy & Betsey, Slaves of Mr. Cuttino		
& Miss Allston	Dec. 21	Do
1823		
Henry Carrebau & Rachel Caps	March 12	Geo: Town
Moses Prince & Sarah Plum	Apr. 3	Do
Brasleman & C. M. Norman	May 11	Do
William Jones & Mary P. Allston	Dec.	Do
1824		
John Gough Lance, M. D. & Rosanna Troy	Feb. 23	Wadesborough, N.C.
Mingo (servant of Mr. Cuttino & Mary		
(servt. of Mrs. Cogdell	Feb. 17	Geo: Town
Shadrack S. Gasque, M. D. & Esther C. Rothmahler	March 4	Do
Stephen Ford, Senr. & Jane Cogdell Thurston	Apr. 8	Do
Charles Mayrant & Caroline Kinloch	May	Kensington
John Derrick & Ann Eliza Reed Mrs. (Doctress)	Nov. 21	Geo: Town
1825		
York & Herriet	Jan. 1	Do
Jim & Jannike	Jan. 8	Do
Anthony B. Shackelford & Elizabeth L. Law	Apr. 19	Black River
1826		
Alwin Ball & Esther McLennen by M. H. Lance	Jan. 24	Black River
George Mitchell & Margaret Collins		
(People of colour) by P. T. Keith	Feb. 9	North Santee
S. C. Ford & H. B. Wilson by P. T. Keith	Feb. 23	George Town
Peter W. Fraser & Mary A. Pawley by M. H. Lance	April XIth	Do
Mathias & Phoebe (people of color) by M. H. L.	Dec. 2	Do
1827		
Samuel Leger & Elizabeth E. Pitman	15 Feby	George Town
Joseph L. E. Eastering & Jane Alexander	15 Feby	George Town
Thomas G. Rice & Esther Ann Verner	11 Apr.	Waccamaw
Raphael Rembert & Elizabeth M. Bailey	12 Apr.	Santee
George Thomas Ford & Mary Warham Toomer	24 Apr.	Geo. Town
Joseph Johnston & Martha Rogers	22 May	George Town
Thos. Lynch Shaw & Nannette Walker	12 Dec.	George Town
Wm. J. Mauldin & Martha Louisa F. Colmar	12 Dec.	George Town
Shadrach Rice & Louisa Linirieux	20 Dec.	Waccamaw
1828 Paul Trapier Keith, Rector		
John Coachman & Charlotte A. Allson	Jan. 10	George Town
Dr. Wm. R. T. Priot & Martha Vaux	Jan. 26	Do
A. W. Dozier & Esther B. Gaillard	March 18	Santee
John Izard Middleton & Sarah McPherson Alston	March 24	Waccamaw
John Alexr Keith & Sarah Brown	Apr. 23	George Town
John Potts & Mary Smith	Apr. 24	Do
Absalom Beasly & Mrs. Sarah Gilchrist	Nov. 20	Do

Names of the Parties	Time	Place of Wedding
Francis Davis & Sarah M. Flint	Nov. 27	Do
George Calhoun Brown &		
Amanda Malvina Fitzallan Greaves	Dec. 20	Britton's Neck
		Marion District
Benjamin Green & Martha E. Marvin	Dec. 24th	George Town

1829

Anthony L. Mariano & Maria N. Church	Jan. 8	George Town
John M. Screven & Margaret P. Coggeshall	Feb. 14	Do
Elias I. Etheridge & Susan Gallevant	May 7	Do
Anthony W. Dozier & Mary C. Cuttino	Dec. 5	Do

1830   **Paul Trapier Keith, Rector**

Cuffee & Phibe (people of color)	Feb. 7	George Town
Peter Tryall & Louisa (people of color)	Feb. 11	Do
Thos. Boston Clarkson & Caroline Heriott	Feb. 25	Do
Will & Hester (people of color)	Dec. 22	Do

1831

Hugh Fraser Grant & Mary Elizabeth Fraser	Apr. 27	Pee Dee

1832 P. Trapier Keith, Rector

Edward Thomas & Mrs. Mary Walker	Apr. 3	George Town
Charles & Martha (col)		North Island

1833

Charles & Martha (col)	Jan. 12	George Town
Frederick & Sarah (col)	March 27	Do
Jas. M. Stanard (of Virginia) and Cleora Harvey	Apr. 3	Do
Benjamin H. King & Martha Caroline Westberry	May 8	Do
Anthony & Patsy (col)	Dec. 14	Do
Pope & Selina (col)	Dec 25	Do

1834

John Potts Ford & Elizabeth Mary Ann Vaux	Jan. 23	Sandy Island,
		residence of Capt. Vaux

1836

William J. Howard & Mary Malvina Westbury	March 10	Geo. Town
Michael Young & Hannah Baxter (free people of color)	March	Geo. Town
Henry Graddock & Sarah Gardiner (free people of color)	Apr. 20	Do
Joseph Michaud & Alithea Smith	Apr. 21	Do
Scipio & Binkey (col)		North Island
Donald L. McKey & Mary Jane Coachman	Nov. 16	George Town
Benjamin Christian & Sarah H. Mitchell	Dec. 25 Xmas	Do
William Hazelton & Elizabeth McNea	Dec. 26	Do

1837

Louis Bausman & Mrs. Ann Watta	June 1	Geo Town
Richard Lucas & Sarah Glenn (free col)	Dec. 7	Do
Charles & Eliza (col)	Dec. 27	Do

Names of the Parties	Time	Place of Wedding
1838		
Josiah Brown & Mary Lewis (col)		Geo Town
Levi G. S. Middleton & Mary Priscilla Gallevant	Jan. 31	Do
John W. Coachman & Mary Helen Ford	March 15	Black River
John Ralston & Elizabeth Dozier	March 29	Geo. Town
Charles Smith & Matilda Tucker	May 21	Geo. Town
William Sparkman & Elizabeth Burgess	Dec. 26	Black River
1839		
James Reese Ford & Martha Elizabeth Henning	Jan. 31	Geo. Town
Door ---- and ---- Harvey [Waverly?]		North Island

1841 Robert Theus Howard, Rector

John (slave of Mr. B. Allston) to	Jan. 12	George Town
Clarinda (slave of Miss Waterman)		
1842		
Dr. George Heriot & Mathilda Smith	Jan. 12	George Town
1843		
Dr. E. B. Brown & E. C. Porter	Feb. 15	Geo. Town
William & Camelia (col)	Feb. 20	Geo. Town
Jerry Pawley & Isabella Knight (free col)	Nov	Geo. Town
Benjamin A. Coachman & Caroline Ford	Dec. 13	Geo. Town
1844		
W. E. Richardson & Sarah Ann Mayrant	March 23	Dover Plantation
J. L. Dickison & Mary Margaret Lester	May 23	Geo Town
Dr. G. F. Lesesne & Hannah Porter	June 13	Geo Town
1846		
Aaron & Molly (col)	Jan	Geo Town
William H. Trapier & Charlotte Pyatt	Dec. 31	Kensington
1847		
Robert Fraser & Sarah McCollough	March 25	Geo Town
James S. Magill & Ella Christian	May 11	Geo Town
1848		
Anglo. T. Coote (England) & M. B. Watts (Ireland)	Jan. 25	Geo Town
John E. Allston & Regina Coachman	Feb. 16	Geo Town
1849		
G. N. Merriman & C. Logan	Feb. 18	In Church
Paul Wigfall (col) & Mildred Tunno (col)	March 21	Geo Town
David W. Richards & Elizabeth M. Leonard (col)	Apr. 25	Geo Town
William B. Steadman & Mary E. Goddard	Dec. 11	Geo Town
Thomas Allston & Anna Meyers (col)	Dec. 19	Geo Town
1850		
Richard T. Walker & Susan Sarah Howard	Jan. 24	Charleston, SC
1851		
James Smith & Eugenia Thomas	May 28	Church

Names of the Parties	Time	Place of Wedding
1852		
Robert H. Clarkson & Mary Charlotte Mayrant	Apr. 7	Dover
Richard G. White & Sarah E. Prior	Apr. 15	Church
A. Toomer Porter & S. Magdalen Atkinson	Dec. 16	Church
1853		
Professor Edward & Miss Matthews	Jan. 14	Privately
Jos. Parker & Lydia Allston (col)	Feb. 22	"
W. W. Shackelford & E. B. Ford	July 6	Church
1854		
Alosso Jackson & Molly Deas (col)	Feb. 15	Privately
Ned & Diana (slaves of Miss Brown& Mr. Porter)	March 15	"
D. S. Stocklin Jr. & Emma Munnerlyn	Aug. 9	"
Deas Wilson & Haga Beckman (col)	Sept. 3	Privately
1855		
Sam Johnson & Louisa Carr (col)	March 14	Privately
A. J. Shaw & Mary E. Walker	May 16	"
R. Stark Heriot & M. Helen Ford	Nov. 6	Church
Dr. John A. Grant & M. Tucker	Dec. 25	Privately
1856		
Robert Thurston & Miss M. R. Ford	Feb. 19	Church
Prof. J. B. White & Miss M. J. Prior	May 6	Church
Col. Francis W. Heriot & Miss S. E. Ford	Nov. 18	Church
1857		
W. F. Joy & Miss M. M. Glidden	Dec. 15	Church
1858		
R. E. Fraser & Mrs. E. C. Brown, A. T. Porter off.	Dec. 16	Privately
1859		
Sherrod & Ella (col)		Privately
George Douglas & Catherine Clark (col)	Aug. 2	Privately
W. G. Dozier & Miss Mary B. Atkinson	Dec. 22	Privately
(By Rev. A. T. Porter)		
1860		
Glennie Heriot & Miss A. G. Coachman	Dec. 20	Church
1861		
Edwin & Peg (slaves)	Nov. 12, '61	
1865		
Bentley Weston to Miss Alice Ward	July 13, '65	Marlboro
Harry Scriven to Marianne Seabrook (col)	Dec. 3, '65	Church
by Rev. A. Glennie		
1866		
Simons Ewbank Lucas to Emilie Anna Herring	March 26	Church
by Rev. Alexr. Glennie		
C. Irvine Walker & A. Orianna Sinclair	June 20	Church
by Rev. A. Glennie		

Names of the Parties	Time	Place of Wedding
1867 by A. Glennie		
Robert Withers Vaux & Eliza Catherine Stoney	Jan. 15	Privately
March Simmons & Minda Wilson (col)	Feb. 3	"
Cleland K. Huger & Susan E. Alston	Feb. 7	in Charleston
Benjamin Cashion & Nancy Means (col)	March 28	Privately
Blair Anderson & Henrietta Porcher Heriot	May 1	Church
William James Sparkman & Martha Emma Heriot	Nov. 20	Privately
1868 by A. Glennie		
Richard Oliver Bush & Margaret L. Barnes	Feb. 12	Privately
Zebedee Small & Eliza Lidaff (col)	March 7	Parsonage
Ross Johnson & Rhoda Wilson (col)	Aug. 2	Parsonage
James A. Bowley & Laura C. Clark (col)	Dec. 28	African Church
1869 by A. Glennie		
Yancey Manney & Jane Knight (col)	Jan. 7	Privately
Edward G. Hume & Anna Maria Ford	March 8	Church
Edwin R. Emery & Ann Eliza Stalvey	Apr. 26	Privately
Joseph Springs & Catharine Merriman	May 6	"
John R. Latta & Kate B. Ralston	Nov. 24	Church
Arthur Middleton Parker & Emma Izard Middleton	Nov. 24	Windsor
1870 by Rev. A. Glennie		
William Henry Lockhart & Civil Pierce	Jan. 2	In Private
Theodore Thorsen & Mrs. Frances Springs	July 4	"
J. Lewis Haenel & Sarah Brahmer	Oct. 26	"
Samuel R. Carr & Emma Matilda Spear	Oct. 23	"
James A. B. Morris & Agnes Caroline Stalvey	Dec. 14	"
John Harleston Read & Annie Elizabeth Stoney	Dec. 22	"
1871		
George Fraser Wilson & Esther Ann Brown	Jan. 12	In Private
by Rev. A. T. Porter		
Ralph M. izard & Esther Jane Read	Feb. 9	"
by Rev. A. Glennie		
Thomas Ford & Ann Elizabeth Ford	May 4	Church
Warner K. Heston & Martha Ivey	July 25	In Private
Stephen Elliott Barnwell & Kate M. Hazzard	Dec. 29	Annandale N. Santee
1872 by Rev. A. Glennie		
Benjamin Huger Ward & Jane McCrady Sparkman	Jan. 25	Dirleton Peedee
Stepney Johnson & Peg Ford (col)	Feb. 1	African Church
Henry Vereen & Susan Mark (col)	Nov. 29	"
Theodore Wilson Tilton & Ida Sampson	Feb. 15	In private
Joseph S. Lawrence & Catherine A. Richardson	Feb. 15	"
Moses Richardson & Mary Allston (col)	March 20	"
James Harvey Jones & Risaltha Eliza Lucas	March 28	African Church
Baxter (col) March 28		
James Divine & Margaret Smith	May 7	In private
Charles Percival Richardson &	Dec 17	"
Mary Catherine Sessions		
1873		
Alfred Jonstone [sic] & Rhoda A. Lee	July 31	Parsonage
Hasford Walker & Elizabeth Harleston Heriot	Oct. 30	Church

Names of the Parties	Time	Place of Wedding
1874		
Stephen E. Woodbury & Sarah A. Stalvey	Jan. 8	In private
George Jackson & Sarah Roux (col)	Jan. 9	Parsonage
Espy Sessions & Ann Eliza Maurice	Feb. 4	In private
Ardolph Blackwell & Sarah Felker	Feb. 8	"
Warren Atkinson & Hess Howard Prior	Apr. 16	Church
George Wetts & Alice Williams	May 3	Parsonage
Robt Lovat Fraser & Catherine Vaux White	May 28	Church
Henry Britton & Mary Caroline Ford	Sept. 3	In private
1875		
James Drayton & Judy Bradley (col)	Apr. 8	In private
Richard Dozier Lee & Mary Elizabeth Dozier	Apr. 22	Church
James Mitchel & Jane Rees (col)	Apr. 29	African Church
Titus Bowling & Julia Smith (col)	July 7	Parsonage
Thomas M. Merrima & Mary L. Tilton	Sept. 23	in Private
Ben Smith & Henrietta Mosella Hartley (col)	Oct. 21	Parsonage
Oscar a. Farris & Mary Margaret Detyens	Oct. 26	in Private
1877		
Albert Hickman & Anna Eliza Detyens	Nov. 1	in Private
Moses Leonard Dorrill & Elizabeth Beckman Andrews	Dec. 19	"
1878		
William Clark & Mary Young (col)	May 20	in Private
Washington Robinson & Sybil Tunno (col)	June 6	"
James Divine & Kothena Caroline Ferril	Aug. 5	"
Nathaniel Baker Tilton & Lillie Adelle Tilton	Nov. 19	"
Jerry Rice & Sallie Williams (col)	Nov. 28	"
Louis A. Butts & Susan Rebecca Dorrill	Dec. 17	"
1879		
Robert M. Cooper & May Nannette Shaw	May 22	in Private
1880		
Allen P. Hazard & Alice B. Tamplet	Jan. 1	Church
John Nickolas Concklin & Hester Hortensia Ellis	Feb. 26	in private
Allen Braswell & Mrs. Frances Thorsen	June 2	"
Thos Mador Gilmore & Julia Forster (by Rev. W. H. B.)	Dec. 17	Church
1881		
Frank F. Gilmore & Alice Forster (by Rev. W. H. B.)	Jan. 11	Church
James R. Parker & Penelope B. Pyatt (by Rev. W. H. B.)	Feb. 17	at home
Saml. Oliver Conyers & Christian Chisolm Ford by Rev. Benj. Allston	Feb. 24	Church
Thomas Jefferson & Ansley Clark (col)	July 25	at home

Rev. J. W. KEEBLE

Wm. Wilburn & Mary Bush Dorrill	July 19, 82	at home

Rev. B. ALLSTON

Walter Hazard & J. Minnie Tamplet	Oct. 17, 82	Church

Names of the Parties	Time	Place of Wedding
1883 Rev. Benj. Allston, Rector		

John Christopher Bauman to Mary Prioleau Ford	Jan. 11	Springwood Pltn.
Oliver Martin Daysher to Annie Susan Anderson	Dec. 18, 1882	
by Rev. J. W. Keeble, recorded by B. A.		

Prince Roberts & Diana Wilson (col)	March 8/ 83	At home
Walter Herbert McDonald & Etta Capers Croft	Aug. 23/83	At home
James Mendenhall Nettles & Mrs. Christina Conyers	Dec. 5/83	Sptingfld pltn.
Samuel Sidney Fraser & Martha Clara Ford	Dec. 18/83	Plantersville Ch'pl
Samuel Holmes Ellis & Mary Elizabeth Smith	Dec. 23/83	At home
John Saville Pyatt & Elliner May Smith	May 20/84	Church
T. Daniel Heyward & E. Selina Johnstone	July 3/84	South Isld. Chapel
Paul E. Twiggs & Emma A. Gilbert	Nov. 27/84	Church
John R. Smith & Mary Ellen Westcot (col)	Jan 29/85	At home
John Gorman & Catherine Williams	March 10/85	Rectory (8 pm)
William Buck Wright & May Alston Congdon	June 18/85	At home (9½ AM)
Benj. B. Russell Jr. & Adelaide Davis	Feb. 13/86	At Church
Louis Laval Williams & Ella Hume Ford	Dec. 27/86	Church

1887
Wm. H. Dorrill & Mary M. Anthony	Aug. 3	At Home

Witnesses: G. E. Sparkman & Josiah Doar; Clergyman, Stewart McQueen

| Jonathan Ingell Hazard & Fanny Wright | Jan. 4, 1888 | At Home |

Witnesses: C. R. Congdon & T. M. Merriman; Clergyman, Stewart McQueen

| Henry D. Esdorn & Civil Lockhart | March 30, 89 | Rectory |

Witnesses: V. Dunbar & V. Douglass McQueen; Stewart McQueen
1890
| George F. vonKolnitz, Jr. & Sara Conover Holmes | Apr. 9th | Church |

Witnesses: Wm. M. Hazzard ___ Wayne; Stewart McQueen

| John A. McInnes & Martha S. McClellan | May 22 | At Home |

Witnesses: G. M. Ford, P. W. McInnes; Stewart McQueen

| Renty Tucker & Nancy Joseph (col) | Sept. 11 | At Home |
| James H. Wilson & Eliza T. Wilson | Oct. 30 | At R. E. Fraser's |

Witnesses: Howard P. Locke & Paul H. Tamplet; Stewart McQueen

| Arthur C. Beach & Rosa B. Smiley (col) | Oct. 30 | At Home |

1891
| Gadsden Morris Ford & Eugenia S. Fitzsimmons | March 2 | At Home |

G. E. T. Sparkman & S. Mortimer Ward; Stewart McQueen

[Because of the unusual format and information, the marriages 1892-1900 (and two others) are found on pages 74-77.]

Names of the Parties	Time	Place of Wedding
1900		
Arthur Oliver Johnson	October Third	P. E. Church
Mary Katharine Meriman	3 P. M.	
B. L. Skinner	Dec. Twenty	Rectory
Mrs. Maria H. Pope	seventh	
Hugh Wilson Fraser	Apr. 18, 1900	At Monticello, Florida
Katherine Archer Parkhill		
1901		
Edgar L. Lloyd	Feb. 9th	Church 3 P. M.
Miss Bernice Sigler		
Joseph A. Truesdell	May 15th	Rectory
Miss Mamie Anderson		
1902		
James Edwin Gardner	Feb. 26th	Private
Miss Mary E. Concklin		
1903		
Edgar L. Lloyd	Jan. 15th	Mr. F. S. Farr's
Miss Maud Storrs Farr		Georgetown, SC
Elliott Maxwell Lucas	June 23d	Church
Miss Anna Manigault Tucker		
Mr. R. C. Snipers, Fla.	Dec. 23d	At Mr. Canon's
Miss Emma Cornelia Coxe		White's Bridge
1904		
Robert P. Shuford	Dec. 14	Georgetown, SC
Miss Florence MacDonald		
1905		
Anthony Pelzer Beckman	April 8th	Church
Miss Frances C. Laveck		
Earnest Humes Duval	April 26th	Church
Miss Mildred Helen McCabe		
Thomas Walter Barfield	July 30th	Private
Miss Evelyn Beckman Rouse		
A. Frank Craven	Dec. 7th	Private
Miss Ida Hathcock		
1906		
John Harvey Holt	June 6th	Private
Miss Louisa S. Willis		
1907		
Wm. Alden James	Jan. 23rd	Church
Miss Ruth Hazard		

Names of the Parties	Time	Place of Wedding
Daniel T. Pope, M. C. Miss Julia Caroline Smith	July 10th	Private
1908 Ben Whaley Miss Lydia Elizabeth Smith	Jan. 25th	Private
Isaac McG. Carraway Miss Mabel H. Young	Nov. 26, 1908	In Church
James Walter Wingate Myrtle Young	Dec. 23, 1908	Private
William D. Jones Miss Annetta Detyens	June 17, '09	Private
Lou Cox Miss Lula Harper	July 26, 1909	Private
John M. Blakely Miss Mary Rose	May 20, 1909	The Rectory
1910 George Thomas Skinner Miss Rhetta Phelps	March 20, 1910	Georgetown, SC
Thomas DeWitt Robeson Miss Martha Selena Ford	April 6, 1910	In the Church
Miss Pearl Marian Merriman James Tyler Adams	April 6, 1910	Private
John Marshall Douthat Louise Oliver	Feb. 1911	Church

Date	Names	Ages	Place

Percy J. Robottom, Rector

Date	Names	Ages	Place
1911 Dec. 22	Charles McCant Bertha Edna Rouse	26 21	Private
Dec. 26	Arthur Middleton Williams Katharine Ward	26 22	Church
1912 Feb. 27	Thomas A. Norman Susan L. McClellan	31 22	Private
1913 Jan. 7	Charles Tamplet, Pauline LaBruce		At Home
Jan. 14	S. E. Lofrton, Gertrude Hurcomb		At Home

1915
Thursday	A. F. Witte, Jr.		At Home
April 8	Hattie McG. Sparkman		
Wednesday	Henry William Davis of Atlanta, Ga, 46		Church
June 23	Sarah I'on Lowndes	35	
Thursday	George W. Smith	29	Rectory
June 24	Myrtle McAlpin	18	
Tuesday	Philip Henry Eve	24	Church
July 27	Martha Fitz-Simons Ford	20	
Wednesday	James Richmon Garreson	33	Church
Aug. 11	Blanche Carrol Conklin	22	

Day and Date	Names	Ages	Residence
Dec. 28, 1892, Holy Innocents. In the Church at 2 PM	John Elliott Bull Jessie Bryan Williams	37 24	Orangeburg, SC Georgetown, SC
Northampton, George-town Co., SC, 8 PM March 15, '93	Charles Weston Rosa Eliza Stark Sparkman	30 22	Georgetown Co.
Thursday after 9th Trinity, Aug. 3, 93. South Island at Home of Mrs. Johnstone	Gardner Brewer Penniman Mary Johnstone	28 22	New York City Georgetown Co., SC
Tuesday, the 27th day of February 1894 At Mr. Detyens	Elias Marion Doar Mary Eleanor Detyens	26 21	Georgetown Co., SC
Thursday 8½ PM May 24. 94 in the Church	Allen McPherson Hamby Jr. & Mary Sparkman Tucker	21 37	Georgetown, SC
Oct. 25th 94 in the Epis. Church 1½ P M	Joseph Yates Snowden Ann Eliza Warley	36 33	Charleston Charleston
Nov. 6th 95 12 AM in the Epis. Church	William Whitfield Gardner Mary Margaret Bush	30 21	Florence, SC Georgetown, SC
Jan. 7th 1896 Mr. Doziers	Edward Capers Haselden Alice Elizabeth Dozier	24 22	Georgetown, SC Waccamaw
Nov. 25 1896 In the Epis. Church	John Stanyarne Wilson Hattie Wilborn Hazard	38 22	Spartanburg, SC Georgetown, SC
June 23d 1896, 2d Wed. after Trinity Epis. Church	Thomas Wilson Brightman Ida Lillian Smith		Georgetown, SC
July 7th 1896 3½ PM Wednesday after 3d Trinity, Epis. Church	Thos Bailey Hamby Emma Amelia Munnerlyn	24 22	Georgetown, SC
Nov. 19, 1897 after 22n Trinity	Hugh Lawson Oliver Etta White Bourke	24 22	Georgetown, SC
Wednesday Dec. 8, 1896 Advent Home.	John Asa Thrall Eunice McDonald	26 20	Georgetown Co.

Parents	Witnesses	Signature
Austin Norman Bull and Elizabeth Elliott Bull, Orangeburg, S. C. & Rev. Jno Bryan Williams, Rector of Parish & Ann Little Skinner Williams, Georgetown	Mrs. G. D. Sellers, Orangeburg, Dr. Mitchell, Charleston, Miss Lizzie Thompson, Summerville, The Congregation.	Performed by Dr. Ellison Capers, Jno. B. Williams, Rector
William Ervin Sparkman, Martha Emma Heriot Sparkman	Housefull, Mr. Ward, Miss LaBruce, Mrs. Rosa, Miss Ward, Mrs. Rosa, Mrs. Hughes, Mr. Hamby	Jno. B. Williams, Rector
Mr. Penniman of New York Mrs. Alice Johnstone of SC	Mrs. Alice Johnstone William H. Johnstone Mary Ely Vaux	Jno. B. Williams
John W. Board James H. Detyens	Mr. L. Walker, Mr. Morgan, Mrs. Dozier, Mrs. Burns, Rev. Mr. Odell & Wife	John B. Williams
A. M. Hamby, Sr. Dr. Sparkman, of Plantersville	Col. Sparkman & sister Dr. Bailey, Mr. Morgan, Mrs. Williams, etc.	Jno. B. Williams
Dr. William Snowden Mary Yates Snowden Jno. C. Warley & Ann Bailey Warley	Dr. Bailey & family, Mr. Snowden Hamphill, Porcher, Ravenel full House	Jno. B. Williams
D. W. Gardner May L. Bush	Mrs. J. R. Congdon, Dr. Garner House full	Jno. B. Williams
Edward W. Haselden & Jessie Tarbox Haselden John F. Dozier & Hattie Gibbes Dozier	Miss Lee, Willie Congdon, Capt. Porter Mr. Tarbox & family	Jno. B. Williams
Col. Wm. Blackburn Wilson Benjamin I. Hazard, Sr.	Col. W. B. Wilson, Jr., Dr. DeFoix, Wilson B. Bishop, B. I. Hazard & family and members of the congregation	Jno. B. Williams assisted by Theo. D. Bratton
	House full, Mr. Brightman's family, etc.	Jno. B. Williams
Ben. Allston Munnerlyn & Anna Jane Wilson Munnerlyn	House full	Jno. B. Williams
Allen McPherson Hamby & Hess Williams Hamby		
Rev. Mr. Oliver & Mrs. Oliver W. O. Bourke & Ida Jeanerettte Bourke	House full	Jno. B. Williams
E[?] B. Thrall, Michigan John J. McDonald, S. C.		John B. Williams

PRINCE GEORGE WINYAH RECORDS 1815-1916

Day and Date	Names	Ages	Residence
Jan. 19, 1898 2 PM Wednesday after 2d Sun in Epiphany	William Lowndes Eliza Bonsall Holmes	25 25	Georgetown Co.
Thursday, Dec. 1st 1898 before 2nd Sunday in Advent, In the Church, Georgetown, SC	James Frederick McLure and Mary Laval Bailey		Union, SC Georgetown, SC
January 2 Church	George Isaac Sprinks Nancy Ann Jepson	27 19	Chicago Georgetown
Dec. 26, 1911 Church	Arthur M. Williams Katie Ward		Charleston Georgetown

Parents	Witnesses	Signature
R. I'On Lowndes & Alice Izard Middleton Lowndes Francis Simmons Holmes & Mary Sarah Hazzard Holmes		John Bryan Williams
Thos. Pierce Bailey & Mary Laval Bailey John William McLure & Jane Pauline McLure		Geo. H. Johnson, D.C. of Washington, D. C.
Wm. & Agnes Sprinks Henry & Alice Jepson		Percy C. Webber, Priest, Boston, Mass.
S. Mortimer Ward Mr. A. M. Williams		Percy J. Robottom, Rector

COMMUNICANTS

[The first lists of communicants are near the beginning of the register. The lists of communicants beginning in 1887 follow the marriages. They are listed together here for the sake of continuity.]

1866

Revd. Maurice Harvey Lance - died 1870
Mrs. M. H. Lance (Sarah Laura) Moved away
Dr. Wm. Randolph Theus Prior - died 1869
Mrs. W. R. T. Prior (Martha)
Sarah Esther Carr
Mrs. Benj. H. Wilson (Julia) moved away 1876
Mrs. J. Rees Ford (Martha Elizabeth) Moved to Prince Frederick
Sarah Ford Henning   "
Anna Henning Ford   "
Martha Clara Ford   "
John Francis Pyatt
Mrs. J. F. Pyatt (Harriet Nowell) died 1869
Joseph Benjamin Pyatt
Mrs. J. B. Pyatt (Joanna) died 1882
Martha Allston Pyatt
Dr. Alexius M. Forster died 1879
Mrs. A. M. Forster (Elizabeth)
Wm. Warham Withers Forster died 1877
Mary W. Forster   moved 1883
Charles W. Forster   moved away 1880   returned '82
Mrs. Richd. Green White (Sarah E.)
Mrs. Stephen Rembert (Sarah Laura)
Mrs. Francis S. Parker (Mary Taylor)
Susan Catherine Brown moved away 1881
Mrs. John W. Coachman (Mary Helen)
Mrs. Jonah Atkinson (Susan)   )
Ann Eliza Atkinson   ) moved 82
Mrs. Martha Pyatt Grant   died 1869
Mrs. James G. Henning (Emma A.) moved away 1877
Emily Anna Henning, married 1866 to S. Ewbank Lucas
Martha Thomas moved away 1872; died 1875
Virginia Caroline Thomas moved away 1869
Mrs. Catherine Merriman, mard. 1869 to Joseph Springs; died 1874
Mrs. Elizabeth Porcher Fitzsimons, moved away 1872, died 1873
Mrs. Catherine Vaux moved away 1873 died 1883
Mrs. Paul Fitzsimons (Martha Selina) moved away died 1884
Anna Alice Ford   "
Eliza Harriet Ford   "
Mrs. Richard Dozier (Elizabeth Jane)
Mrs. Paul Tamplet (Hannah E.) died 1870
Mrs. Henry F. Heriot (Georgie)
Dr. Thos Pierce Bailey
Jonathan Bailey - moved away 1876
William McKnight never attends
Richard Oliver Bush
Mrs. Alexr. Glennie Heriot (Anna Glen)
Mrs. David Henry Smith (Eleanor Elizabeth) moved away 1872; returned 1878
Elizabeth Matilda Smith - moved away 1872 (Mrs. Oliver) married & joined Baptist
Eliza Catherine Stoney - married 1867 to Robt. W. Vaux & removed
Annie Elizabeth Stoney - married 1870 to J. Harleston Read & removed
Elizabeth Harleston Heriot - married 1873 to Hasford Walker

Mrs. Charles S. Stockman (Caroline) -moved away 1872
Mrs. J. Harleston Read (Esther Jane) died 1877
Eleanora Withers Read moved away
Mary E. Y. Powelson - married 1867 to Rev. Alexr Glennie & removed 1880
Ralph Izard Middleton
Mrs. R. I. Middleton
R. I. Middleton Junr - moved away 1870
Alice Izard Middleton - married 1870 to Richd I'on Lowndes & removed
Mrs. Fraser   ) Moved away 1868
Mrs. Wm. C. Johnstone)

ADDED IN 1868

Mrs. Richd. O. Bush (Margaret L.)
Mrs. Willis Jacobs (Mary Ann) removed 1876
Benj. H. Wilson died 1876
Mrs. Blair Anderson (Henrietta Porcher) removed to Baltimore 81
Hesse Howard Prior - married 1874 to Warren Atkinson
Francis W. Forster moved 1881 returned '82
Julia Forster married T. M. Gilmore 1880 & removed
Ann Elizabeth Ford - married 1871 to Thos Ford & removed
Thomas Ford moved away 1873
William Prior White moved away 1872
Mrs. David Risely (Georgie)
Mrs. McCusker
Mrs. Wm. H. Dorrell (Alafair)
Joseph Charles Brown moved away 1870
Mrs. John F. Dozier (Harriet) moved away 1871 returned '80

COMMUNICANTS 1868

Mrs. Elizabeth S. Shackelford died 1870

ADDED IN 1869

Mrs. Benj. H. Read (Mary)

ADDED IN 1870

Catherine Vaux White - married 1874 to R. Lovatt Fraser
Hannah E. Harral, married & moved away 1871
Dr. Richard Green White died 1875
Alexius M. Forster, Junr. moved away 1876 died 1881
Mrs. St. J. P. Ellis (Mary Lesesne) died 1873
Thomas Gregg   ) moved away 1871
Mrs. T. Gregg   )
Mrs. L. P. Miller removed 1874 Died 1877
Mrs. S. Sydney Fraser (Sarah) Died 1877
Esther Ann Brown - married 1871 to G. Fraser Wilson - Died 1879

ADDED IN 1871

Mrs. Horace Waldo (Julia) removed 1876
Mrs. Waldo Senr - died 1873
Mrs. Hazzard Senr - moved
Martha Ivey - married 1871 ot Warner K. Heston moved

Mrs. Theodore Thorden (Frances) married A. Brazwill '80
Mrs. Thurston (Maria Reese) Died 1876

ADDED IN 1872

Mrs. James Divine (Margaret) died 1872
Mrs. Annette Nelson - moved away 1875
Mary Elizabeth Dozier - married 1875 to Richd. D. Lee & removed

ADDED IN 1873

Mrs. Wm. O. Bourke (Ida C.)
Mrs. Saml. R. Carr (Emma Matilda) removed 1884
Jessie Minnie Tamplet (married Walter Hazard 1882)
Alice Bonneau Tamplet - married 1880 to A. P. Hazard
Penelope Bentley Pyatt   married James R. Parker
Rebecca Dennis married to ____ Gogherty 1878
Mrs. Wm. H. Trapier (Charlotte) removed 1873
Mrs. Alexs. M. Forster Junr. (Mary) removed 1877 returned & died 1879
Dr. Hasford Walker Died 1879
Sarah Thurston - moved away 1876
James Divine Suspended reinstated Jan '85
Mrs. Joseph M. Brown (Eveline H.) removed 82
Mrs. T. P. Bailey (Maria L.)

ADDED IN 1874

Alice Forster   married Frank F. Gilmore, 81
Catherine Ann Ford   removed
Emma Elizabeth Springs - removed 1874 (married Lachicotte)
Mrs. Sarah Haenel - removed 1875
Mrs. Sarah A. Bleckwehl removed 83
Mrs. Isaac Carr (Sarah B) Died 1879
Dr. R. Stark Heriot - died 1875
Mrs. R. Stark Heriot (Martha Helen) removed 1876
Warren Atkinson
R. Lovatt Fraser Died 1879
Mrs. Edwin M. Tilton (Amelia C.) removed 1881

ADDED IN 1875

Susan Dorrill - married Louis A. Butts 1878
John P. Hazzard
Alexr Glennie Heriot
Emilie B. Atkinson
Mary J. Atkinson
Ella Atkinson
Hannah M. White
Anne E. Detyens - married Albert Hickman 1877 - Died 1879
Mrs. James H. Detyens (Mary Ann) never comes
John Haenel - removed 1877
Wm. H. Felker removed
Mrs. Thos Merriman (Mary L.)
Mary A. Robinson - died 1878
Kothena C. Ferril - died 1878
Mary E. Heriot - removed 1877

Eliza S. Heriot - removed 1877
Florine S. Rembert
Moses L. Dorrill
Mary B. Dorrill (married Wilburn & removed)
Julia L. Waldo - removed 1870
Sarah L. Ferrill

ADDED IN 1876

Cornelia Waldo - removed 1876
David Risley

ADDED IN 1877

Mrs. Elliot Hazzard
Wm. H. Dorrill
John W. T. Dorrill

COMMUNICANTS 1877

Francis F. Gilmore   removed 1882
Madora T. Gilmore   removed 83
Rutledge Parker
Mrs. Rutledge Parker (Charlotte)
Mary Etta Jacobs removed 80
Mary Walter Hiort
Emilie Read (married Fox & removed)
Mrs. McCusker previously entered
Florence Adelle Tamplet
Mrs. D. Lynch Pringle (Caroline)
Mrs. Edio G. Hume (Anna Maria) removed returned 1884

ADDED IN 1878

Mrs. Conchlin

ADDED IN 1879

Mrs. LeG. G. Walker (Catherine T.)
LeGrand G. Walker
Mary Shaw   removed
Hester H. Ellis - mraried John N. Concklin 1880
Mrs. M. Haig   removed
Mrs. B. F. D. Perry   removed 1880

ADDED IN 1881

Mary Alston Congdon
Mary M. Ford
Mary M. Haig removed
Jane Anne Tilton removed 81
Robert E. Fraser
Wilson Millar removed 81
George LaBruce removed 81
John N. Conklin
Adriana Congdon (Mrs. George R.)
Maria L. W. Bailey (Mrs. T. P.) previously admitted

ADDED IN 1882

James R. Parker
Eleanor May Smith
Esther Holbrook Smith
Mary Eveline Wallace
Anseley Jefferson (colored)

ADDED IN 1883

Anne E. Ehney   removed 1883
Julia J. Anderson

ADDED IN 1883

Sallie Bonneau Wilson
Anna Josephine White   removed 1883
Anna Jane Munnerlyn (Mrs. B. A.)
Julia Caroline Smith
Clara O. Elliot
Rosa Murrel (colored)
Louise G. Allston (Mrs. B) by removal
Wm. C. Lloyd   "   )
Mrs. Wm. C. Lloyd   "   ) removed 1883
Mrs. Chs. Forster   "
Miss Warley   "   Removd 1883
Mrs. Henry Heth (Harriet S).   "   in 81
Mr. S. R. Carr being hopelessly ill was admitted to communion June 14/83. He went away
              in Aug. & died shortly after in New Port, R. I.

ADDED IN 1884

Benj. A. Munnerlyn
Walter Hazzard
John S. Pyatt
Mrs. Elizabeth M. Rouquie
Mrs. Eugenia A. Holsenbach
____ Byrd Dorrill

ADDED IN 1886. March 28

Mrs. Laura C. Bowley (col)

ADDED IN 1887. April 24th

Miss Mary Eleanor Detynes

This Record by Rev. Jno. B. Williams Jan. 1893

Day and Date	No.	Names	C. A. R.	
July 1, 1887	1	Charles P. Allston	C	
"	2	Mrs. Charles P. Allston	C	
"	3	Mrs. Susan Atkinson	C	died 94
"	4	Eliza Atkinson	C	Gone to California 95
"	5	Mrs. Emily B. Atkinson	C	withdrawn
"	6	Miss Emily B. Atkinson	C	
"	7	Miss Mary Atkinson	C	
"	8	Miss Ella R. Atkinson	C	removed '94
"	9	Dr. T. P. Bailey, Sr.	C	
"	10	Mrs. T. P. Bailey	C	
"	11	Mrs. W. O. Bourke	C	
"	12	R. O. Bush	C	died 94
"	13	Mrs. R. O. Bush	C	went to Augusta 96
"	14	Miss Sarah A. Carr	C	returned to Georgetown 95
"	15	Mrs. Mary Coachman	C	died 95
"	16	Alex. Glennie Heriot	C	Removed to Charleston 95
"	17	Mary W. Heriot	C	Charleston in 95
"	18	Mrs. Alex. Glennie Heriot	C	Moved to Charleston 95
"	19	Mrs. G. R. Congdon	C	
"	20	John N. Conchling	C	'94
"	21	Mrs. John N. Conckling	C	died in 93
"	22	Mrs. Mary E. Conckling	C	Died Feb. 3 and was buried Feb. 4th 4 PM Jno. B. Williams
"	23	Mrs. J. H. Detyens	C	died 94
"	24	Mary E. Detyens, Doar	C	
"	25	W. H. Dorrill	C	
"	26	Bird Dorrill	C	Gone to Baptists
"	27	R. E. Fraser	C	died 95
"	28	Mrs. C. V. Fraser	C	
"	29	Mrs. A. P. Hazard	C	withdrawn
"	30	Walter Hazard	C	"
"	31	Mrs. Elliott W. Hazzard	C	
"	32	John Potter Hazzard	C	
"	33	Miss Etta Jacobs	C	
"	34	Mrs. M. Merriman	C	
"	35	B. A. Munnerlyn	C	
"	36	Mrs. B. A. Munnerlyn	C	
"	37	W. Wilson Munnerlyn	C	moved to Atlanta
"	38	Mrs. A. M. Parker	C	
"	39	Mrs. Jas. R. Parker	C	died in 1886
"	40	John S. Pyatt	C	
"	41	Mrs. John S. Pyatt	C	
"	42	Joseph B. Pyatt	C	
"	43	Mattie Pyatt	C	
"	44	Mrs. Stephen Rembert	C	
"	45	Florine Rembert	C	died in N. Y. '96
"	46	Mrs. E. E. Smith	C	
"	47	Miss E. H. Smith	C	
"	48	Miss Julia C. Smith	C	
"	49	Miss Clara M. Tamplet	C	

PRINCE GEORGE WINYAH RECORDS 1815-1916

Day and Date	No.	Names	C. A. R.	
July 1887	50	Miss Florence A. Tamplet	C	
"	51	J. Charles Tamplet	C	withdrawn
"	52	Mrs. S. E. White	C	
"	53	Miss Hannah White	C	
"	54	LeGrand G. Walker	C	
"	55	Mrs. LeGrand G. Walker	C	died 94
"	56	Mrs. M. E. Tucker Hamby	C	married in 93
"	57	Mr. S. M. Ward	C	
"	58	Mrs. S. M. Ward	C	
"	59	David Risley	R	Philadelphia died Sep. 1895
"	60	Mrs. David Risley	R	Gone to N. Y. 96
"	61	Sallie B. Wilson	C	
"	62	Alice R. LaBruce died	C	Drown in the reat Oct. 13th Storm 1893
April 8, 1888		Under Rev. S. McQueen & Bh. Howe		
"	63	Thos P. Bailey, Jr. 94	C	Moved away
"	64	Robert S. Bailey	C	
"	65	Mary Laval Bailey	C	
"	66	Eliza E. Fraser	C	died Jan. 18 '96
"	67	Benj. I. Hazard, Sr.	C	
"	68	Sarah F. Hazard	C	
"	69	Allen P. Hazard	C	withdrawn
"	70	Ruth A. Hazard	C	
"	71	Hattie W. Hazard	C	
"	72	Mrs. Emily C. (Benj. I. H. Jr.) Hazard	C	
"	73	Elliott W. Hazzard	C	died in 1896
"	74	Anna Remel Heriot	C	Gone to Chalreston Feb. 95 returned 95.
"	75	William A. James	C	withdrawn
"	76	Mary T. Parker	C	
"	77	Mary E. Rembert	C	
"	72	Victoria Smith Collins	C	withdrawn
"	73	St. John P. Ellis	C	died years ago W.
Nov. 17, 1887		Under Rev. S. McQueen & Bh. Howe		
"	74	Henrietta W. Bourke Oliver	C	
"	75	Mary M. Bush	C	Married Mr. Gardner in 95 & went to Florence
"	76	Benj. I. Hazard Jr.	C	withdrawn
"	77	Annie J. Munnerlyn	C	
"	78	Emma A. Munnerlyn Hamby	C	
"	79	Herbert L. Smith	C	
"	80	Rebecca W. (Greer) Smith	C	
"	81	William Percy Smith	C	
"	82	Ida L. Smith Brightman	C	

NEGROES

July 1887	83	Laura C. Bowley	C	
"	84	Amesby Jefferson	C	
"	85	Rachel Huger	C	
By Removal		Renty Tucker	C	

Day and Date	No.	Names	C. A. R.	
Nov. 1889	86	Mrs. J. Harleston Reid	C	Charleston
"	87	William B. Reid	R	" removed to Flat Rock 1893

By Confirmation under Rev. S. McQueen & Bh. Howe

April 12, 1891	86	Julia L. Allston	C	died 96 Feb.
"	87	James H. Detyens	C	
"	88	Jonathan I. Hazard	C	
"	89	Fanny (Mrs. J. I.) Hazard	C	
"	90	Emma A. Twiggs	C	moved away 92
"	91	William C. White	C	moved away

By Confirmation under Rev. S. McQueen & Bh. Howe

March 27, 1892	92	J. Harleston Reid	C	
"	93	Mary Helen Coachman	C	
"	94	Genevieve Maud McKinlay	C	moved away

1893	93	Eliza Stark Sparkman, Mrs. Rosa	C	
	94	Julia Bonham Sparkman	A	Columbia, S. C.
	95	Wilson Miller	C	
	96	Miss Marietta Jacobs	C	Away moved

By Confirmation under Rev. Jno. B. Wliliams and by Bh. Capers

Dec. 20, 1893		George Reynolds Congdon	C	died Dec. 24, 93 ten days after Baptism etc.
"		William Pryor Congdon	C	
"		Annie Estelle Young	C	
		Mary Catherine Merriman	C	
		Florence Lester Bush	C	Gone to Augusta 96
		Mary Eva Walker	C	
		Fannie Espeth Ferris	C	Darlington, Dec. 94
		Samuel Fraser	C	
		Thomas Emile Arrowsmith	C	Gone to Darlington Dec 94
		Georgie Alberta Congdon	C	
		Virginia Caroline Walker	C	
		Susan Lowndes Allston	C	
		Gilbert Johnson	C	
		Elza Eveline Johnson	C	
		Gilbert Lester Johnson	C	

April 1894		Mrs. Vaux	A	Charleston, 94
"		Minnie Vaux Whitford	A	"

April 1894		David Bailey	C	
		Howard Sank Risley	C	Gone to N. Y. 96
		Allen McPherson Hamby	C	
		John David Whitford	C	
		Harriet Gibbes Dozier	C	Gone to N. Y.
		Sarah Freeborn Hazard	C	
		Annetta Detyens	C	
		Maria Williams Bailey	C	

Feb. 9, 96		Mrs. J. H. Detyens	C	
"		Catherine Ward Pyatt	C	

PRINCE GEORGE WINYAH RECORDS 1815-1916

Day and Date	Names	C. A. R.
Feb. 9, 96	Robert Vaux Read	D
Oct. 96	Anna Ramell Herriot	returned from Charleston 96
"	Maria Rees Herriot	Charleston
"	Anna Glenn Herriot	"
March 26, 1898	Geo. E. Fourd, Confirmed in St. Stephens, Jocksonsutle, Feb. 21, 1897	
"	Elizabeth Agnew	Prince Frederick Parish
April 8, 1898	Arthur Williams Hamby	Harry Ravenel Lucas
	John LaBruce Ward	Catherine Louize Walker
	William Buck Sparkman	
	Dr. W. E. Sparkman	received 1898
	Mrs. W. E. Sparkman	
1887	Charles Pettigru Allston	C
	Mrs. Chas. P. Allston	C
	Dr. Thos. P. Bailey	C
1881	Mrs. Thos. P. Bailey	C
	Mrs. W. O. Bourke	C
	Mrs. W. O. Bush	C — Removed to Augusta May 96
	Mrs. Geo. R. Congdon	C
	Mrs. Mary E. Conckling	C
	Mrs. Mary E. Detyens Doar	C
	William H. Dorrill	C
	Mrs. C. V. Fraser (Miss White) [check here]	
	Mrs. Elliott W. Hazzard (Miss Johnstone)	
	Mrs. John Potter Hazzard	C
	Etta Jacobs	C
	Mrs. M. Merriman	C
July 27, 1884	B. Allston Munnerlyn	C
	Mrs. A. M. Parker	C
" 1884	Jno. S. Pyatt	C
April 10, 1881	Mrs. Jno. S. Pyatt (Miss Smith)	
	Jos. B. Pyatt	C
	Mrs. Stephen Rembert	C
	Florina Rembert (dead)	C — died in New York June 2d 96
1850	Mrs. David Smith	C
April 15, 1882	Miss E. H. Smith	C
1883	Julia C. Smith	
	Clara M. Tamplett	C
	Florence A. Tamplett	C
	Mrs. S. E. White	
	Miss Hannah White	C
	LeGrand Walker	C
	M. E. Tucker Hamby	married 2 time 1894
1888	Sallie B. Wilson	
"	Mary L. Bailey	
88	Ben. I. Hazard, Sr.	
"	Sarah F. Hazard	
"	Hattie W. Hazard	
"	Anna Jane Munnerlyn	
1888	Mrs. Benj. I. Hazard, Jr.	
	Major Elliott W. Hazard, dead	died in Asheville, N. C. June 2d, '96
	Mary T. Parker	

Day and Date	Names	C. A. R.	
	Mary E. Rembert		
	Victori Smith Collins		
	Rebecca R. Gogarty		
1889	Alice E. Dozier Haselden		married Mr. Haselden 1896
	Rev. McQueen & Bh. Howe		
	Henrietta Bourke		
	Annie J. Munnerlyn		
	Emma A. Munnerlyn		
	Herbert L. Smith		
	Rebecca W. Greer Smith		
	W. Percival Smith		
	Ida L. Smith Brightman		
1886	NEGROES		
	Laura C. Bowley		
	Anesly Jefferson		
	Renty Tucker		
1889	Mrs. Harleston Read		
1891	Rev. McQueen & Howe, Bishop		
	James H. Detyens		
	Jonathan Hazard		
	Fannie Hazard		
1892	J. Harleston Read		
	Mary Helen Coachman		
	Eliza Sparkman Rosa		
	Julia Bonham Sparkman	R	Columbia
Dec. 10, 1893	Rev. Jno. B. Williams & Bh. Capers		
	William Pryor Congdon		
	Annie Estelle Young		
	Mary C .Merriman		
	Florence Lester Bush		Augusta, May '96
	Mary Eva Walker		
	Samuel Fraser	C	
	Georgia Alberta Congdon	C	
	Virginia C. Walker	C	
	Susan Lowndes Allston	C	
	Gilbert Johnson	C	Methodists
	Elzy E. Johnson	C	"
	Gilbert Lester Johnson	C	"
	Eliz. Smith Oliver	C	
	Hugh Fraser	R	
1894			
	Mrs. Vaux	R	Charleston
	Mrs. Minnie Vaux Whitford	R	"
1894-5	Rev. Jno. B. Williams & Bh. Capers		
	David Bailey	C	Gone to Sweanee '96
	Howard Sark Risley	C	
	Allen McP. Hamby	C	

Day and Date	Names	C. A. R.	
	Jno V. Whitford	C	
	Harriet Gibbes Dozier	C	Gone to New Jersey Oct. 96
	Sarah Freeborn Hazard	C	
	Annetta Detyens	C	
	Maria William Bailey	C	
Feb. 9th 95-96	Jno. B. Williams & Bh. Capers		
	Mrs. J. H. Detyens	C	Presbyterians
	Catherine Ward Pyatt		
	Robert Vaux Read	C	
1895			
	Mrs. Hagadorn	R	N. Y.
	Mrs. Gardner	R	"
	Gen. Hagadorn	R	"
	Mr. Whitton	R	England, Returned to England, Aug. 96
	Mrs. Whitton	R	"
1896			
	Miss Sparkman	R	returned to Plantersville
	Miss Bessie Sparkman	R	Oct. 96
	Eliza		
	Miss Lila Holmes Holmes	R	
	John Allston	R	
	Elliot Hazzard, Jr.	R	
Oct. 96	Anna Ramell Harriott	R	Charleston
"	Maria Rees Harriott		
"	Anna Glenn Harriott '97		
"	Miss Etta Jacobs		Returned from Conn. '96
March 24, 1897	William Twigg Hazzard Holmes	R.	Church
"	Richd. Lowndes Allston	C	"
	Bachman Doar	C	Methodists
	Catherine Bryant Hawkins	C	Baptists
	Elizabeth Blanche Homer	C	"
	Ethel Walker	C	Church
	Geo. G. Foard		1898
	Mrs. Agnew		
April 8, 98	Arthur Williams Hamby		1898
	Henry Ravenel Lucas		"
	John LaBruce Ward		"
	Catherine Louize Walker		"
	Wm. Buck Sparkman		"
	Dr. Wm. E. Sparkman		"
	Mrs. W. E. Sparkman		"
April 19, '98	Mrs. A. A. Springs by transfer from Wilmington, N. C., Rev. Rob. Strange		

The following namse are taken from the <u>Confirmation Records</u> elsewhere in this book. So far as I am able to ascertain no record of Communicants has been kept since the above date, namely April 19, 1898. John S. Lightbourn, Rector-- July 1916.

1899
Bryan, Norman	Gone
Bryan, Reid Whitford	Gone - Charleston
Merriman, Thomas	Dead
Ward, Emma Sparkman	Gone
Sparkman, James Ritchie	Gone - Columbia
Smith, David Thomas	

1900
Pyatt, Maham Ward	
Young, (Mrs.) Laura J.	Dead
Young, Henning William	
Springs, Holms Buck	
Tucker, James Sparkman	Gone - Washington, D. C.
Tucker, Claudia Allen	" "
Tucker, George Eugene	" "
Ward, Bentley Douglas	
Morris, Charles Ellis	Gone, Manning, S. C.
Conklin, Mary Ann Eliza	
Hazard, Paula Elizabeth	
Fraser, Rees Ford	Gone, Charleston
Forgeson, Theodore M.	
Fraser, (Mrs.) Katherine (Parkhill)	
Read, J. Harleston	
Johnson, Arthur O.	Gone - Florida

1901
Bryan, Elizabeth Sherwood	Gone
Hazard, Minnie Tamplet	
Rouquie, Agnes Jane	Gone
Tilton, Lillian Constance	Gone
Petrie, Eleanor Josephine	Gone
Dozier, Kate Hampton	Gone
Gardner, Katherine	Gone - Charleston
Young, Sarah Lauretta	
Youne, Lena Rebecca	
Congdon, George Reynolds	
Congdon, (Mrs.) Rosa Lohr	
Oliver, Hugh Lawson	
Springs, Maurice	Dead
Merriman, Robert	Gone - Columbia
Emerson, Elhanan Victor	

1901
Springs, Maurice	
Merriman, Robert	
Springs, Albert Adams	Gone to N. Y.
Morris, William Freeman	
Congdon, Charles S.	
Congdon, (Mrs.) Minnie (Brock)	
Bailey, C. Williams, Dr.	Dead

1902
Ward, Katherine LaBruce   Mar. A. M. Williams
Young, Julia Isabel
Bailey, (Mrs.)   Gone - New Bern, N. C.

1903
Daggett, Thomas Shepherd
Daggett, (Mrs.) Clara
Daggett, Edna
Arrowsmith, Philip Heller   Gone - Lake City, S. C.
LaBruce, George H.   Gone
Pyatt, John Saville, Jr.
Doty, Emily G.   Gone
Smith, Herbert Lee, Jr.
Brantom, (Mrs.) Hattie

1904
Walker, (Miss) Le Grand   Dead
Young, Myrtle Josephine   Mrs. Isaac Carraway
Hazard, Lucile G.
Sparkman, Hatie M.   Mar. --- Witte
Concklin, Nicholas

1906
Hyman, Mary Pender
Wright, Alberta   Mar. - Mazyck - Charleston
Pyatt, May
Butler, Theodosia
Butler, (Mrs.) Jessie Theodosia
Whitford, Bird   Gone - to Charleston
Springs, St. Julian Lachicotte   Gone
Hazard, Jonathan Ingell, Jr.
Hazard, Frank Arthur
Hazard, Karl Benjamin
Young, Charles LeRoy
Merriman, Geo. Congdon   Gone
Barr, Capers Gamewell, Jr.
Butler, LeRoy   Removed

1907
Carraway, John G.
Carraway, Isaac McG.
Carraway, Janie M.
Carraway, Elizabeth   Mar. Frank Siau
Holleman, William H.   Gone - Columbia
Smith, William Henry   Gone - N. Y.
Congdon, George Reynolds, Jr.
Ward, Allen Rutledge   Gone
Concklin, James Albert   Gone
Bryan, (Mrs.) Herman   Gone - Charleston ?
Walker, William Hasford
Hucks, John Johnston
Moorer, Morgan Preston, M. D.   moved to Asheville
Young, Mabel Helen
Doar, John Walter
Carraway, John Herman

Dorrill, Corneliua A.   Gone
Dorrill, John W.
Morris, Douglas L.
Carraway, Haskell
Beckman, Herman Decatur, M. D.
1909
Doar, Lula Mary   Dead
Holmes, William Wigg Hazzard   Gone - Mt. Pleasant, S. C.
Ward, Joshua   Gone
Collins, Julian Horner
Rosa, Delmar
Fruttiger, (Mrs.) Florence Marian Gone
Pyatt, Charlotte Josephine

No record of Confirmations fr. 1909 till January.
1912
Smith, Helen
Haselden, Alice Marie
Ward, Alice
Carraway, Ruth   Married Green
Emerson, Bertha   "   Brockinton
Riggs, Ernest
Young, Alvah
Collins, Alberta   Married Bowen[?]
Lefaendahl, Peter August   Dead
Munnerlyn, Lucy Middleton   Married Wendt
Hucks, Robert
Young, (Mrs.) Fred
Cains, Park
Cains, Arthur
Cains, Ruth
Cains, (Mrs.) M. J.
Webber, Clarence P.
Rosa, William S.
Doar, Minnie Bachman
LaBruce, Arthur
Pyatt, Edward N.
Adams, Pearl Merriman   Gone - Columbia
Young, Louis M.
Pyatt, Henry S.
Ford, Wentworth, F.

No record of Confirmations from 1912 till November
1915
Hillard, Maria Nash
Weber, Edith Waldo
Oliver, Henrietta Hunt
Doar, Eleanor Clyde
Rosa, Louise Delmar
Munnerlyn, Benjamin
Doar, LeRoy Henning
Rosa, James Richard
Doar, William Walter
Oliver, Virginia Bourke   Married & moved
Garrison, William Richmond   Gone - Petersburg, Va.

PRINCE GEORGE WINYAH RECORDS 1815-1916

BURIALS

Burials in 1816 by the Revd. Mr. Lance

Surname	Christian Name	Age	Time of Burial
Crosby	Moses G.	45 to 50	January 17th
Walker	William	15 years	March 3d
Lincon	Benjamin (mulatto child)	8 weeks	March 13th
Course	Charles B.	26 years	March 20th
Smith	John	75 years	April 18th
Whitehurst	James	7 years	April 30th
		Revd. Mr. Fraser performed. M. H. Lance being absent	
Heriot	Mary Ouldfield	20 months 15 days	May 16, M. H. Lance
Cheesborough, Esther		56 years	September 20
Futhey	Doctor John	23 years	September 25
Bogle	James L.	21 months	November 5

Burials in 1817

Surname	Christian Name	Age	Time of Burial
Smith	Robert	53	April 25
Tucker	Mrs. Susan	--	May 10
Martin	Mrs. Elizabeth	73	June 11
Smith	Paul	15	September 6
Croft	Ann	8	September
Shackelford	Mary Julia	9 months	October 26
Tucker	George Heriot	21 years	December 28

Burials in 1818

Surname	Christian Name	Age	Time of Burial
Blyth	Dr. Joseph	60 years & 7 months	January 4
Hillin			January 17
Benjamin	Mrs. Ann		July 31
Prior	David	61	
Shackelford	Mrs. Martha	58	September 8
Dubois	Samuel Abraham	18	October 5
Withers	John	3 months	December 24

Burials in 1819

Surname	Christian Name	Age	Time of Burial
Brown	Charles Major	57	April 27th
Carr	Joseph Blythe	Infant	July 4th
Pawley	Susan Mrs.	43	July 28th
		burried at Waccamaw by Revd. Gibbs	
Shackelford	Hannah Martha	14 months	August 5th
Bogle	James Dr.		August 6th
		I was absent at the time	
Pyatt	Joseph	32	August 12th
Walker	Mary Mrs.	48	September 8th
Henning	Thomas William	4 yrs. 1 m. 14 days	September 8th
Allston	Sarah W. Mrs.	23	September 14th
		Service performed at Waccamaw by Revd. H. Gibbes	
Withers	John	Service at Waccamaw by Revd. Mr. Gibbes	
Larebour	John B.		

Burials in 1820

Surname	Christian Name	Age	Time of Burial
Lance	Lambert	7 ms. & 18 days	January 16th 2d Epiph.
Wragg	Erasmus Rothmahler	28	January 26
Brown	Juliet		April 16
Heriot	Sarah Mrs.	66	June 5
Thurston	Samuel J.	64	June 13
Cheesborough, Charles William		Infant	June 15
Heriot	John Futhey		July 18
Smith	Emma Mrs.		September 2
Pyatt	John Francis		September 9
Norman	Eliza Mrs.	42	October 12

Burials in 1821

Anderson	James		January 2
McColough	Sarah		April
Taylor	Archibald	70	May 22
Prince	Mrs.		August 13th
McDonald	Esther	–	September 18th
Pinckney	Mrs. Rebecca		September 23d

Burials in 1822

Scott			February 6th
Hucks	Daniel		
Lance	Sarah	1 yr 11 mths	August 28th
Edmunds			October 22d
Cheesborough, Elizabeth		14 yrs 8 mths	November 4th
Shackelford	John W.		
Gourdin	unbaptized female child	18 days	December 22d

1823

Carr (Isaac)	Unbaptized male child	23 days	January 12th
Carr (Thos)	Edmund Hayne	3 years	February 20th
Ford	Dr. George		February 17th
Singletary	Mrs. Elizabeth		February 28th
Shackelford	Richard	40	April 18th
Huger	Honble Benjamin	50 interred at Waccamaw	
Kinloch	Cleland	intered at Stateburg	
Keith	Major John		
McClenan	Murdoch.	23	November 6th
	service by the Revd. Mr. Fraser		
Simons	Eleanor		December 14th
Taylor	John Man	37	December 20th
	service by the Revd. Mr. Taylor		

1824

Smith	Mrs. Elizabeth		January 6th
Simons	Mrs. Sarah service by the Revd. Mar. Taylor		do 7th
McClenan	Mrs. Mary E. M.	18	Do XIth
	service by the Revd. Mr. Fraser		

Surname	Christian Name	Age	Time of Burial
Allston			
Shackelford	John	64	March
Withers	Elizabeth	54	April 12th
Shackelford	Mrs. Jane H.		October 20th
Allston	Mrs. Charlotte A.		Do

1825

Surname	Christian Name	Age	Time of Burial
Shackelford	Mrs.		June 4th
James	Dr.		October 4th
McKensie			October 13th

1826

Surname	Christian Name	Age	Time of Burial	Clergyman
Croft	John		February 10th	P. T. Keith
Dailey	Mrs. Jane Thompson	22	February 18th	M. H. Lance
Porter	Francis	61	February 23d	M. H. Lance
Rothmahler	Miss E.	old	March 6th	M. H. L.
Lester	John Cosia (unbaptized)	5 weeks & 2 days	April 2d	M. H. L.
Coggeshall	Mrs. Margaret E.	24	April 9th	M. H. L.
Gourdin	Elizabeth Allston (unbaptized)	6 ms. 19 days	April 15th	M. H. L.
Henning	Thomas	50 yrs.	April 24th	M. H. L.
Taylor	Robert Andrew		September 22nd	P. T. Keith
Green	Richard S.	26 yrs.	October 13th	P. T. K.
Anderson	Mrs. Charlotte Keith	17 yrs.	October 20th	P. K. Keith

1827

Surname	Christian Name	Age	Time of Burial	Clergyman
Cogdell	Miss Anna	86 yrs	January 1827	M. H. L.
LaBruce	Joseph P.		March 14th	P. T. K.
Ford	Mrs. Sarah		April	M. H. L.
Withers	Robt. F.		April 14th	M. H. L.
Cambridge	Margaret Ann	4 weeks	April 23rd	P. T. K.
Christian	John Shackelford		Novr. 5th	P. T. K.
Ford	William	19	Novr. 10th	P. T. K.
Johnson	William at North Santee	8	Novr. 19th	P. T. K.

1828 (P. Trapier Keith, Rector)

Dozier	Mrs. Esther B. service held in G. Town on the 27th April, buried at Santee
Smith	Samuel	29 yrs 9 mth	July 28th
Wayne	Abraham (colored)		April or May
Potter	Obadiah	about 49 yrs.	October 2nd
	Old Kate (col)		June or July
Porter	John	32	October 25th	J. Fraser
Haight			
Prince			
Shackelford	Clara		Dec. 17th buried next day at Sampit P. T. K.

Rector absent during summer and autumn

1829 P. Trapier Keith, Rector

Surname	Christian Name	Age	Time of Burial
McKab	Alexander		January 31st
Thomas	Thos. Burrington (buried in the country)		February 11th
McKab	Mrs.		February 12th
Taylor	John		February 23rd (by Revd. Mr. Fraser)
Shackelford	Anthony Bonneau		February 26th (by Revd. Mr. Lance)
Wragg	Dr. John	43 yrs & 4 moths.	March 18th
Walker	LeGrand G.	30 yrs.	March 27th
Walker	Mrs. wife of Peter W.	28 yrs.	March 28th (buried in the country)
Porter	John Senr. (buried in the country)	72 yrs.	April 6th (by Revd. Mr. Fraser)
Gasque	Erasmus Rothmahler		
Lester	Bannister		
Gasque	John Wragg		
Hall	Thos. (North Island)	7 months	September 15th
Hall	John (N. Isd)	33 yrs	September 21st
Hall	William (N. Isd.)	12 yrs & 5 mths	September 22nd
Pawley	Miss Sarah		buried at Waccamaw
Wragg	Mrs. Eleanor		October 29th
Potter	John		October 30th

1830

Hall	Mrs. John (Baptist yard)		
Hall	--- --- (Baptist yard) child		
Carr	Carr Isaac (Methodist yard)		
Gasque	Mary child		

1831

Romney	Mrs. Louisa	36 yrs, 2 mths 10 days	March 1st (buried in the country)
Chapman	Julia Agnes	about 4 years	July or August (buried in the Baptist Cem.)
Jones	Thomas L.	about 30 yrs.	Septr. or Oct.
Briggs	Mrs.	about 37 yrs	October 24th
Gasque	Samuel Wragg	about 11 months	November 9th

Burials in 1832 by P. Trapier Keith, Rector

Palmer	William G.	32 yrs	January 23rd (in Methodist yard)
Warham	Mrs. Mary	74 yrs.	March 22nd (at Sampit)
Swanston	Mrs.		April 11th
Trapier	William Windham	55 yrs & 5 mths.	September 28th
Maxwell	Ella		October 8th
Elkel	Mrs.		November 4th
Ford	Miss Anna M.	16 yrs	November 29th (in the country)

1833

Hume, Mrs. wife of Dr. Alex. Hume		37 or 38 yrs.	January 4th buried at Santee
Read Rose (col)			January 20th
	Chas (col) (servant of Mrs. Cogdell	20 yrs.	May 22nd
Berton	Daniel V., M. D.		
Rutlege	Robert Smith		November 18th (at Santee)

Surname	Christian Name	Age	Time of Burial
Tait	Mrs. Hannah	69 yrs 9 mths	November 25
Ford	Mrs. Margaret	73 yrs 8 mths	November 27th (in the country)

1834

Ford	Richard W.	12 or 14 yrs	Died at North Island in summer

1835

Summer & autumn of this year more than usually sickly in Geo. Town

Ford	Thomas		Feby 9th in the country
	Frank (col child)	about 2 yrs	August 7th (at North Island)
	Tom (white sailor)		August 25th (do)
Gasque	Mrs. Esther C.	about 37 yrs	August 27th
	Charles (white sailor)		August 30th (at North Island)
Atkinson	Eliza	4 or 5 yrs	Sept. 30th (buried in the country)
Coachman	John	between 60 & 70 yrs.	October 4th (Do)

1836

Linerieux	Francis (Methodist family)	about 18 yrs	January 7th (buried in the country)
Walker	Peter (do)		January 7th (do)
Porter	Miss Ansey	15 yrs.	January 13th
North	John Gough	about 32 yrs	February 14th (in Charleston)
Jones	Mrs. Mary O.	about 40 yrs.	March 21st (body carried into the country)
Shackelford	John W.	about 50 yrs.	March 23rd
Brown	Wm. Tennent	35 yrs 3 mths 12 days	March 28th
Tarbox	John (Methodist family)		April 4th
Thomas	Dr. Edward Gibbes	61 yrs	April 6th (body carried into the country)
Inglis (col)	George Warren	1 yr & 25 days	April 26th
Thomas		10 days old	
Roux	Mrs. Elizabeth		July
Heriot	John Ouldfield		September 3rd
Thomas	Washington		November
Coxe	Elizabeth	about 8 yrs	December 29th

1837

Henning	Mary Ann (and with her, her infant, ten days old)		January 1st
Mitchell	Thomas Rothmahler	54 or 55 yrs	February 15th
Thomas	Mrs. Mary		June 21st
Gasque	Dr. S. S.	about 39 yrs.	October 18th
Hawkins	Eliza Emeline	4 yrs & 7 mths	December

1838

Marsh	Emerina	2 yrs & ___	January 22nd
Wood	Ann Eliza	4 or 5 weeks	March 29th
Grosvener	Selina	1 yr & four mths	April 2nd
Prior	Mrs.		
Magill	Mrs.		

Surname	Christian Name	Age	Time of Burial
Lecesne	Joseph		November 26th
Waring	Mrs.		December 12th

1839

	Charles (col) adult		January 7th
Shackelford	Mary	15 or 16	
	Emma (col) child		
	Moll (col) adult		
Walker	Mary Catharine	10 yrs	November 5th
Heriot	Thomas	about 48	November 12th
Ford	Samuel	5 yrs & 9 mths	December 2nd

1840

Cogdel	Mrs. Esther	94 yrs under 7 days	January 5th
Taylor	George		January 15th
Blyth	Mrs. Elizabeth F.	78 yrs	January 20th
Young	Mrs.,	about 60 yrs	April 14th
Smith	Sarah Heriot	7 mths)	
Smith	Charles		) all in summer and autumn
Brown	Mrs. Susan		) during Rector's absence
Smith	Mrs. Rebecca		)
Ford	Thomas		November 17th

Burials 1841, Robert Theus Howard, Rector

Coachman	Mrs. Sarah	30 yrs	February 5, 1841
Davis	Mrs. Mary B.	28 yrs & 11 mths	February 15, 1841
Herriott	Mrs. William Frances	44 yrs	April 10, 1841
Henning	Mrs. Anna B.		July 31, 1841
Chapman	Mr. William		August 5, 1841
Porter	Mr. John		September 9, 1841
Thomas	Mrs. Emily		September 17, 1841
Sarah Taylor	Miss		May 29, 1842
Coachman	Mr. Benjamin		1842
Taylor	Miss E. A.	about 54	January 24, 1843
Gaillard	Mr. William S.	38 yrs & 2 mts	March 20, 1843
Howard	Goverman Kortright	4 months	April 5, 1843
Keith	Mrs. John A.		August 20, 1843
Henning	Martha Emma		June 21, 1843
Martha (col)	Deas Wilson		1843
Henning	Thomas		13th August 1844
Wakefield	Miss		
Heriot	Dr. George	about 40 yrs	November 24, 1844
Ford	Maria Caroline	near 18 months	January 7, 1845
Robert George Mitchell (col)		10 yrs	January 23, 1845
Sparkman	William E.		February 3, 1846
Wilmot	Thomas Townsend	10 mnts & 28 dys	February 19, 1846
Tom Happy	the property of Mrs. B. Allston about 75 yrs		March 21, 1846
Dickison	Mrs. Mary Margaret	in 24th year	October 2, 1846
McClennan	Archibald	in 83rd year	November 4, 1846 Santee
Prior (infant)	Dr. W. W. Prior	just lived	December 20, 1846 Geo Town

Surname	Christian Name	Age	Time of Burial
		1847	
Withers	Francis	78 yrs	November 27) died in
Allston	Benjamin	83 yrs	November 27) in Charleston
		1848	
Allston	Dr. William	76	February 6 Church in Geo Town
Hillen	Mrs.	81	March 22 Methodist Ch
		1849	
Mitchell	Frederick (col)		February 11, 1849
Pawley	Jerry (col)		April 5, 1849
Henning	James Green	4 yrs 8 mo. 21 dys	November 3, 1849
Atkinson	Louisa Catharine	8 yrs	1849
Atkinson	Jonah (died in Charleston		1849
Postin	A. Matilda	14 yrs	December 17, 1849
Finklea	I. W.	about 35	December 23, 1849
Bankhead	Nancy (col)		March 5, 1850
Ford	Mrs. Jane		June 15, 1850
Fraser	Mrs. Sarah	24 yrs	December 18, 1850
Trapier	Miss Sarah Cruger	30 yrs	May 9, 1851
Walker	Hasford	26 yrs	September 7, 1851
Thomas	Edward	45 yrs	December 30, 1851
		1852	
Ford	Stephen		
Brown	Toomer Porter	6 years	September 17, 1852
Trapier	Paul (died in Charleston)		
Smith	Basil Manly	10 years	January 10, 1853
Taylor	Anna (col)	65 years	January 14, 1853
Smith	Sarah Edith	6 months	July 18, 1853
King	Benjamin	59	June 21, 1854
Stewart	Jane McGuiman	2 yrs 8 mths	September 5, 1854
Ford	Robert Thurston	24 yrs. 9 mths	October 12, 1854
Stewart	Robert McGuiman		October 15, 1854
Prior	Emma Margaret	13 yrs & 4 mths	October 27, 1854
Forster	Francis	6 yrs	November 13, 1854
Tamplet	William Wilson	2 yrs & 4 mos.	April 5, 1855
King	Benjamin		June 18, 1855
Lester	William	30 yrs.	September 21, 1855
Ford	Stephen Charles	52 yrs	July 29, 1855
Ford	John Potts	44 yrs & 6 mos.	February 13, 1856
Shaw	Archibald James	8 days	May 26, 1856
Richardson	George W.	About 40 yrs.	August 19, 1855
Edmonston	Jessie Coffin	16 yrs.	August 23, 1856
Atkinson	Jane	2 days old	September 26, 1856
Richardson	Franklin Augustus	8 yrs 24 mo.	November 7, 1856
Silvy	slave of Mrs. I. Carr	50 yrs	February 9, 1857
Allston	Annie (coloured)	65 yrs	March 8, 1857
Bush	Emily Leighton	10 mos. & 9 days	April 20, 1857
Tucker	Mrs. Benjamin	65 years	May 11, 1857

Surname	Christian Name	Age	Time of Burial
Howard	Robert Lee	4 mos & 8 days	June 16, 1857
Brown	Miss Catherine		1857
Trapier	Miss Elizabeth S.		1857
Coachman	Helen Frederine	5 yrs 9 mos. 19 dys	January 1, 1858
Brown	Dr. E. B.	49 years	January 5, 1858
Screven	Henry (col)	21 years	January 29, 1858
Allston	Laura (col)	30 years	March 28, 1858
Ella	slave of Mrs. James Smith	5 yrs.	June 3, 1858
Fraser	Samuel William	11 yrs & 6 mos.	June 20, 1858
Tuttle	Moses	67 yrs.	March 26, 1859
Alex Slave	of I. G. Henning, Sr.	5 yrs	June 14, 1859
Tamplet	John Paul	13 days	July 16, 1859
Prior	Dr. Percival E.	24 years	July 21, 1859
Allston	Thomas Hern (col)	7 years & 3 mos.	September 13, 1859
Exum	Mary R.	68 yrs.	March 12, 1860
Fraser	Mrs. Elisa C.	35 yrs, 10 mos. 11dys	May 12, 1860
Carr	Miss S. E. W.	36 yrs & 9 months	September 14, 1860
Rothmahler	Erasmus B.	57 years	February 4, 1861
Dosier	Wm. Gaillard	_8 months	June 4, 1861
Tharp[?]	(Con Soldier) Wingate	18 yrs	January 1862
Duncan	" Hosey A.	30 yrs	February 7, 1862
Matthews	" R. M.	16 yrs	February 7, 1862
Sauls	" John R.	20 yrs	February 15, 1862
Matthews	" Moses	27 yrs	March 23, 1862
Gordon	" Willis James	30 yrs	March 29, 1862
Ashby	" John S.	29 yrs	April 4, 1862
Ward	Florence	4 or 5 yrs	May 1865
Pyatt	Josephine Charlotte	7 yrs	September 2, 1865

By Revd. A. Glennie

Surname	Christian Name	Age	Time of Burial
Trapier	Genl. James Heyward	50 yrs	December 22, 1865
Ward	Mayham	28 yrs 2 m.	February 20, 1866
Bush	Caroline F.	15 yrs	March 24, 1866
Lester	Margaret	76 yrs	November 22, 1866
Cook	Mary P.	36 yrs	November 30, 1866
Forster	Theodore Herbert	9 yrs 8 mo.	December 10, 1866
Trapier	Mrs. Hannah Shubrick	84 yrs. 1 m. 29 d.	January 21, 1867
Parker	Arthur Middleton	42 yrs. 8 m. 26 d.	June 25, 1867
Davis	Isaac Dunbar	12 yrs	August 13, 1867
LaMotte	Mrs. Lucy Louiza	80 yrs	August 22, 1867
Carr	Mrs. Sarah Rose	51 yrs	August 25, 1867
Bowland	John R.	39 yrs	September 9, 1867
Parker	Dr. Francis S.	52 yrs	September 13, 1867
Johnstone	Wm. Clarkson	4 yrs 7 mo.	November 27, 1867
McCormick	William Bramwell	2 yrs 4 mo.	December 12, 1867
Rembert	Robert	10 yrs 10 mo.	March 4, 1868
McCormick	Sarah	30 yrs	July 11, 1868
James	Robert Wilson	13 yrs	August 1, 1868
James	James Washington	12 yrs	August 18, 1868
Tucker	William Hyrne	43 yrs 10 mo. 11 d.	November 20, 1868
	(Parish Ch. All Saints)		
Miner	Ann	34 yrs 2 mo 6 d.	December 4, 1868
Dozier	Mary Blake	33 yrs 3 mo. 16 d.	December 14, 1868

Surname	Christian Name	Age	Time of Burial
Tucker	Joseph Ramsey (Prince Fredks. Pedee)	39 yrs	March 39, 1869
Prior	William Randolph Theus	64 yrs 2 mo. 9 d.	April 4, 1869
	Harriet Glennie (col)	16 yrs	May 5, 1869
Ford	Junius Wilson (Peedee)	28 yrs 7 m. 17 d.	May 17, 1869
Stone	Charles	30 yrs.	June 11, 1869
Ford	George T. (Plantersville)	63 yrs	July 6, 1868
Webb	Henry W.	37 yrs	August 20, 1869
Baker		35 yrs	August 21, 1869
Lambert	Richard	6 yrs	August 21, 1869
Alston	Charles (Parish Ch. All Saints)	43 yrs	October 3, 1869
Thorsen	Julia Ann	20 yrs. 6 mo. 18 d.	October 4, 1869
Ellis	Thomas	7 yrs. 6 mo. 3 d.	October 19, 1869
Grant	Martha Pyatt	42 yrs.	November 10, 1869
Baxter	Alexr. George (col)	39 yrs 7 mo.	December 2, 1869
Keightley	Mrs. P. K.	37 yrs.	December 20, 1869
Trapier	Emma Heyward (died in Charleston)	16 yrs 21 days	January 17, 1870
Hasell	Mrs. Catherine (Cruger) (Parish C. All Saints)	62 yrs	January 30, 1870
Heriot	Mrs. Matilda (Tucker)	53 yrs.	February 5, 1870
Trapier	Mrs. Mary Thomasine (Ford) (died in Charleston)	31 yrs 6 days	March 15, 1870
Shackelford	Mrs. Elizabeth S.	75 yrs	March 30, 1870
Tamplet	Mrs. Hannah E.	40 yrs 5 mo. 10 d.	April 2, 1870
Thorsen	William Julius	7 mo. 24 d.	May 22, 1870
Wooddard	Mrs. Priscilla	48 yrs	May 29, 1870
Middleton	Ralph Izzard	1 yr. 4 mo. 29 d.	June 20, 1870
Stalvey	John Daniel	4 yrs. 5 mo. 7 d.	July 1, 1870
Vaux	Wm. Percival (Plantersville)	51 yrs. 6 mo. 20 d.	August 29, 1870
Wilson	Hagar (col)	85 yrs	October 10, 1870
Springs	Joseph H.	45 yrs	October 15, 1870
Riley	Eleanor Jane	22 yrs 10 mo. 8 d.	October 24, 1870
Heriot	Charles Julian	25 yrs 4 mo. 24 d.	October 28, 1870
Rhodes	Thomas	6 days	November 2, 1870
Fishburne	Benjamin Clay	35 yrs	November 9, 1870
Lance	Revd. Maurice Harvey	77 yrs 5 mo.	November 18, 1870
Potts	Mrs. Mary (died in Charleston)	74 yrs	December 8, 1870
Long	Joshua	59 yrs	December 13, 1870
Ford	Jessie Helen	9 yrs	December 27, 1870
Parker	Emily Rutledge	23 yrs	December 27, 1870
Pierce	Mary	30 yrs	February 10, 1871
Tamplet	Paul	41 yrs. 8 m. 11 d.	March 5, 1871
Lockhart	William Henry	23 yrs. 1 m 4 d.	April 6, 1871
FitzSimons	Paul	39 yrs	April 14, 1871
Prior	William Murray	31 yrs. 3 mo. 1 day	May 18, 1871
Conklin	Mary Elizabeth	18 yrs. 1 mo. 22 d.	July 28, 1871
Graham	Arthur Edward	9 mo. 24 d.	July 31, 1871
Collins	Frances Isabella	1 yrs. 9 mo.	August 7, 1871
Johnson	infant son of Ross & Rhoda (col)	1 day 18 hrs.	August 9, 1871
Heriot	Helen Fredrine	5 mo. 17 days	August 22, 1871
Rumley	Williametta A.	4 yrs 9 m. 26 d.	August 30, 1871
Welsh	Mary Elizabeth	2 yrs. 7 m. 9 d	September 3, 1871
Ford	Mrs. Hannah B.	65 yrs. 6 m. 20 d.	October 7, 1871
Johnson	Ella (col)	36 yrs.	October 14, 1871

Surname	Christian Name	Age	Time of Burial
West	Sarah Adeline	7 yrs.	October 28, 1871
Lance	Sarah (col)	80 yrs.	November 21, 1871
Pyatt	infant dau. of Jos. B. & Joanna P.	3 hrs.	November 25, 1871
Sullivan	R. W.	62 yrs. 10 m.	January 11, 1872
Smith	Addie May	1 yr.	January 11, 1872
Gatt	William	30 yrs	January 26, 1872
Winslow	Edward (col)	42 years	April 2, 1872
Gainey	Sarah (col)	22 years	April 29, 1872
Trapier	Hannah Mary	54 yrs.	May 1, 1872
Smith	James (died in Charleston)	74 yrs.	May 22, 1872
Detyens	Mrs.	54 yrs.	November 7, 1872
Ford	Frederick Wentworth	60 yrs.	November 30, 1872
Read	John Harleston	1 yr. 5 mo.	February 23, 1873
Waldo	Mrs. S. C. St.	73 yrs.	March 29, 1873
Risley	George Ezra	5 mo. 16 d.	June 7, 1873
FitzSimons	Mrs. Elizabeth Porcher	67 yrs.	June 16, 1873
Williams	Mrs. Marianne	65 years	June 22, 1873
Carr	John Magill	49 yrs. 3 m. 8 d.	July 18, 1873
Thompson	Anna Malvina	1 yr. 11 mo.	July 24, 1873
Dorrill	Elizabeth Sarah (col)	22 yrs. 5 m. 27 d.	August 9, 1873
Byrd	Cleland Kinloch	49 yrs. 9 m. 3 d.	August 14, 1873
Ford	Joseph Walter	8 yrs. 7 m. 2 d.	August 28, 1873
Simmons	Wilson (col)	1 yr. 8 m. 26 d.	September 13, 1873
Ford	Stephanus	43 yrs. 5 m. 5 d.	October 17, 1873
Ellis	Mrs. Mary Lesesne	38 yrs. 8 m. 12 d.	November 20, 1873
Ford	Martha Georgeana	42 yrs. 22 days	December 3, 1873
Morse	Albert Dunbar	9 months	December 20, 1873
Markley	Mrs. Amelia	28 yrs. 10 m. 22 d.	December 26, 1873
Heriot	Francis Withers	49 yrs. 8 mo. 8 d.	December 29, 1873
Richardson	Mrs. Mary Catherine	21 yrs. 12 d.	January 8, 1874
Ford	Elizabeth Shackelford	14 yrs. 6 m. 28 d.	January 10, 1874
Jones	inf. dau. of W. H. Jones (col)	4 days	February 18, 1874
Waldo	Katey (col)	83 yrs.	May 11, 1874
Springs	Mrs. Catharine	49 yrs.	June 16, 1874
Vaux	Paul FitzSimons	6 mos. 22 days	June 18, 1874
Capel	Louis Frederick	8 mo. 4 days.	September 11, 1874
Horry	Elias	12 yrs.	September 24, 1874
Manigault	Edward	58 yrs.	October 4, 1874
Haenel	John Louis	9 mos. 12 days	October 22, 1874
Thomas	Martha C.	64 years	January 8, 1875
Lucas	Alethea	2 mos. 29 days	February 3, 1875
Trapier	Henry (d. in Charleston)	24 yrs.	April 5, 1875
White	Richard Green	48 yrs. 11 m. 9 d.	May 21, 1875
Fraser	Robert Ellison	5 mo. 10 d.	June 29, 1875
Tucker	Joseph (col)	40 yrs.	August 31, 1875
Lother	James	32 yrs.	September 30, 1875
Waldo	Andrew (col)	75 yrs.	October 3, 1875
Heriot	Robert Stark	44 yrs. 10 m. 10 d.	November 5, 1875
Ford	Mrs. Mary Warham	65 yrs.	November 6, 1875
Henning	John Shackelford	22 yrs. 15 days	November 19, 1875
Doar	Mrs. Martha Prior	22 yrs.	December 14, 1875
Stalvey	Mrs. Elizabeth	66 yrs. 98 m. 22 d.	January 19, 1876
Vernon	Mrs. Maria Elizabeth	26 yrs. 7 m. 13 d.	April 21, 1876
Vaux	John Stoney	3 mos. 19 d.	June 29, 1876

Surname	Christian Name	Age	Time of Burial
Welsh	William Waff	1 mo. 13 d.	July 4, 1876
Ahrens	Gabriel	27 yrs. 10 m. 3 d.	November 5, 1876
Dorrill	William Henry·	13 yrs. 8 mo. 20 d.	February 11, 1877
Sparkman	Mrs. Martha Emma	34 yrs. 11 mo. 10 d.	March 12, 1877
Butler	R. G.	35 yrs.	March 19, 1877
Read	Mrs. Esther Jane	54 yrs. 98 m. 5 d.	March 26, 1877
Detyens	Sarah Eliza	1 yr. 3 mo. 13 d.	July 3, 1877
Fraser	Sarah M. (Mrs.)	35 yrs. 1 mo.	August 31, 1877
Bryan	Joseph	47 yrs.	October 6, 1877
Munnerlyn	William C.	64 yrs.	December 7, 1877
Conklin	Nicholas	67 yrs.	March 2, 1878
Harvey	William	40 yrs.	August 6, 1878
Bossard	Mrs. Matilda A.	76 yrs. 2 m. 9 d.	August 13, 1878
Smith	Andrew	8 days	September 16, 1878
Shaw	Judge Archibald James	49 yrs 11 mo. 13 d.	October 5, 1878
Bourke	William Jeannerette	5 yrs. 2 mo. 2 d.	October 12, 1878
Anderson	Clarence Eugene	3 yrs. 4 mo. 4 d.	October 18, 1878
Divine	Mrs. Kothene Caroline	22 yrs. 2 mo. 9 d.	October 27, 1878
Walker	Legrand Guerry	2 yrs. 11 mo. 2 d.	November 7, 1878
Heyward	Murchison	18 years	November 7, 1878
Murrel	Joseph (col)	60 years	November 8, 1878
Morse	Virginia Leolan	2 yrs. 9 m. 17 d.	December 10, 1878
Tilton	Robert Allston	22 yrs. 9 m. 1 d.	December 22, 1878
Britton	Henry Forster	3 yrs. 6 mo.	December 29, 1878
FitzSimons	Pauline	14 yrs. 2 m. 15 d.	January 4, 1879
Hickman	Mrs. Anna Eliza	18 yrs. 1 m. 13 d.	January 17, 1879
Smith	Emma Sarah (d. Charleston) 59 yrs.		March 28, 1879
Avant	William Green	77 yrs. 1 mo.	April 4, 1879
Barnwell	Mrs. Kate M.	31 yrs. 10 mo. 18 d.	April 13, 1879
Fraser	Robert Lovat	29 yrs. 7 m. 23 d.	June 13, 1879
Fraser	Florence	11 mo. 2 d.	June 18, 1879
Carr	Mrs. Sarah B. (died in Plantersville)		July 10, 1879
Merriman	Lilian Maud	1 yr. 2 mo. 9 d.	July 10, 1879
Forster	Dr. Alexius Mador	63 yrs. 10 m. 15 d.	July 31, 1879
Forster	Mrs. Mary P.	32 yrs. 1 mo.	October 11, 1879
Bourke	Anna Tilton	1 mo. 33 d.	November 9, 1879
Trapier	Wm. Shubric (d. Charleston) 30 yrs. 3 m. 5 d.		November 20, 1879
Bailey	Allard Belin	4 yrs. 10 m. 8 d.	November 29, 1879
Walker	Hasford	31 y. 4 m. 14 d.	December 9, 1879
Hucks	Wilmot Jenkins	10 yrs.	January 11, 1880
Waring	William H.	40 yrs.	April 21, 1880
Glennie	Rev. Alexander (at Charlotte, Va.)		November

(All Saints Wac.)

Benj. Allston, temp'y Rector

Parker	Daniell Hayes	25 y. 8 m. 7 d.	March 25, 1881
Bailey	Laval Williams	5 9	July 24, 1881
Conyers	Samuel Oliver	23 9 7	October 16, 1881
Forster	Alexis Mador	34 5 24	October 31, 1881
Anderson	infant of Clarence Anderson's		December 29, 1881
Walker	Wm. W.		
Pyatt	Mrs. Joanna		June 4, 1882
Hazelden			Nov.
Bourke	Jessie J. Viola		Nov.

Surname	Christian Name	Age	Time & Place of Burial
	Benj. Allston, Rector		
Gibson	Mrs. Florence Lee	41 yrs.	Died Macon, Ga. Feb 7.
			interred Feb. 11, 1883
Ehney	Peter T.	40 y. 10 m. 2 d.	March 21, 1883
Pedrick	Robert (from Pedericktown, NJ)	16 yrs.	April 12, 1883
Jefferson	Thomas (col)	80 yrs.	April 16, 1883
Rembert	Herbert	23 yrs.	June 9, 1883
			(murdered June 7)
Collins	Joseph E.	40 y. 9 m. 22 d.	August 6, 1883 (M. E. C. Cemty.)
Wallace			August 7, 1883 (M. E. C. Cemty.)
Vaux	Christopher F.		February 25, 1884
Mayrant	Sarah Ann	17 minutes	July 14, 1865 Entered by request
Mayrant	William H.	47 yrs.	March 17, 1886 of daughter. No
			Rector at time of death. B. A.
Mitchell	Charles Williams	21 yrs 8-9 d.	July 9, 1884 Methodist Cemetery
Williams	Francis	64 years	July 19, 1884 Bapt. Cemetery
Mitchell	Eliza M. Cokry	52 yrs.	July 23, 1884 Methodist cemetery
Parker	(Mrs.) Charlotte Mead	3 yrs	Sept. 11, 1884 Church yard
Hume	(Mrs. Anna Helen	25 yrs. 1 m 3 d	Sept. 25, 1884 Pr. Fredk Chpl
Dorrill	Mrs. Alafair Delilah	53 yrs 11 mo 2 d.	Sept. 27, 1884 Ch. Yard
Pyatt	John Francis	67 yrs & 64 d.	October 20, 1884 Ch Yard
Anderson	George Congdon	44 y. 9 m 9 d	October 23, 1884 at residence
Palmer	Asa Benoin	50 y. 5 m. 18 d.	October 27, 1884 at residence
Middleton	Arthur de Lancey	34 y. 6 m. 9 day	December 12, 1884 at Church
Saunders	Liddy Joanna	13	March 22, 1885 at Residence
Saunders	Elizabeth		March 25, 1885 "
Canes	Martin Van Buren	17 y. 7 m 3 d.	April 3, 1885 "
Risley	Samuel Morse	3 yr 3 mo.	April 7, 1885 Church
Thomas	James	52 yrs	April 23, 1885 at residence
Hazard	Walter Rowland	9 mos.	June 21, 1885 residence
Parker	Mrs. Mary T.		September 7, 1885 at church by Lay Reader
Ward	Mayham Lee	24 yrs.	October 14, 1885 Church
Wilburn	William	31 yrs.	November 2, 1885 Church
Butts	Oliver I.	29 yrs. 2 mos 10 days	March 29, 1886 Church
Price	Martha LaBruce	76 yrs.	April 5, 1886 Residence
Hazard	Benjamin Ingell	7 mos. 26 days	July 19, 1886 Church
Rouquie	Elizabeth Snow	33 years	September 23, 1887 Church
Clayter	William		September 13, 1887 Cemetery
Nettles	Oliver Gregory	2 mos.	October 30, 1887 Ch. Yard
Huger	David (negro)		November 5, 1887 residence
Hazard	Oliver Perry	8 yrs 7 mos 6 d.	November 24, 1887 Ch. Yd.
Cooper	C. (Mrs.)	80 yrs.	December 3, 1887 Meth. Cem.
Hume	John A.	65 yrs.	December 10, 1887 Hume Plantn.
Parker	Rutledge	37 yrs	April 1, 1888 Ch. Yard
Hazard	Allen Presbrey	9 mos. 27 days	September 1, 1888 Ch. Yard
Ellis	St. John P.		December 5, 1888 Ch. Yard
Hazard	Jessie Minnie	33 yrs.	January 8, 1889 Ch. Yard
Lowndes	R. I'on	44 yrs.	May 13, 1889 Ch. Yd
Detyens	Joseph Morgan	1 months	July 19, 1889
Conklin	Maria Amelia	2 yrs &	October 9, 1889 Bp Grave y'd
Hazard	Lena May	19 yrs. &	October 26, 1889 Ch Y'd
Merriman	Louise	6 yrs & 6 mos.	November 1, 1889 Ch Y'd

Surname	Christian Name	Age	Time & Place of Burial	
Bush	Eunice M.	19 yrs.	April 15, 1890	Ch. Y'd
Krengel	Oswald Richard	2 weeks	June 4, 1890	Meth. Cem.
Wright	Wm. Buck	3 mos &	June 25, 1890	Ch. Yd.
Macusker	Mrs. F. W.	78 yrs.	July 10, 1890	Ch. Yd.
Phillips	William	7 mos &	July 16, 1890	Meth. Cem.
Richardson	T. N.	42 yrs.	July 26, 1890	Meth. Cem.
White	John	34 yrs.	September 7, 1890	Ch. Yd.
Divine	James	68 yrs.	September 27, 1890	Ch. Yd.
Detyens	Eliza	6 yrs.	November 1, 1890	Meth. Cem.
Springs	Fanny		December 23, 1890	"
Pyatt	Harriet Elinor	2 mos.	March 17, 1891	Ch. Yard
Krengel	Mrs. George		June 2, 1891	Meth. Cem.
Porter	Susan Magadalen		June 19, 1891	Ch. Yard
Izard	Ralph S.		November 4, 1891	Ch. Yard
Read	Annie S.	17 yrs	March 5, 1891	Ch. Yard

The Burial Service was read over the Remains of all persons whose Names are herein recorded beginning with Mrs. Elizabeth Snow Roquie (Sept. 23rd/ 1887) & those following ending with inclusive by the Rector, Rev. Stewart McQueen, From July 1st 1887 to June 1st 1892, 4 yrs. & 11 mos.

Conckling   Mary E.   34 yrs.   February 4, 1893   Baptist Grounds
     died Feb. 2d, 93. Mrs. Conckling was communicant of P. E. Church.
                                  John B. Williams, Rector

Trapier   Marion Heyward   41 years 6 mos.   February 9, 1893   Church Yard
        Died in Aiken Feb. 7th. service read by Rev. Mr. Edgerton, Daughter of Rev. Mr. Trapier, Rector of St. Michaels Charleston. Jno. B. Williams

Munnerlyn   Benjamin   25 years   March 18, 1893   Church Yard
        in Savannah from a blow by a pile-driver. Son of Major B. A. & Mrs. Munnerlyn.
                                    Jno. B. Williams

Johnstone   William C.   65 years Charleston, from this Church March 1893
        Died March 15 93, suddenly of hear-failure. Buried in Charleston March 26th 93.
                                  Jno. B. Williams

Lance   Mrs. Sarah Laura, widow of Rev. Mr. Lance. 82 years. Church Cemetery.
        March 1893. March 18, 93 in Charleston, S. C. March 21st, 93. Buried in Georgetown, S. C. By Rev. A. Toomer Porter

Tilton   Edward M. 1893-4   64 years. Church Cemetery, April 10th, 1893.
        April 9th 1893 Charleston. Father of Mrs. Merriman, Buried April 10th 93.
                                  John B. Williams

Atkinson   Susan Ann   86 years.   Church Yard, July 13, 1893
        July 12, 1893 A. M. Heart Failure in Georgetown. Relict of J. M. Atkinson.
                                  John B. Williams

Skinner   Anne Rebecca   16 mo.   Cemetery, October 21, 1893.
        Died Oct. 20th 93. Parents: Mr. & Mrs. Benjamin Skinner.
                                  John B. Williams

Gargoty   Alphonsius   10 days December 6, 1893. Cemetery, Methodist.
Dec. 5th 93. Thomas Gogarty. Rebecca Ward Gogarty.
                                   John B. Williams

Lucas   Anna Maria   5 months   Episcopal Grounds. Dec. 22, 1893
Dec. 23d, 93. Infant child of E. M. Lucas & wife.
                                   John B. Williams

Congdon   George Reynolds   53 years   Dec. 27, 1893. Episcopal Grounds
Christmas Eve, 5 P. M. 1893   John B. Williams

Gargorty   Douglas   15 mo.   Feb. 14, 1894. Feb. 13, '94.
Thos. Gargoty, Rebecca Ward Gargoty. Jno. B. Williams

Surname	Christian Name	Age	Time & Place of Burial
Ford	James Rees	40	December 16, 1893 Episcopal Cemetery
Rembert	Stephen	63	Episcopal Grounds April 1, 1894
Bush	Oliver Arnold	25	Epis. Grounds June 20, 1894
Walker	Kate T.	40	August 12, 1894 Epis. Cemetery
Walker	May	1 Day	July 16, 1894 Epis. Cemetery
Detyens	Mary E.	44	Methodist Cemetery October 1, 1894
Hazzard	Thomas Edward	57	October 24, 1894 Epis. Cemetery
Bush	R. O.	80	October 19, 1894 4½ P. M. Episcopal Cemetery
Merriman	Thos.	14	Episcopal Cemetery November 5, 1894 4 P. M.
Donaldson	Robert J.	58	November 22, 1894 Friendfield on the Waccamaw, in the woods
Tilton	Amelia Catherine	62	Episcopal Cemetery February 8, 1895 4 P. M.
Hazard	Hattie Gwendolyn	7 mo.	Episcopal Cemetery July 13, 1895
Hazard	Alice Bonneau Tamplet	35	July 10, 1895 Episcopal Cemetery
Fraser	Robert Ellison	79	July 28, 1895 6 P. M. Episcopal Cemetery
Risley	David	71 yrs.	Sept. 18, 1895 Epis. Cemetery
Young	Milley Hilton	Infant	Aug. 1895
Coachman	Mary Helen Ford	76	Epis. Cemetery Oct. 19, 1895. 1 P. M.
Trapier	Rev. Richard S.	85	Epis. Cemetery Oct. 26, 1895
Fraser	Eliza Ellison	25	Epis. Cemetery Jan. 31, 1896

Time of Death	Cause of Death	Clergyman
December 14 Albany, Ga.	Consumption	John Bryan Williams
Saturday night March 31, '94	Exhaustion & weakness	John B. Williams
June 19, 94	Consumption	John B. Williams
Aug. 22, 94	Kidney Trouble	by Rev. Mr. Guerry in absence of Rector, Jno. B. W.
July 15, 94		Without service. Jno. B. Williams
Sep. 30, 94	Paralysis	Jno. B. Williams
Oct. 23, 94 S. Island	Paralysis of Brain	Jno. B. Williams
Oct. 28, 94 Sunday morning about 7 o'clock	Old age	Jno. B. Williams
Nov. 4, 94. 6 P. M. Georgetown, S. C.	Rapid case of fever	Jno. B. Williams
Nov. 21, 94	Paralysis resulting from Hemorrhagic Fever.	John B. Williams
February 7, 95 Georgetown, S. C.	Apoplexy	John B. Williams
May 9, 9 P. M. 1895	Inflamation	Jno. B. Williams
July 12, 95 12½ P. M.	Consumption	Jno. B. Williams
July 28, 95 A. M.	Heart Failure	Jno. B. Williams
16 Sep. 95	Congestive Chill	Rev. Mr. Guerry
Aug. 95	Spinal troubles	Jno. B. Williams
Oct. 18, 95 Charleston	Old Age	John B. Williams
Oct. 22, 95 Highlands, N. C.	Old Age	Rev. Mr. Campbell of St. Paul's, Charleston
Jan. 28, 11 ½ A. M. Father's House	Pneumonia	John B. Williams

Surname	Christian Name	Age	Time & Place of Burial
Middleton	Thomas	60	Charleston, Middleton Estate, Ashley River.
Allston	Julia Lowndes	• 20	Feb. 17, 1896 Episcopal Cemetery
Pyatt	Edward Nowell	31	Episcopal Cemetery April 1, 1896
Merriman	Desdemona	19 mo.	May 4, 1896 Epis. Cemetery
Hazzard	Elliott Waight	52 years	Epis. Cemetery June 4, 1896 12 A. M.
Rembert	Florine S. Rembert	30 yrs.	Epis. Cemetery June 5, 1896
Brunson	Ella Reed	50	Epis. Cemetery June 19, 1896
McKusker	F. W.	65	Epis. Cemetery July 23, 1896
Taylor	Charlotte Ellis	47	December 8, 1896 1 P. M. Methodist Cemetery.
Vernon	Laurence	25	December 28, 1896 Sampit, Private Grounds.
Hagadorn	Gen.	81	Georgetown, S. C. January 2, 1897
Nowell	Lionel C. Nowell	60	Buried, January, 7, 1897 Epis. Cemetery
Vernon	Jas. Hamilton	23	January 20, 1897 Sampit
Vernon	Henry	30	Father's Home, Sampit January 28, 1897
Allston	Adele Petigru Allston widow of Gov. Allston	86 Born Nov 11, 1810	Epis. Cemetery Nov. 27, 1896
Hooper	Jessie Lee	2 yrs. 7 mo.	In the Country. Oct. 8, 1897
Izzard	Esther Jane	49	Nov. 16, 1897
Hazard	Ben. I.	67	Cemetery of Epis. Thursday 5½ P. M.

Time of Death	Cause of Death	Clergyman
Feb. 6, 96	Found dead in bed from natural causes	Jno. B. Williams
Feb. 15, 96 Charleston.	Pneumonia	Rev. Ben. Allston
May 31, 1896 New York	Pneumonia	Rev. Jno. B. Williams
May 3, 96 3 A. M.	Pneumonia	Jno. B. Williams
Monday June 1, 96	Tuberculosis of Throat	John B. Williams
Monday, June 2d 96 New York	Peritonitis	Jno. B. Williams
June 17, 96 near Florence	Gastritis	John B. Williams
Tuesday, July 21, 96 Farmersville[?], Va.	Apoplexy	Jno. B. Williams
Dec. 5, 1896 Charleston, S. C.	Hemorhage	John B. Williams
Dec. 27th, 96	Paralysis of Heart from Grippe	Jno. B. Williams
Died Jan. 1, 1897	Old Age	Jno. B. Williams
Died July 1896 Berkeley Springs, Va.		John B. Williams
Jan. 19, 97 Georgetown	Pneumonia	John B. Williams
Jan. 27, 1897 11 P. M.	Grippe and Pneumonia	John B. Williams
Died Nov. 26, 1896 Chicora Plantation		Rev. Mr. Guerry & Rev. Ben. Allston
Died Oct. 7, 97	Chronic Malarial Fever	Jno. B. Williams
Nov. 15, 1897 at Harleston Reed's	Creeping Paralysis	Jno. B. Williams
Church April 21, 1898	Died April 19, 1898 Heart Disease	John B. Williams

PRINCE GEORGE WINYAH RECORDS 1815-1916

Surname	Christian Name	Age	Time & Place of Burial
Sparkman	Dr. Geo. Eugene	43	Episcopal Cemetery 1 P. M.
Johnson	G. Lester	30	Episcopal Cemetery 4 P. M. September 23, 1898

Time of Death	Cause of Death	Clergyman
May 30, 1898	Died May 29, 1898 2 A. M. Congestion of Brain	John B. Williams
Sept. 22d, 1898 Georgetown, S. C.	Cancer	Rev. L. F. Guerry

Rev. G. H. Johnston, D. D., Rector.

Surname	Christian Name	Age	Date

1899

Surname	Christian Name	Age	Date
Henning	Miss Sarah G. F.		July 10th
Ballenberger	Sparkman	2 days	Aug. 18th
Nettles	Elizabeth Edmonstone	3 months 21 days	Nov. 6th
Nettles	Julian Chisholm	54 8 m. 15 d.	Nov. 25th
Ruggles	Hubard Laten	3 m. 23 d.	Dec. 9th

1900

Surname	Christian Name	Age	Date
Ford	George Gilliard	71 y. 5 m.	Jan. 19th

1901

Surname	Christian Name	Age	Date
Rembert	Mrs. Laura Sarah	70 years	Feb. 25th
Du Vernat	Richard Charles	1 y. 1 mo. 27 d.	May 26th
Lloyd	Mrs. Bernice	24 y. 5 m. 7 d.	Nov. 4th
Pierson	Mrs. J. H.	60 yrs.	Dec. 3d
Andrews	Miss Mary	48 yrs.	Nov. 29th
Rogers	Mrs. D. K.	71 yrs.	Dec. 3d

1902

Surname	Christian Name	Age	Date
Porter	A. Toomer, D. D.	74 y. 1 m. 29 d.	March 30th
Wills	Harry Oliver	20 mo. 25 d.	May 11, 1902
Skinner	Lee Taloe	7 mo. 15 d.	May 28, 1902
Lucas	Mrs. Henrietta	45 y. 7 d.	Nov. 11, 1902
Congdon	George, Sr.	66 yrs.	Sept. 24, 1903
Tucker	Henry M., M. D. Anna Jane	70 yrs.	Jan. 10, 1904
Munnerlyn	Mrs. Benja. A.	65 yrs.	July 15, 1904
Bailey	Thomas P., M. D.	72 yrs.	July 19, 1904
Bourke	Mrs. Ida C.	63 yrs.	Oct. 29, 1904
Walker	Mrs. Ethel Anna	21 yrs.	Oct. 29, 1904
Fraser	Saml Sydney	76 yrs.	Nov. 25, 1904
Bellune	son of M. S. Bellune & wife	1 yr. 3 mos.	Dec. 30, 1904
Hazzard	Capt. Miles Wm.		Dec. 31, 1904
Farr	Raymond S.		Feb. 28, 1905
Read	Mrs. J. Harleston		April 29, 1905
James	Mary Elizabeth		March 16, 1905
Jefferson	Mrs. Emily[?] (col)	74 yrs.	June 24, 1905
Lubs	H. Dedrick	72 yrs.	Sept. 7, 1905
Merriman	Thomas M.	58 yrs.	Nov. 18, 1905
Porter	Walter C.	43 days	Dec. 23, 1905
Lubs	Sarah A. C.	83 yrs.	Jan. 13, 1906
LaBruce	John	56 yrs.	Jan. 21, 1906
Lucas	Elliot Maxwell	65 yrs.	Feb. 25, 1906
Gardner	John James	15 days	Jan. 2, 1907
Dozier	John F.		Jan. 29, 1907
Ford	Wm. Rees	61 yrs.	Feb. 1, 1907
Lawrence	Abram (col)	101 yrs.	June 10, 1907

Surname	Christian Name	Age	Date
White	Hannah Mary	48 yrs. 26 d.	June 22, 1907
Bryan	Herman	49 yrs. 41 d.	July 26, 1907
Bailey	Maria L.		Nov. 6, 1907
Ford	J. Rees	94 yrs.	Nov. 10. 1907
Young	Fritz	69 yrs.	Oct. 12, 1909
McDaniels		5 mos.	April 28, 1911

Percy J. Robottom, Rector

Date	Name	Age	Date of Death
1912			
Feb. 15	Robert Sparkman	45	Feb. 13
Feb. 16	V. V. Nunnely	36	Feb. 15
Feb. 25	Mrs. Herbert Smith	43	Feb. 23
March 21	John Nicholas Concklin	60	March 19
April 27	Louis LaBruce	72	Apr. 25
May 1	Allston Read	75	Apr. 29
May 12	Mrs. P. Wright	39	May 6
June 27	J. Louis Haenel	66	June 26
Nov. 11	Mrs. J. Logan Merriman	26	Nov. 10
Nov. 21	Susan McClellan Norman	23	Nov. 20
July 1914	Julia Cornell		July 1914
July 21	Ball Caines		July 22
July 29	Dolly Caines		July 30
	Josephine Ford		
Oct. 20	E. M. Sparkman		Oct. 21
Nov. 26	Mary Elizabeth Concklin		Nov. 27
Dec. 13	Nellie Johnson		Dec. 14
Dec. 28	Mrs. William C. Johnstone		Dec. 30, 1914
June 21, 1913	Albert Nicholson Johnston		June 22
June 25, 1913	Renty Tucker (col). The old Sexton of the Church 83 yrs old. Faithful & loyal Communicant. Buried with honors.		
Sept. 1913	Benjamin Skinner	16	Sept. 2
Oct. 4, 1913	Albert Springs (Captain)	62	Oct. 6
1915			
Jan. 26	Anne Henning Ford	72	Jan. 24
Died in Charleston, S. C.			
Feb. 17	Mrs. A. E. Gould		Feb. 28
Died in Hendersonville, N. C.			
March 19	Mrs. Lola Hosier Snow		March 19
July 14	Thomas Ford	76	July 18
July 17	William Henry Dorrell	86	July 18

COMMUNICANTS

Names	Date	How Received
Fraser, Hugh Wilson, Jr.	Dec. 13, 1916	Confirmation
Walker, John Tull	"	"
Smith, Buford Colclough	"	"
Bull, Joseph Lawrie	"	"
Pyatt, Julia Bossard	"	"
Emerson, Hilda Witherspoon	"	"
Gardner, Mary Catharine	"	"
Edmonds, Frederick William	"	"
Boyt, John	"	"
Boyt, (Mrs.) Blanche (Eliason)	"	"
Skipper, Retha Lee	May 23, 1917	"
Ford, Frederick Wentworth	May 24, 1917	"
Russell, Sarah Lois	Dec. 12, 1817	"
Doar, Elias Marion	"	"
Munnerlyn, William Wilson	"	"
Ford, Ellen Hume	"	"
Hilliard, Katherin Haren	"	"
Wood, Alan 3rd	Mar. 6, 1919	Transfer fr. Calvary Ch., Conshohocken,Pa.
Doar, Virginia Elizabeth	April 4, 1919	Confirmation
Fraser, Lily Ellison	"	"
Ford, Alexander Hume	"	"
LaBruce, Allard Flagg	"	"
Doar, Bachman	"	"
Gardner, William Albert	"	"
Oliver, Hugh Lawson, Jr.	"	"
Fraser, (Mrs.) Harriet Aldridge (Gibson)	"	"
Campbell, William Archibald	"	"
Gaillard, Dr. William Minott	"	"
LaBruce, (Mrs.) Esther (Richardson)	Jan. 29, 1920	Tran. fr. Prince Frederick's, Pee Dee
Carraway, Edward Haselden	April 28, 1920	Confirmation
Brock, Lillian May	"	"
Doar, (Mrs.) Anne (Chewning)	"	"
Johnston, Nellie Geraldin	"	"
Pyatt, Joseph Benjamin Allston	"	"
Wingate, James Walter	"	"
Waddell, Doris Margaret Louise	"	"
Rosa, Helen	Feb. 9, 1921	"
Rosa, Julia Allison	"	"
LaBruce, Lucy Tucker	"	"
Ward, Frances McCrody	Feb. 9, 1920[sic]	"
Hilliard, John McCarten	"	"

Memoranda

Removed, Lives in Georgia

Removed, Lives Columbia, SC. Transferred Christ Ch: Greenville, SC, May 1936. Transferred back to Pr: George Church Winter of 1946-57.

Married Harold Kaminski Dec. 1925
Married Rev. Jno. A. Pinckney Oct. 8, 1931, and moved to Allendale, SC
Transferred to St. Andrews, Mt. Pleasant 3-11-80
Transferred to St. Luke's Church, Charleston, SC, May 20, 1918
Removed to Middletown, Delaware transferred to Trinity Ch: Wilmington, Del. Apr. 26 1948
"
Gone
Died Dec. 5, 1939
Married Arthur L. Dellinger. Transferred Jan. 3 '37 to Ch. of the Holy Comforter, Sumter

Removed to Jacksonville, Fla.
Married Clarence V. Steinhart Dec. 27, 1944
moved Transferred Calvary, Wadesboro, NC, Feb. 1, 1961

Married J. V. Nielsen, lives Charleston, Transferred Ch: of the Holy Communion, Feb. 10, 1938
Removed to West Palm Beach, Fla. about 1926
At sea (literally)

Transferred to Christ Ch: Charlotte, NC. Nov. 15, 1949
Moved to New York City, Transferred to Holyrood Church, N. Y. C. May 27, '34
Died Nov. 38, 1939

Died May 27, 1930
Mar. J. Herman Carraway

Gone
Removed to Tappahannock, Va.
Married Robt. A. Clyburn, Oct. 27, 1924. Lives in New York City. Transferred to Holyrood Ch: NYC Mar. 31, 1941
Died Sept. 14, 1939

Died in Georgetown, SC. Jan. 23, 1943
Removed

Married Richard B. Powell, Aug. 2, 1944.

Names	Date	How Received
Ward, Frances McCrody	Feb. 9, 1920[sic]	"
Hilliard, John McCarten	"	"
Cranwell, Henry Arthur	"	"
Cranwell, Lelia Mary (Mrs. H. A.)	"	"
Cranwell, Jack Pierpont	"	"
Cranwell, James Logan	"	"
Cranwell, Mary Alice	"	"
Hucks, Myrtle DeMichell	"	"
Wendt, Adelbert Thomas	Feb. 27, 1921	"
Lee, Iva	March 26, 1922	"
Bowers, Florence Emily	"	"
LaBruce, Eugene Fitzsimmons	"	"
LaBruce, Grace Dennis (Mrs. Eugene)	"	
Clark, (Mrs.) Lila (Johnston)	Oct, 15 1922	At her request
Trenholm, Alfred G.	Dec. 29, 1923	
Gardner, Annie Bertha	May 3, 1925	By Confirmation
Fraser, Wm. Lesesne	"	"
Mercer, Mabel	"	"
Couturier, Anna Sinkler	"	"
Vaughan, Alice M.	"	"
Grisillo, Screvin Wm.	"	"
Jacobs, Wm. Napoleon	"	"
Johnstone, James V.	"	"
Overton, Louis L.	"	"
Bruorton, (Mrs.) Enid Ford	"	"
Fraser, Ellen Aldridge	June 27, 1925	"
Plowden, Edwin Ruthven	May 11, 1876	Presbyterian
Oliver, (Mrs.) Martha Benn	"	By Confirmation
Clerc, George Edward	"	"
Young, Wm. Coleman	"	"
Campbell, Jas. Archibald	"	"
Wingate, Mable Virginia	"	"
Johnstone, Francis E. Jr.	"	"
Walker, Mrs. Julia Tull	May 1926	Trans. from Holy Tr. Ch. W. P. B. Fla.
Hayes, Leonard	Aug 1926	
Witte, Franz D.	Aug 1926	Transfer
Witte, (Mrs. F. D.) Hattie S.	Aug 1926	"
Boyd, (Mrs.) Marian Godfrey	July 1926	"
Boyd, Chas. W. Jr.	July 1926	"
Boyd, Gilespie Godfrey	July 1926	"

Memoranda

Married June 4, 1930 to Russell E. Davis, Transferred to All Saints, Waccamaw
Lives near Plantersville, S. C. Feb 19, '31. Oak Grove
Transferred to St. Paul's., Summerville, S. C., Dec. 27, 1921
   "
    "
    "
    "

Married Julian Albergotti (1929) moved to Charlotte, N. C.
Removed. Lives in New York
Removed

Moved from place to place so much, does not know where she was last registered.
By transfer from Ch. of Good Shepherd, Columbia, SC
Transferred to Holyrood Church, N. Y. C. May 27, '34

Married Legare Hamilton
Married H.E. Padgett Transferred to the Church of the Epiphany, Eutawville, SC. 10-12-8-
Married T. Cordes Lucas; lives on Santee. Died Mar., 28, 1936
Removed to Charleston, SC
Removed to St. Alban's, Kingstree, S. C. Died Kingstree about 1938
Died March 3, 19276

Removed to Columbia, SC. 1926 Transferred to Trinity Ch: Cola 1930
Married 1933 to Lieut. Andrew O'Meara, U. S. A. Lives in Army posts

Married 2nd Herbert L. Smith Dec. 20, 1946
Lives Huber, Georgia

Married Sept. 20, 1926 to Chas. A. Holland of Florence, SC. Left the Church Feb. 29, 1952

Married Oct. 1932 to Charles Schovenling. Divorced 1933
Died Mar. 31, 1937
Removed to Charleston about 1931
   "
Died May 22, 1947
Removed to Florence, SC
Removed to Natchez, Miss. 1950

Names	Date	How Received
Boyd, Elizabeth	July 1926	Transfer
Bull, Henry DeSaussure	Sept. 1, 1924	Transfer from
Bull, (Mrs. H. D.) Gertrude C.	"	Transfer from
Chas. W. Glover, Capt. U. S. A.	May 29, 1927	By Confirmation
Jno. Percival LaBruce	"	"
Lucile Meggett King	"	"
Jas. Ritchie S. Siau	"	"
Geo. Thos. Ford, Jr.	"	"
Ora Belle Hucks	"	"
Mary Jacobs	"	"
Agnes L. Emmerson	"	"
Mattie McK. Couturier	Apr. 29, 1928	By Confirmation
Dorothy Edna Gardner	"	"
Lillian L. Johnstone	"	"
Elizabeth H. Ford	"	"
Mrs. Mary Eliz. Panton	"	"
Kenneth W. Karnes	"	"
(Mrs. K. W.) Edyth W. Karnes	"	"
Miss Julia Cornell	July 8, 1928	
(Mrs. C. W.) Catherine Glover	July 8, 1928	Transfer from Mississippi
Richard C. Patton	Apr. 19, 1929	
Julian L. Johnson	May 26, 1929	By Confirmation
Virginia Rhem	"	"
Myrtle H. Carraway	"	"
Helen H. Gardner	Mar 16, 1930	By Confirmation
Henley Chapman, Jr.	"	"
John H. Bull	"	"
(Mrs. Leroy) Margaret White Doar	June 13, 1930	Transfer from Trinity Ch: Portland, Conn.
E. Olin Gardner	Jan. 18, 1931	By Confirmation
Paul L. Baker	"	"
Harriett McG. Witte	"	"
Richard Lowndes Allston	Feb. 26 ,1932	Confirmed 1897
J. Chas Tamplet, Jr.	Feb. 28, 1932	By Confirmation
G. LaBruce Tamplet	"	"
Wm. A. Johnstone	"	"
Dorothy C. Sinclair	"	"
Agnes Lula Gardner	"	"
Margaret Bourne	"	"
Caroline K. Bull	"	"
Gertrude C. Bull	"	"

Memoranda

Married Oct. 14, 19836 to Jesse P. Thomas
Calvary Church, Fletcher, N. C. Rector
Calvary Church, Fletcher, N .C.
Left. Capt. in U. S. Army. Transferred to Ft. Bragg, N. C. Transferred to St. Wilford's Ch: Marion, Ala., June 23, 1941
Transferred to St. Philips Ch: Charleston, S. C. June 13, '46. Married Bacot A. Wayne Oct. 8, '29

Captain U. S. A. Accidentally killed Dec. 30, 1943
Married Norman H. Nutall: lives elsewhere. Transferred S. Martin's Charlotte, NC Feb. 18, 1944.
Removed to St. Alban's, Kingstree, SC
Married August 1935 to Lee C. Ballard, Jr.
Married July 22, 1937 to Wm. E. Lesesne. Lives Greelyville, SC
Transferred Holy Rood Church NYC, May 27 '34
Married June 2, 1946, to Jas. B. Bagwell, Jr. of Charleston
Transferred to Trinity Ch: Columbia, SC Sept. 9, 1935

Left
Left
Transfer from Our Savior Rock Hill, SC. Confirmed there May 16, 1920. Married C. P. Jamison
See Capt. C. W. Glover above, Line 4. Transferred to St. Wilford's Ch: Marion, Ala.
Transfer from St. George's Hempstead, L. I., NY. Returned to NY. Ordained to ministry in Kentucky.
Transferred to Trinity Church, Columbia, SC, April 27, 1944.
Married Roy Hinson, resident Kingstree, SC
Married Aug. 15, 1943 to J. Francis Powell of Andrews, SC
Transferred Holyrood Church, N. Y. C., May 27 '34
Transferred to All Saints Ch: Hamlet, NC, Nov. 3, 1937
Transferred to S. Stephens Ch: Oak Ridge, Tenn. July 3, 1947.
Lives Kingstree, SC
Lives Columbia, SC
Living in Greenwood, SC, Transferred to Greenwood, SC
Married July 1, 1937 to George S. King. Lives in Columbia, SC
Transferred to All Saints Ch: Waccamaw, Feb. 26, 1932
Died August 30, 1951

Married Hunt 1942. Transferred St. Cyprians, Lufkin, Texas, Oct. 1, 1946
Transferred Holyrood Church, N. Y. C. May 27, '34
Married Dec. 1948 in Pr. George to J. Taylor Marion of Charlotte, NC
Married to Peter E. Grannis, July 31, 1943. Lives Windsor, Conn.
married to LaVern B. Terrell, Dec. 18, 1945

PRINCE GEORGE WINYAH RECORDS 1916-1936

Names	Date	How Received
Fritz Young Mercer	Feb. 5, 1933	Confirmed Feb. 5, 1933
Frederick Edward Rembert	"	"
Margaret Bentley Fraser	"	"
Sarah Victoria Bourne	"	"
Isabelle Mercer	"	"
Mildred Chapman	"	"
(Mrs. H. L.) Sallie Knox Smith	Jan. 28, 1934	Confirmed Jan. 28, 1934
Mattie Deveaux Ford	"	"
Pauline F. Tamplet	"	"
Frank William Wolfe, Jr.	"	"
Barbara Evelyn Thieleu	Feb. 3, 1935	Confirmed Feb. 3, 1935
Kathryn Waller Doar	"	"
William Lander Mahan	"	"
(Mrs. D. M.) Marguerite R. Oswald	"	"
James D. Hazzard	"	"
Jane Louis Gaegan	"	"
Mary Frances Richardson	"	
Benjamin William Bourne	Feb. 24, 1935	Conf. at Prince Fredericks, Feb. 24, 1935
C. Beaufort Albrecht	Aug. 16, 1935	Trans. from St. Lukes Ch. Chaston
Helen Walker (Mrs. C. B.) Albrecht	"	"
W. Whiteford Hayne	Jan. 19, 1935	"
(Mrs. W. W.) Margaret W. Hane	"	"
Jos. L. Bull, Sr.	Feb. 19, 1936	Confirmed Feb. 16,1936
(Mrs. J. L. Jr.) Emily Bull	"	"
Josephine Lee	"	"
(Mrs. Wm. W.) Julia Poag Doar	Mar. 8, 1936	" Mar. 8, 1936
Esther Richardson LaBruce		Confirmed May 25, 1924
Francis LeGrand Moorer		Confirmed May 25, 1924
Herbert Michel Hucks		Confirmed May 25, 1924
Susan L. Allston	old book	Confirmed Dec. 10, 1893
Herbert Michel Hucks, Jr.		Confirmed May 25, 1924
Rosa M. Hucks		Confirmed May 25, 1924

Memoranda

Trans. to St. Johns Ch: Florence, SC, Mar. 14, 1950
Married July 28, 1942 to Alfred Huger of Charleston
Married Nov. 6, 1941 to Hugh Callahan of Rutherfordton, NC
Married Neal E. Thomas, Sept. 12, 1944
Transferred to All Saints Ch: Hamlet, NC, Nov. 3, 1937
Died April 10, 1945; last res. Georgetown, SC
Transferred to Trinity Ch: Columbia, SC Sept. 9, 1935
Married Oct. 28, 1939 to John A. Witsell. Trans. to S. Philips Ch: Chaston Nov. 13, 1942

Transferred to Gethsemane Ch: Minneapolis, Minn.
Lives Tappanannock, Va.

Married November 1941 to Buck Wait. Transferred to Augusta, Ga., Jan. 13, 1955
Married, living Washington, DC. Transferred to Trinity Church there Mar. 13, 195

Transferred to Ch. Ch. Mount Pleasant, Feb. 29, 1952
    "   "

Dead.

Married Dr. Philip E. Assey, May 24, 1942
Confirmed at St. Peter's Chapel, Mar. 8. '36, for Pr. George.
Mar. J. E. Simpkins, Transferred to Ch. of the Advent, Sptburg, SC, Sept. 16, 1945
Transferred to the Ch: of the Good Shepherd, Augusta, Ga., Dec. 3, 1945
Died May 27, 1948
Transferred to St. Michael's Church Charleston, SC. May 25, 1946
Transferred to Trinity Church, Edgefield, SC, May 13, 1949
Married S. Salters McClary, June 14, 1934. Left the Church

BAPTISMS

Names	Sex	Parents	Sponsors
Harriet McGillivray Witte	F	Franz Witte	Mr. & Mrs. W. L. Sparkman
		Harriet (Sparkman) Witte	Mr. & Mrs. A. F. Witte, Sr.
George LaBruce Tamplet	M	John L. Tamplet	Paula E. Hazard
		Pauline (LaBruce) Tamplet	W. W. Munnerlyn
Hilda Witherspoon Emerson	F	E. Victor Emerson	Mrs. Chas. W. Mercer wit.
		Annie (Young) Emerson	Miss Lena Young
Agnes Lauretta Emerson	F	E. Victor Emerson	Fritz Young
		Annie (Young) Emerson	Mrs. Chas. W. Mercer
John Ellison Boyt	M	John Boyt	Alexander Boyt
		Blanche (Ellison) Boyt	Mrs. Adelaide L. Crane
Lucy Poe Sparkman	F	W. B. Sparkman	Mrs. A. T. Witte
		Lucy (Poe) Sparkman	Mrs. F. J. P. Cogswell
			E. H. Sparkman
James Richmond Garrison	M	James Richmond Garrison	Mrs. J. A. Perry
		Blanche (Conklin) Garrison	Dr. W. M. Gaillard
			Capt. Dewitt C. Conklin
William Andrew Johnstone	M	Francis Elliott Johnston	Andrew Johnston
		Eleanor (Nicholson) Johnston	Wm. H. Johnston
Margaret Bentley Fraser	F	Benjamin P. Fraser II	Mrs. James M. Dick
		Bessie (Lesesne) Fraser	Emily Fraser
			S. M. Ward
Myrtle Helen Carraway	F	Isaac McG. Carraway	Mrs. Jas W. Wingate
		Mable (Young) Carraway	Maria Jane Carraway
Paul Tamplet	M	J. Charles Tamplet	Col. Holmes R. Springs
		Pauline (LaBruce) Tamplet	S. M. Ward
			James H. DuPre
Armier Franz Witte	M	A. Franz Witter	Dr. W. B. Sparkman
		Hattie (Sparkman) Witte	Dr. J. R. Sparkman
			Martha F. Fitzsimmons
			Mrs. C. W. Rosa
Agnes Lula Gardner	M	J. Edward Gardner	
		Annie (Concklin) Gardner	
Iredell Hilliard, Jr.	M	Iredell Hilliard	Parents
		Mary McCarter Hilliard	Maria Noah Hilliard
			John Boyt
Harriet Aldridge (Gibson) Fraser		Adult	James H. Fraser
			Mrs. Hugh W. Fraser
William Archibald Campbell	M	Adult	Mrs. W. A. Campbell
			Mrs. Campbell
Walter Hazard Tamplet	M	John C. Tamplet	Thomas Bailey Hamby
		Pauline LaBruce Tamplet	Mrs. Emma Hamby
			Dr. LaBruce Ward
Sarah Victoria Bourne	F	Burness Bourne	Mrs. M. J. Collins
		Alberta Collins Bourne	Miss Anna Bourne
			Burness Bourne
Julia Allison Rosa	F	Franz D. Rosa	The Parents witnesses
		Daisy (Chamberlain) Rosa	
Mary Alice Cranwell	F	Henry Arthur Cranwell	The Parents witnesses
		Lelia Mary	
Mattie Devoe Ford	F	G. Thomas Ford	Martha Fitzsimmons
		Katherine Devoe Ford	Katherine V. Ford
			James V. Croskeys
John Sparkman Moyer	M	Clarence Alvin Moyer	Dr. Raymond Banryholtzer
		Lucia (Cary) Moyer	Mary E. Carns

Date Place of Birth	Date, Place of Baptism	Officiating minister
June 13 Georgetown, SC 1916	July 30 Church 1916	John S. Lighthourn
June 3 Georgetown, SC 1916	Aug. 6 Parents' Residence 1916	John S. Lighthourn
June 28 Georgetown, SC 1902	Nov. 28 Prince George Ch 1916	John S. Lighthourn
Oct 30 Georgetown, SC 1913	Nov. 28 Prince George Ch. 1916	John S. Lighthourn
July 26 Georgetown, SC 1916	Jan. 28 Prince George Ch 1917	John S. Lighthourn
Greenville, SC	March 4 At the residence 1917 of Dr. & Mrs. W. E. Sparkman	John S. Lighthourn
March 2 Georgetown, SC 1917	Ap. 7 Prince George Ch 1917	John S. Lighthourn
Nov. 7 Estherville Plantation 1915 Georgetown Co., SC	June 25 Prince George Ch 1917	John S. Lighthourn
May 15 Georgetown, SC 1917	June 26 Prince George Ch 1917	John S. Lightbourn
May 29 Georgetown, SC 1914	June 26 Prince George Ch 1917	John S. Lightbourn
Nov. 14 Georgetown, SC 1917	July 6 Prince George Ch 1918	John S. Lightbourn
Mar. 23 Georgetown, SC 1918	Sept. 14 Prince George Ch 1918	John S. Lightbourn
Mar. 18 Georgetown 1918	Nov. 1 Private baptism at 1918 home. Child ill	John S. Lightbourn
Jan. 18 Georgetown, SC 1917	Jan. 21 Prince George Ch 1919	John S. Lightbourn
Aug. 8 Loudon Co., Virginia 1882	Apr. 3 Prince George Ch 1919	John S. Lightbourn
Jan. 14 Marion, SC 1888	Apr. 4 Prince George Ch 1919	John S. Lightbourn
Aug. 15 Georgetown, SC 1919	Dec. 26 Prince George Ch 1919	John S. Lightbourn
Sept 21 Georgetown, SC 1919	Easter Even, Apr. 3, 1920 Prince George Winyah Church	John S. Lightbourn
Jan. 4 Georgetown, SC 1903	Quiquagesima, Feb. 2, 1921 Prince George Winyah Church	John S. Lightbourn
Dec. 4 Marshall, Texas 1907	Quiquagesima, Feb. 2, 1921 Prince George Winyah Church	John S. Lightbourn
July 28 Andrews, SC 1919	March 13, 1921 Prince George Ch.	John S. Lightbourn
Nov 1 Georgetown, SC 1900	March 26, 1921, Easter Even Prince George Ch	John S. Lightbourn

Names	Sex	Parents	Sponsors
Pauline Fitzsimmons Tamplet	F	Jules Charles Tamplet Pauline (LaBruce) Tamplet	Mr. & Mrs. C. W. Rosa Naimi Tamplet Hazard Justine W. LaBruce
Catherine Amelia Collins	F	William J. Collins Sophy (Groverman) Collins	Mr. & Mrs. Henry Groverman Mrs. Amelia Collins Wolfe
Karteryn Waller Doar	F	E. Marion Doar, Jr. Anna (Chewning) Doar	E. Conway Chewning Mrs. Herman Schenk E. Clyde Doar
Frank William Wolfe	M	Frank W. Wolfe M. Amelia (Collins) Wolfe	Frank S. Collins Frank W. Wolfe (father) Mrs. W. J. Collins
Benjamin William Bourne	M	Burness Bourne Alberta (Collins) Bourne	Burness Bourne (father)
Irma Marie Grisillo	F	Joseph Grisillo Mabel (Johnson) Grisillo	Mr. & Mrs. Ernest R. Blumberg
Edward Theodore Grisillo	M	Joseph Grisillo Mabel (Johnson) Grisillo	Mr. & Mrs. Ernest R. Blumberg
Maud Adele Grisillo	F	Joseph Grisillo Mabel (Johnson) Grisillo	Mr. & Mrs. Ernest R. Blumberg
Ernest Grace Grisillo	M	Joseph Grisillo Mabel (Johnson) Grisillo	Mr. & Mrs. Ernest R. Blumberg
William Capers Green	M	Marion C. Greene Ruth (Carraway) Greene	John G. Carraway E. Capers Haselden Mrs. E. Capers Haselden
Eugene Fitzsimmons LaBruce	M	Eugene F. LaBruce Grace (Dennis) LaBruce	In Extremis (Died April 4, 1922)
Ernest Richard Blumberg	M	Ernest Richard Blumberg Grace (Barrett) Blumburg	Mrs. Fred Ford The Parents
William Lander Mahon	M	William Lander Mahon Marie (Haselden) Mahon	William L. Mahon, Sr. E. C. Haselden Mrs. E. C. Haselden
Mary Katherine Witherington	F	Mardison S. Witherington Alice (Ward) Witherington	Mrs. A. R. Williams Mrs. W. H. Darby Dr. J. LaBruce Ward
William Wilson Wendt	M	Adelbert Thomas Wendt Lucy (Munnerlyn) Wendt	In Extremis

Presented Nov.16 '24 Name changed to Wilson Adelbert Wendt, H. D. Bull Rector

Names	Sex	Parents	Sponsors
Charlotte Daggett Plowden	F	Edward Ruthven Plowden Edna Daggett Plowden	Wm. Henry Thomas Emma Beaty Thomas Mary Daggett Keels
Edith Conklin Gardner	F	Jas. Edw'd Gardner Anna Conklin Gardner	Thomas D. Smoak Mary K. Smoak Bessie L. Fraser
Penelope Bentley Parker	F	James Rose Park Sallie DeSaussure Parker	Mr. Mahom Pyatt Mrs. J. R. Parker Mrs. DeSaussure Parker
Marian Jean LaBruce	F	Eugene F. LaBruce Grace D. LaBruce	Dr. W. E. Sparkman Mrs. J. C. Tamplett Mrs. F. W. Ford
Jacqueline Abegail Morris	F	John F. Morris Mrs. Jno. F. Morris	Mrs. W. B. Ruddick Dwight B. Morris Miss Alice Vaughan
Jane Carraway Higgins	F	Thos. W. Higgins Maria Jane (Carraway) Higgins	Mrs. J. L. Bull Mrs. F. L. Siau Mr. Isaac McG. Carraway
Marion Carlile Green, Jr.	M	Marion Carlile Green Ruth (Carraway) Green	Mrs. J. L. Bull J. Herman Carraway Jno. G. Carraway

Date Place of Birth	Date, Place of Baptism	Officiating minister
Feb. 24 Georgetown, SC 1921	May 22, 1921, Trinity Sun. Prince George Winyah Church	John S. Lightbourn
April 16 Georgetown, SC 1921	May 29, 1921 Prince George Winyah Church	John S. Lightbourn
May 19 Georgetown, SC 1921	July 10, 1921 Prince George Winyah Church	John S. Lightbourn
Nov. 1 Georgetown, SC 1921	Apr. 15, 1922, Easter Even Prince George Winyah Church	John S. Lightbourn
March 7 Georgetown, SC 1922	Apr. 15, 1922, Easter Even Prince George Winyah Church	John S. Lightbourn
June 9 Beaufort, SC 1914	Apr. 15, 1922, Easter Even Prince George Winyah Church	John S. Lightbourn
June 20 Charleston, SC 1916	Apr. 15, 1922, Easter Even Prince George Winyah Church	John S. Lightbourn
June 3 Charleston, SC 1919	Apr. 15, 1922, Easter Even Prince George Winyah Church	John S. Lightbourn
Dec 20 Georgetown, SC 1921	Apr. 15, 1922, Easter Even Prince George Winyah Church	John S. Lightbourn
Aug 20 Georgetown, SC 1922	Mar. 4, 1923 Prince George Winyah Church	John S. Lightbourn
Mar. 26 Georgetown, SC 1922	Apr. 1, 1922, Easter Day At Home	John S. Lightbourn
Nov. 25 Georgetown, SC 1922	May 24, 1923 Prince George Winyah Church	John S. Lightbourn
Nov. 17 Spartanburg, SC 1922	June 17, 1923 Prince George Winyah Church	John S. Lightbourn
Feb. 8 Goldsboro, NC 1923	July 1, 1923 Prince George Winyah Church	John S. Lightbourn
Dec. 31 Georgetown, NC 1923	Dec. 31, 1923 At Home	John S. Lightbourn
Sept 22 Georgetown, SC 1923	April 19, 1924 Pringe George Winyah Church	Melville K. Bailey
Jan 22 Georgetown, SC 1923	April 19, 1924 Prince George Winyah Church	Melville K. Bailey
Feb. 19 1924	June 27, 1924 Prince George Winyah Church	C. W. Boyd
Oct. 9 Georgetown, SC 1924	Nov. 9, 1924 Prince George Winyah	H. D. Bull
Nov. 2 Georgetown, SC 1924	Dec. 14, 1924 Prince George Winyah	H. D. Bull
Jan. 22 Georgetown, SC 1924	Feb. 15, 1925 Prince George Winyah	H. D. Bull
Sept. 19 Balsam, NC 1924	Feb. 15, 1925 Prince George Winyah	H. D. Bull

Names	Sex	Parents	Sponsors
Fritz Young Mercer	M	Charles Wood Mercer Mrs. C. W. (Young) Mercer	Fritz Young Wit: Roy Young Miss Sadie Young
Charles Wood Mercer, Jr.	M	Same	Same
William Napoleon Jacobs	M	Long dead	Mrs. W. Napoleon Jacobs Wit: Mrs. Jos. L. Bull Miss Theo Butler
Mabel Mercer	F	Sam'l E. Mercer Mrs. S. E. Mercer	Mr. H. W. Young Wit: Mrs. Henly Chapman Parents
Henrietta Reeves Witte	F	Mr. Franz Witte Mrs. Franz Witte	Father Mrs. Jas. Sparkman Mrs. Buck Sparkman
Harriett Horry Pyatt	F	Edward Nowell Pyatt Harriett Lowndes Pyatt	Miss Charlotte Pyatt Miss Charlotte Cain J. Saville Pyatt
Margaret Middleton Munnerlyn	F	Mr. Ben Munnerlyn Mrs. Ben Munnerlyn	Mrs. A. J. Went, Miss Theo Butler, Chas. Douglass Springs, Douglass Morris
Julian Lester Johnson	M	Julian Lester Johnson Louise Rosa Johnson	Mrs. M. B. Glenn Clarence P. Lachicotte Heyward Brockinton
Robert Edward Mahan	M	Wm. L. Mahan Marie H. Mahan	Mrs. E. C. Haselden Mrs. Wm. L. Mahan Mr. Wm. L. Mahan
Edward Haselden Carraway, Jr.	M	Edward H. Carraway Ellen S. Carraway	Isaac McG. Carraway Herbert L. Smith Mrs. Jno. T. Howell
Sarah DeSaussure Parker	F	Jas Rose Parker Sallie DeSaussure Parker	Miss Martha A. Pyatt Miss Catharine W. Pyatt Mr. R. C. DeSaussure
Sarah Fairbanks Bull	F	Henry DeSaussure Bull Gertrude C. Bull	Francis Kinloch Bull Miss Sarah Smith Mrs. A. E. Cornish
Carmel Edithe Karnes	F	Mr. Kenneth Karnes Mrs. Karnes	Mrs. E. M. McLeod Miss Florence Ward
Thomas Jefferson Karnes	M	Same	Same
Sharon Karnes	F	Same	Same
Mary Bull Pinckney	F	Frank D. Pinckney Mary B. Pinckney	Mrs. Caroline Kinloch Bull Mrs. Alice Adams Peterman Jno. Adams Pinckney
Edna Ruthven Plowden	F	Edward Ruthven Plowden Mrs. Edna D. Plowden	Mrs. Minnie D. Steele Mrs. Susie D. Smith Thos. D. Daggett
James Capers Mahon	M	Dr. W. C. Mahon Mrs. Marie Mahon	Jas. W. Wingate Mrs. J. W. Wingate E. C. Haselden
Burness Bourne	M	Burness Bourne Mrs. Alberta Bourne	Mrs. Frank Wolfe Parents
Raymond Coates Marjenhoff	M	 Mrs. Bissonette Marjenhoff	Dr. W. M. Gaillard Rev. H. D. Bull Mrs. H. D. Bull

Date Place of Birth	Date, Place of Baptism	Officiating minister
Age 15 yrs. Georgetown, SC Nov. 2, 1909	Mar. 19, 1925 Residence, Georgetown, SC	H. D. Bull
Age 17 yrs. Georgetown, SC	Mar. 19, 1925 Residence, Georgetown, SC	H. D. Bull
Age about 50 Kingstree, SC	April 29, 1925 Residence, Georgetown, SC	H. D. Bull
Age 13 yrs Georgetown, SC	May 2, 1925 Prince George Winyah	H. D. Bull
June 6, 1922	Sept. 6, 1925 Prince George Winyah	H. D. Bull
July 30, 1925	Sept. 27, 1925 Prince George Winyah	H. D. Bull
Oct. 7 Charleston, SC 1925	Dec. 27, 1925 Prince George Winyah	H. D. Bull
Nov. 22 Georgetown, SC 1924	Oct. 3, 1926 Prince George Winyah	H. D. Bull
Sept. 4 Georgetown, SC 1926	Oct. 3, 1926 Prince George Winyah	H. D. Bull
May 2 Georgetown, SC 1926	Oct. 31, 1926 Prince George Winyah	H. D. Bull
June 11 Columbia (?), SC 1926	Jan. 2, 1927 Prince George Winyah	H. D. Bull
Nov. 23 Georgetown, SC 1926	Jan. 16, 1927 Prince George Winyah	H. D. Bull
Dec. 12 Charleston, SC 1921	April 16, 1927 Residence, Georgetown, SC	H. D. Bull
Mar. 4 Georgetown, SC 1924	April 16, 1927 Same	H. D. Bull
Dec. 27 Georgetown, SC 1926	April 16, 1927 Same	H. D. Bull
Dec. 14 Orangeburg, SC 1927	April 1, 1928 Prince George Winyah	H. D. Bull
Sept. 15 Georgetown, SC 1927	April 7, 1928 Prince George Winyah	H. D. Bull
Feb. 19 Georgetown, SC 1928	April 7, 1928 Prince George Winyah	H. D. Bull
April 25 Georgetown, SC 1927	April 7, 1928 Prince George Winyah	H. D. Bull
1927 Georgetown, SC	April 7, 1928 Prince George Winyah	H. D. Bull

PRINCE GEORGE WINYAH RECORDS 1916-1936

Names	Sex	Parents	Sponsors
Alice Vaughan Lucas	F	Mr. T. Cordes Lucas Mrs. T. Cordes Lucas	Russell M. Doar Mrs. Russell M. Doar Mrs. Fred W. Ford
Dorothy Tyler Crawford	F	Richard T. Crawford, Jr. (decd) Mrs. R. T. Crawford, Jr.	Rev. H. D. Bull Mrs. H. D. Bull Mrs. A. E. Cornish
Martha Allston Parker	F	Jas. Rose Parker Sallie DeS. Parker	Mrs. R. C. DeSaussure Mrs. Henry W. Davis B. A. Pyatt
Sarah Baker Harrison	F	Frank Pinckney Harrison Mrs. Sarah B. Harrison	Parents
Hugh Hamilton Sisson	M	An Adult	Wit: Mrs. Isabel Sisson Mrs. W. M. Layton
Anne DuBois Doar	F	E. Marion Doar, Jr. Mrs. Anne W. Doar	LeRoy H. Doar Mrs. Minnie Doar Miss Caroline Waller
David Tooker Johnson	M	Julian L. Johnson Mrs. Louise R. Johnson	Miss Helen Rosa Jos. B. Johnson Thos W. Williamson
John Philip Hurcomb (also entered in register of All Saints Waccamaw, belongs there)	M	John Philip Hurcomb Florence G. Hurcomb	Father Jos. T. Rosa Mrs. D. C. Simpkins
George LaBruce	M	Eugene F. LaBruce Grace La Bruce	Miss Elizabeth C. LaBruce J. Chas. Tamplet Geo. H. LaBruce
Hugh Lawson Oliver III	M	Hugh Lawson Oliver, Jr. Martha B. Oliver	F. Wentworth Ford Edw. H. Carraway Mrs. E. H. Carraway
Jane Morris Munnerlyn	F	Benj. Munnerlyn Margaret S. Munnerlyn	Mrs. Douglas Morris Mrs. Thos. B. Hamby Wilson Munnerlyn
Hildegarde Gertrude Morris	F	Caleb Carrualt Morris Mary Lee Morris	Mrs. L. W. Doolan Miss Caroline Morris D. B. Morris
Walter Scott Sinclair, Jr.	M	W. Scott Sinclair, Sr. Mrs. W. S. Sinclair (nee Savage)	Parents Wit: Johs. John Leland Mrs. H. D. Bull
Celesta June Smith	F	Zachary Taylor Smith Mrs. Z. T. Smith	Rev. C. F. Collins (Proxy) Mrs. C. T. Collins " Mother
Dorothy Clark Sinclair	F	W. Scott Sinclair, Sr. Mrs. W. S. Sinclair, Sr.	S. B. Alsop Mrs. S. B. Alsop Mother
Julian Shepherd Albergotti, Jr.	M	Julian S. Albergotti Myrtle H. Albergotti	Wm. Albergotti Herbert M. Hucks, Jr. Rosa Hucks
Henry DeSaussure Bull, Jr.	M	Rev. H. D. Bull Mrs. H. D. Bull	F. Kinloch Bull Miss Julia Rees Father
Harriett Oliver Plowden	F	E. R. Plowden Mrs. E. R. Plowden	Miss Harriett E. Plowden Mr. S. Oliver Plowden Mrs. S. Oliver Plowden
LeRoy Henning Doar, Jr.	M	LeRoy H. Doar Margaret Doar	Parents E. Marion Doar, Jr.
Paul Livingston Baker	M		Mrs. C. W. Rosa Wit: D. D. Rosa
Virginia Ann Bourne	F	Mr. Burness Bourne Mrs. Burness Bourne	Parents and Mrs. F. W. Wolfe

Date Place of Birth	Date, Place of Baptism	Officiating minister
1928 Georgetown, SC	July 8, 1928 Prince George Winyah	H. D. Bull
June 11 Georgetown, SC 1928	July 8, 1928	H. D. Bull
Jan. 29 Columbia, SC 1928	July 22, 1928 Pr. George Winyah	H. D. Bull
June 30 1928 Age 34 years Virginia	Sept. 26, 1928 Myrtle Beach, SC Dec. 27, 1928 home of W. M. Layton, Georgetown, SC	Rev. E. W. Gamble of Selma, Ala. Entered here: isolated church people H. D. Bull
Oct. 8 Georgetown, SC 1928	Dec. 23, 1928 Prince George Winyah	H. D. Bull
Aug. 4 Georgetown, SC 1928	Mar. 30, 1929 Prince George Winyah	H. D. Bull
Feb. 8 Georgetown, SC 1929	April 9, 1929 _ Prince George Winyah	H. D. Bull
April 19 Georgetown, SC 1929	Aug. 4, 1929 Prince George Winyah	H. D. Bull
April 14 Georgetown, SC 1929	Aug. 25, 1929 Prince George Winyah	H. D. Bull
Jan. 15 Jacksonville, FL 1929	Sept. 8, 1929 Prince George Winyah	H. D. Bull
Feb. 9 Georgetown, SC 1929	Oct. 6, 1929 Prince George Winyah	H. D. Bull
Age about 14	Feb. 12, 1930 Prince George Winyah	H. D. Bull
Sept. 18 Georgetown, SC 1929	Mar. 2, 1930 Prince George Winyah	H. D. Bull
Age 10 Georgetown, SC years	June 1, 1930 Pr. George Winyah	H. D. Bull
May 20 Charlotte, NC 1930	July 31, 1930 Pr. George Winyah	H. D. Bull
June 30 Charleston, SC 1930	Aug. 3, 1930 Prince George Winyah	H. D. Bull
1929 Georgetown, SC	Aug. 10, 1930 Residence, Georgetown	R. B. Herbert (Irregularly tho validly baptized)
Sept. 13 Georgetown, SC 1930 Age about 18 Florida	Oct. 12, 1930 Prince George Winyah Jan. 16, 1931 Res: Mrs. C. W. Rosa, Georgetown, SC	H. D. Bull H. D. Bull
Oct. 19 Georgetown, SC 1930	April 5, 1931 Prince George Winyah	H. D. Bull

PRINCE GEORGE WINYAH RECORDS 1916-1936

Names	Sex	Parents	Sponsors
Herbert Smith Carraway	M	Edward H. Carraway Ellen (Smith) Carraway	Wm. H. Smith Dr. G. T. Howell Mrs. G. D. Oswald
Mary Cordes Lucas	F	Mr. T. Cordes Lucas Alice V. Lucas	Mrs. Elleanor Ball Lucas Gaillard " Charlotte Cordes Lucas LaFaye Grange Simons Lucas
Helen Louise Johnson	F	Julian L. Johnson Louise R. Johnson	Mrs. Julian L. Johnson Miss Julia Rosa Mr. D. D. Rosa
Lupton Allemong Wilkinson, Jr.	M	Mr. & Mrs. Lupton A. Wilkinson	Will H. Hayes) Mrs. Ethel Calkins) Wit J. H. Carraway)
Donald Ray Kermon	M	Mr. Wm. M. Kermon Mrs. Wm. M. Kermon	Par. & Mrs. H. D. Bull witnesses Private, child sick
Edward Gerald Kermon	M	Mr. Wm. M. Kermon Mrs. Wm. M. Kermon	Par. & Mrs. H. D. Bull witnesses Private
Katherine Daughdrille Glover	F	Capt. Chas. W. Glover, USA Mrs. Chas. W. Glover	Mrs. Cato (Ellen) Glover Lieut. Cato Glover, USN Miss Lyda Daughdrille
Mary Murray Wayne	F	Bacot Wayne Lucile King Wayne	Maham W. Pyatt Julia King Emily F. Fraser
Isabelle Mercer	F	Sam E. Mercer Mrs. S. E. Mercer	Fritz Young Miss Lena Young Mrs. Harold Kaminski
Elizabeth Izard Bull	F	Rev. H. D. Bull Mrs. H. D. Bull	Mrs. C. W. Boyd Mrs. G. T. Skinner B. A. Pyatt, M. D.
Frederick Edward Rembert	M		Fritz Y. Mercer Alvah Young, wit.
William Allen Sinclair	M	Mr. & Mrs. W. Scott Sinclair	Mr. John Leland Mrs. John Leland Father
Catherine Hume Lucas	F	T. Cordes Lucas Alice V. Lucas	Mr. & Mrs. Jas. D. Lucas Mrs. F. Wentworth Ford
Francis Rufus Bourne	M	Mr. & Mrs. Frank R. Bourne	Mrs. Fred W. Ford Miss Barbara Bell
Melissa Bourne	F	Same	Same
Ruth Burn Oliver	F	H. Lawson Oliver Martha B. Oliver	Mrs. F. Wentworth Ford Hugh L. Oliver Mrs. Hugh L. Oliver
Richard Bruce Jayroe	M	Mrs. W. H. Jayroe Mrs. Jayroe	Private: very ill (Meth)
John Doar Nielsen	M	Johannes V. Nielsen, Jr. Virginia Doar Nielsen	John Walter Doar Miss Emily Tyell[?] Father
John Francis Bourne	M	Burness Bourne Mrs. Burness Bourne	Parents Mrs. F. W. Wolfe
Joseph Allison Johnson	M	Julian L. Johnson Louise (Rosa) Johnson	Parents Mrs. F. D. Rosa
Charles Williamson Glover, Jr.	M	Capt. Chas. W. Glover, USA Catherine D. Glover	Cato D. Glover Williamson A. Glover Carlotta Daughdrill

Date Place of Birth	Date, Place of Baptism	Officiating minister
Dec. 6. Florence, SC 1930	April 19, 1931 Prince George Winyah	H. D. Bull
Nov. 24 Charleston, SC 1930	July 5, 1931 Prince George Winyah	H. D. Bull
May 29 Georgetown, SC 1931	Aug. 2, 1931 Prince George Winyah	H. D. Bull
Sept. 18 1917	Dec. 20, 1931 Prince George Winyah	H. D. Bull
Nov. 29, 1931, Res: St. James St., Georgetown	Feb. 5, 1932, Res. St. James St.	H. D. Bull
Sept. 29, 1830, Res: St. James St., Georgetown	Feb. 5, 1932, Res. St. James St.	H. D. Bull
Dec. 2 Fayetteville, NC 1930	Mar. 26, 1932 Prince George Winyah	H. D. Bull
June 5 Charleston, SC 1931	June 5, 1932 Prince George Winyah	H. D. Bull
Mar. 19 Georgetown, SC 1919	Jan. 1, 1933 Prince George Winyah	H. D. Bull
Nov. 18 Charleston, SC 1932	Jan. 1, 1933 Prince George Winyah	H. D. Bull
Age. c23 Georgetown, SC	Feb. 4, 1933 Prince George Winyah	H. D. Bull
Feb. 8 Georgetown, SC 1933	April 15, 1933 Prince George Winyah	H. D. Bull
Sept. 2 North Santee, SC 1932	April 23, 1933 Prince George Winyah	H. D. Bull
4 years old	July 8, 1933 Res. Santee, near Georgetown	H. D. Bull
2 years old	July 8, 1933 Same	H. D. Bull
June 26 Georgetown, SC 1933	Oct. 15, 1933 Prince George Winyah	H. D. Bull
July Georgetown, SC 1933	Dec. 12, 1933 Residence, Georgetown, SC	H. D. Bull
Sept. 9 Kensington 1933	Dec. 25, 1933 Res. Kensington, Georgetown, SC	H. D. Bull
Aug. 29 Georgetown, SC 1933	Mar. 31, 1934 Prince George Winyah	H. D. Bull
April 14 Georgetown, SC 1933	Mar. 31, 1934 Prince George Winyah	H. D. Bull
Dec. 26 Fort Bragg, NC 1933	April 15, 1934 Prince George Winyah	H. D. Bull

PRINCE GEORGE WINYAH RECORDS 1916-1936

Names	Sex	Parents	Sponsors
James Marion Doar	M	LeRoy H. Doar Margaret W. Doar	E. Marion Doar, Sr. Jas. G. L. White Mrs. Minnie McCracken
Barbara Marie Raftelis	F	Jas. M. Raftelis Josephine J. Raftelis	Parents Mrs. B. P. Fraser
Esther Marie LaBruce	F	Allard Flagg LaBruce Marie H. LaBruce	Mrs. D. M. Oswald Miss Esther LaBruce Legere LaBruce
Lawrence Petigru LaBruce	M	Lawrence Petigru LaBruce Julia O. LaBruce	Miss Charlotte Orr G. A. LaBruce J. Herman Carraway
Joseph Laurie Bull III	M	Joseph L. Bull II Emily B. Bull	Joseph L. Bull I Clayton W. Bailey Mrs. Ruth M. Williams
Joy Anne Bull	F	Joseph L. Bull Emily B. Bull	Mesdames Joy E. Bailey & J. L. Bull, Sr. John C. Bull
Jane Louis Gargan	F	Mr. & Mrs. John H. Gargan	Mr. & Mrs. Geo. S. Clark Mr. & Mrs. Louis L. Overton
John Carraway Bull, Jr.	M	John Carraway Bull Cora Lee K. Bull	Mr. & Mrs. Jos. L. Bull, Sr. Jos. L. Bull, Jr. Mrs. P. D. Kitchens
Arthur Manigault Labruce, Jr.	M	Arthur Manigault LaBruce Julia Gantt LaBruce	Mrs. Leonard Ravenel J. Percy LaBruce S. Saltus McClary Jesse Thomas
Joyce Ann West	F	Herbert West Mrs. Hessie West (deceased)	Rev. H. D. Bull Mrs. H. D. Bull
Katherine Elliott Jacobs	F	Capt. J. Elliott Jacobs Gertrude Bourne Jacobs	Mrs. T. E. Hough Mr. & Mrs. B. P. Fraser
George Edward Clerc, Jr.	M	George Edward Clerc E. Bessie Clerc	Edward L. Clerc Phillip Courtenay Mrs. H. Lawson Oliver
William Walter Doar, Jr.	M	Wm. Walter Doar Julia P. Doar	Father J. Walter Doar Mrs. Virginia D. Nielsen
Mary Jane Doar	F	Leroy H. Doar Margaret W. Doar	Mrs. W. D. Bartlett Mrs. Frank Whitlock Father
Bacot Allston Wayne	M	Bacot Allston Wayne Lucile King Wayne	Stephen W. King C. Neyle Fishburn Mrs. Esther Wayne Jenkins
Benjamin Jas. Berry, Jr.	M	Benj. J. Berry Bernice H. Berry	E. C. Haselden Wm. L. Mahon, Jr. Mrs. August R. Cotton

PRINCE GEORGE WINYAH RECORDS 1916-1936

Date Place of Birth	Date, Place of Baptism	Officiating minister
Dec. 28　　SC 1933	May 6, 1934 Res. E. M. Doar, Jr., Georgetown	H. D. Bull
Jan. 16　Charleston, SC	June 10, 1934	H. D. Bull
1934 Jan. 31　　SC 1933 or 1934[?] May 10 Anderson, SC 1934	Prince George Winyah June 15, 1934 "Arundel," Georgetown Co., SC June 15, 1934 "Arundel," Georgetown Co., SC	H. D. Bull H. D. Bull
Sept. 21, 1931	Jan. 3, 1935 Residence, Georgetown, SC	H. D. Bull
Dec. 21　Georgetown, SC 1934	Jan. 3, 1935 Residence, Georgetown, SC	H. D. Bull
Aug. 27, 1931	Jan. 12, 1935 Prince George, Georgetown, SC	H. D. Bull
Sept. 21　Raleigh (Hospital) 1934　　　NC	Feb. 22, 1935 Prince George, Georgetown, SC	H. D. Bull
Dec. 13　Charleston, SC 1934	Mar. 24, 1935 Prince George, Georgetown, SC	H. D. Bull
Nov. 10　Georgetown, SC 1934	Apr. 20, 1935 Prince George, Georgetown, SC	H. D. Bull
May 17　Richmond, Indiana 1934	July 13, 1935 Prince George, Georgetown, SC	Rev. J. M. Dick for rector
July 9　Georgetown, SC 1935	Sept. 22, 1935 Prince George, Georgetown, SC	H. D. Bull
Mar 9　Rock Hill, SC 1935	Dec. 22, 1935 Residence, Georgetown, SC	H. D. Bull
Jan. 18, 1935	Jan. 19, 1936 Prince George, Georgetown, SC	H. D. Bull
July 3　Charleston, SC 1935	April 26, 1936 Prince George Winyah	H. D. Bull
Dec. 7　Chicago, Ill. 1935	Sept. 6, 1936 Prince George Winyah	H. D. Bull

CONFIRMATIONS

Full Name	Sex	Date and Place of Birth	Baptism
Fraser, Hugh Wilson, Jr.	M	Feb. 4, 1904 Georgetown, SC	Church
Walker, John Tull	M	Jun. 17, '04 "	"
Smith, Buford Colclough	M	Sep. 9, '01 "	"
Bull, Joseph Lowrie	M	May 19, '03 "	"
Pyatt, Julia Bossard	F	Feb. 27, '00 "	"
Emerson, Hilda Witherspoon	F	Jun. 28, '02 "	"
Gardner, Mary Catharine	F	Sept. 26, '05 "	"
Edmonds, Frederick William	M	Sept. 26, 1876 England	"
Boyt, John	M	Dec. 6, 1873 "	"
Boyt, Mrs. Blanche Ellison	F	Dec. 28, 1884 Del.	Presbyterian
Skipper, Rutha Lee	F		Methodist
Ford, Frederick Wentworth	M		Church
Russell, Sarah Lois	F		Methodist
Doar, Elias Marion	M		"
Munnerlyn, William Wilson, Jr.	M		Church
Ford, Ellen Hume	F		"
Hilliard, Kathrine Karnes	F		"
Doar, Virginia Elizabeth	F	13 yrs	Church
Fraser, Lily Ellison	F	13 yrs	"
Ford, Alexander Hume	M	12 yrs	"
LaBruce, Allard Flagg	M	14 yrs	"
Doar, Bachman	M	12 yrs	"
Gardner, William Albert	M	15 yrs	"
Oliver, Hugh Lawson, Jr.	M	20 yrs	"
Fraser, Mrs. Harriet Aldridge (Gibson)		36 yrs	"
Campbell, William Archibald	M	31 yrs	"
Gaillard, Dr. William Minott	M	47 yrs	"
Carraway, Edward Haselden	M	25 yrs	Church
Brock, Lillian May	F	39	Methodist
Doar, Mrs. Anne Chewning	F	26	Baptist
Johnson, Nellie Geraldin	F	18	Church
Pyatt, Joseph Benjamin Allston	M	58	"
Wingate, James Walter	M	34	Methodist
Haselden, Edward Capers	M	48	"
Waddell, Doris Mayrant Louise	F	23	Presbyterian
Cranwell, Henry Arthur	M	59	Disciples
Cranwell, Mrs. Kelia May	F	38	"
Cranwell, Jack Pierpont	M	16	"
Cranwell, James Logan	M	15	"
Cranwell, Mary Alice	F	13	Church
Hilliard, John McCarter	M	18	"
Hucks, Wyatt D. Michell	F	15	Roman Catholic
LaBruce, Lucy Tucker	F	15	Church
Rosa, Helen	F	15	"
Rosa, Julia Allison	F	14	"
Ward, Frances McCrady	F	17	"
Wendt, Adelbert Thomas	M	26	Roman Catholic

Date Place of Confirmation	Presented By	Bishop Confirming
Dec. 3, 1916, Prince George, Winyah	John S. Lightbourn	Rt. Rev. William A. Guerry
"		
"		
"		
"		
"		
"		
"		
"		
May 23, 1917, "	John S. Lightbourn	Rt. Rev. William A. Guerry
May 24, 1917, Private at Home		
Dec. 23, 1917, Prince George Winyah	John S. Lightbourn	Rt. Rev. William A. Guerry
"		
"		
"		
Apr. 4, 1919, Prince George Winyah	John S. Lightbourn	Rt. Rev. W. A. Guerry
"		
"		
"		
"		
"		
"		
"		
Apr. 28, 1920, Prince George Winyah	John S. Lightbourn	Rt. Rev. William A. Guerry,
"		
"		
"		
"		
"		
"		
Feb. 9, 1921 Prince George Winyah	John S. lightbourn	Rt. Rev. W. A. Guerry, D.D.
" "		
" "		
" "		
" "		
" "		
" "		
" "		
" "		
" "		
" "		

Feb. 27, 1921 St. Paul's Charleston. This confirmation took place thus because Mr. Wendt was called away at the time the class was presented.

Full Name	Sex	Date and Place of Birth	Baptism
Lee, Iva	F	16	Methodist Church
Bourne, Florence Emily	F	15	"
LaBruce, Eugene Fitzsimmons	M	30	Church
LaBruce, Mrs. Grace Dennis	F	21	Disciples
Bull, John Carraway	M		Church
Fraser, Jas. Hamilton Jr.	M		"
Fraser, Richard Parshill	M		"
Fraser, Benj. Porter, 3	M		"
Fraser, Bessie Lesesne	F		Church
Gardner, Edward Earl	M		Roman Catholic
Hucks, Herbert Michel	M		Church
Hucks, Herbert Michel, Jr.	M		"
Johnston, Lois Leona	F		"
Hucks, Rosa Marguerita	F		"
LaBruce, Laurence Pettigru	M		"
LaBruce, Legare Richardson	M		"
LaBruce, Esther Richardson	F		"
Moorer, Francis LeGrand	M		"
Bruorton, Mrs. Enid Ford	F	Adult	Presbyterian
Couturier, Anna Sinkler	F	Age 13	Church
Fraser, Wm. Lesene	M	Age 14	Church
Gardner, Annie Bertha	F	Age 13	Church
Grisillo, Screvin William	M	Age 13	Church
Jacobs, Wm. Napoleon	M	Adult	Church from Judaism
Johnston, James Vance	M	Adult	Methodist
Mercer, Mabel	F	Age 13	Church from Baptist
Overton, Louis Linde	M	Adult	Methodist
Vaughan, Alice May	F	Adult	Lutheran
Fraser, Ellen Aldridge	F	Age c18 Georgetown, SC Apr. 15, 1911	Prince George
Plowden, Ed: Ruthven	M	Age c40 Summerton, SC	Presbyterian
Martha B. Oliver (Mrs. H. L)	F	Age c25 , Ala.	Presbyterian
George Edward Clerc	M	c14	Methodist
William Coleman Young	M	c12 Georgetown, SC	Prince George Winyah
James Archibald Campbell	M	c12 Charleston, SC	St. Philips Ch: Charleston
Mabel Helen Wingate	F	c14 Georgetown, SC	Prince George Winyah
Francis E. Johnstone, Jr.	M	c15 Belle Isle, SC	Prince George Winyah
Chas. Williamson Glover	M	c32 Ala.	Methodist
Jno. Percival LeBruce	M	c30 Georgetown Co., SC	Church
Lucile Megett King	F	c22	Presbyterian
James Ritchie S. Siau	M	c17 Georgetown, SC	Methodist
Geo. Thomas Ford, Jr.	M	c15	Church
Ora Belle Hucks	F	c13 Georgetown, SC	Church
Mary Jacobs	F	c12 Kingstree, SC	Church
Agnes L. Emmerson	F	c14 Georgetown, SC	Church
Mattie McKelvey Couturier	F	c12 Eutawville, SC	Church
Dorothy Edna Gardner	F	c13 Georgetown, SC	Church
Lillian Lee Johnstone	F	c14 Santee, SC	Church
Elizabeth H. Ford	F	c15 SC	Church
Mary Elizabeth Panton (Mrs.)	F	c35 SC	Methodist
Kenneth W. Karnes	M	28 Illinois	Methodist
Edythe S. (Mrs. K. W.) Karnes	F	27 England	Ch: of England
Myrtle Helen Carraway	F	15 Georgetown	Church

Date	Place of Confirmation	Presented By	Bishop Confirming
Mar 26, 1922	Prince George Winyah	John S. Lightbourn	Rt. Rev. K. J. Finlay, D.D.
"	"		
"	"		
"	"		
May 25, 1924	Prince George Winyah	Rev. C. W. Boyd	Rt. Rev. W. A. Guerry
"	"		
"	"		
"	"		
"	"		
"	"		
"	"		
"	"		
"	"		
"	"		
"	"		
"	"		
"	"	Hugh W. Fraser	
May 3, 1925	Prince George Winyah	Rev. H. D. Bull	Rt. Rev. W. A. Guerry
"	"		
"	"		
"	"		
"	"		
"	"		
"	"		
"	"		
"	"		
"	"		
June 27, 1925	"	H. D. Bull	Rt. Rev. W. A. Guerry, D.D.
May 11, 1926	Prince George Winyah	H. D. Bull	Rt. Rev. E. A. Penick, D.D.
"	"		
"	"		
"	"		
"	"		
"	"		
May 29, 1927	"	H. D. Bull	Rt. Rev. W. A. Guerry, D.D.
"	"		
"	"		
"	"		
"	"		
"	"		
"	"		
"	"		
Apr. 29, '28	Pr. George Winyah	H. D. Bull	Rt. Rev. W. A. Guerry, D.D.
"	"		
"	"		
"	"		
"	"		
"	"		
"	"		

Full Name	Sex	Date and Place of Birth		Baptism
Virginia Rhem	F	14	Rhem's, S. C.	Bapt: Roman Catholic
Julian Lester Johnson	M	c30	Georgetown	Methodist
Helen Vivian Gardner	F	c13	Georgetown, SC	Church
John H. Bull	M	12	Charleston, SC	Church
Henley Chapman, Jr.	M	12	SC	Church
E. Olin Gardner	M	26	Georgetown, SC	Church
Paul L. Baker	M	c18	Florida	Methodist
Harriett McG. Witte	F	14	Georgetown, SC	Church
J. Chas. Tamplet, Jr.	M	16	"	Church
G. LaBruce Tamplet	M	15	"	Church
Wm. A. Johnstone	M	16	"	Church
Dorothy C. Sinclair	F	11	"	Church
Agnes Lula Gardner	F	14	"	Church
Margaret Bourne	F	12	"	Church
Gertrude C. Bull	F	12	Charleston, SC	Church
Caroline K. Bull	F	13	"	Church
Fritz Young Mercer	M	23	Georgetown	Mar 19, 1925 Georgetown
Frederick Edward Rembert	M	c23	Georgetown	Feb. 4, 1933 Pr. George
Sarah Victoria Bourne	F	Sept. 21, 1919 Georgetown		Apr. 3, 1920 "
Isabelle Mercer	F	Mar 19, 1919 Georgetown		Jan. 1, 1933 Pr. George
Margaret Bentley Fraser	F	May 15, 1917 "		June 2, 1917 "
Mildred Chapman	F	Age 13	Sumter	Church
Sallie Knox Smith (Mrs. H. L.)	F	Adult	Ky.	Methodist
Pauline F. Tamplet	F	Feb. 24, 1921 Georgetown		May 22, 1921 Church
Mattie Devaux Ford	F	July 28, 1919 Georgetown?		Mar. 13, 1921 Church
Frank William Wolfe	M	Nov. 1, 1921 Georgetown		Apr. 15, 1922 Church
Barbara Evelyn Thieleu	F	Age 21	Minneapolis	Congregational
Marguerite R. Oswald (Mrs. D. M.)	F	Adult	Sumter, SC	Presbyterian
James D. Hazzard	M	Age c18		Presbyterian
Mary Frances Richardson	F	Age c12		Church
Jane Louis Geagan	F	Age 14		Jan. 23, 1935 Church
Kathryn Waller Doar	F	Age 13	Georgetown	July 10, 1921 Church
Wm. Sander Mahan	M	Nov. 17, 1922 Spartanburg, SC		Jan. 17, 1923 Church
Jos. L. Bull, Sr.	M	Age c60	Maryland	Church
(Mrs. J. L. Jr.) Emily Bull	F	Age c30		Methodist
Josephine Lee	F	Age c30		Methodist

Date Place of Confirmation	Presented By	Bishop Confirming
May 26, '29 Pr. George Winyah	H. D. Bull	Rt. Rev. A. S. Thomas
" "		
" "		
Mar. 16, '30 Pr. George Winyah	H. D. Bull	Rt. Rev. A. S. Thomas
" "		
" "		
Jan. 18, 1931 Pr. George Winyah	H. D. Bull	Rt. Rev. A. S. Thomas
" "		
" "		
Feb. 28, 1932 Pr. George Winyah	H. D. Bull	Rt. Rev. A. S. Thomas, D.D.
" "		
" "		
" "		
" "		
" "		
" "		
" "		
Feb. 5, 1932 Pr. George Winyah	H. D. Bull	Rt. Rev. A. S. Thomas, D.D.
Jan. 28, 1934 Prince George Winyah	H. D. Bull	Rt. Rev. A. S. Thomas, D.D.
Feb. 3, 1935 Prince George Winyah	H. B. Bull	Rt. Rev. A. S. Thomas, D. D.
Feb. 16, 1936 Prince George Winyah	H. D. Bull	Rt. Rev. A. S. Thomas, D.D.

PRINCE GEORGE WINYAH RECORDS 1916-1936

BURIALS

Full Name	Sex & Age	Last Residence	Date of Death
Weber, Arthur Putnam	M 44	Charleston, SC	Aug. 9, 1916
Wilson, Sarah B.	F 81	Georgetown, SC	Sept. 18, 1916
Hemmingway, Jane (Scott) (Mrs.)	F 41	Hemmingway, SC	Dec. 6, 1916
Read, Lynch (Deas)	F 38	Georgetown, SC	Jan. 30, 1917
Hazard, Benjamin Ingell	M 56	Georgetown, SC	Feb. 27, 1917
Walker, William Hasford	M 26 y 4 m	Georgetown, SC	Mar. 20, 1917
Tucker, Henry M.	M	Georgetown, SC	Nov. 5, 1917
LaBruce, E. Mortimer	M 51	Georgetown, SC	Nov. 15, 1917
Conklin, DeWitt C.	M 64	Georgetown, SC	Nov. 22, 1917
Ward, Katherine (LaBruce)	F 60	Georgetown, SC	Jan. 9, 1918
Skinner, Mrs. Georgianna	F 48	Andrews, SC	Jan. 31, 1918
Bowman, Mrs. Minnie Ford	F 60	Jacksonville, FL	Mar. 1, 1918
Parks, Harold W.	M	Georgetown, SC	Mar. 25, 1919
Johnson, Gilbert	M 50	Georgetown, SC	Mar. 29, 1919
*Johnston, Rev.			
George Harbaugh, D.D.	M 85	Georgetown, SC	Sept. 29, 1918
Kent, Harry Watson	M 36?	Washington, D. C.	Oct. 13, 1918
Kent, Mrs. Reba	F ?	Washington, D. C.	Oct. 20, 1918
Detyens, Marion Doar	F 3	Hopewell, Va.	Oct. 25, 1918
Read, J. Harleston	M 46	Georgetown Co.	Nov. 29, 1918
Smith, Mrs. Sally Elizabeth	F 38	Georgetown, SC	Dec. 3, 1918
Jacobs, Ruth	F 16	Georgetown, SC	Dec. 4, 1918
Dawley, Mrs. Maria	F 70	Georgetown, SC	Dec. 8, 1918
Cooper, Charles Richard	M 11 mos.	Georgetown, SC	Nov. 8, 1918
Ford, Mrs. Anne Eliza Ford	F 64	Plantersville, SC	Feb. 19, 1919
Atkinson, Mary Julia	F	Berkeley Springs, WV	Mar 22, 1919
Doar, Thomas Watts	M 43	Columbia, SC	Apr. 26, 1919
LaBruce, (Mrs.) Katherine Fitzsimmons	F 58	Georgetown, SC	May 9, 1919
Carraway, James F.	M 69	Georgetown Co.	Oct 24, 1919
Collins, William Joseph	M 2 days	Georgetown, SC	Dec. 27, 1919
Jeppson, John	M 42	North Island	Feb. 7, 1920
Young, Mrs. Mary (Cherry)	F 20	Georgetown, SC	Feb. 19, 1920
Young, George F.	M 43	Georgetown, SC	Feb. 25, 1920
Carraway, Lanier	M 31 y 4 mos	Georgetown, SC	Mar. 12, 1920
Ford, Eliza Harriet	F 79 y 3 mos	Georgetown	Mar. 28, 1920
Hazard, Florence Adel (Tamplet)	F	Georgetown, SC	Aug. 31, 1920
Walker, LeGrand G.	M 70	Georgetown, SC	Oct. 25, 1920
Tucker, Mrs. Ann Manigault	F 78	Georgetown, SC	Nov. 6, 1920
Kent, Mrs. Claudia Johnson (Hucks)	F 40	Georgetown, SC	Nov. 8, 1920
Verner, Mrs. Mary Deas (Young)	F 18	Georgetown, SC	Nov. 10, 1920
Houck, Mrs. Mata G.	F 71	Georgetown, SC	Mar. 8, 1921
Munnerlyn, William Wilson	M 52	Georgetown, SC	Mar. 20, 1921
Hucks, Robert Hern Collins	M 73	Georgetown, SC	May 10, 1921

*Dr. Johnston was Rector of this parish from 1899-1911. From 1911 to his death he was on the retired list, living in Georgetown. His mental failure was truly distressing. All through these years of helplessness he was cared for by his only daughter, Miss Anna Johnston whose patience was of a beautiful & extraordinary type. Dr. Johnston's remains were taken to Philadelphia for burial after the service in the old Parish Church in which the Rev. J. E. H. Galbraith of Waccamaw took part with the Rector.

Cause of Death	Place of Interment	Date of Burial
Acute ____ of Heart	Parish Church Yard	Aug. 11, 1916
Infirmities of old age	Parish Church Yard	Sept. 18, 1916
Tuberculosis	Union Church, Georgetown	Dec. 7, 1916
Blood Poison	Parish Church Yard	Jan. 31, 1917
Pneumonia	Parish Church Yard	Feb. 28, 1917
Tuberculosis	Parish Church Yard	Mar. 21, 1917
Paralysis	Parish Church Yard	Nov. 6, 1917
Apoplexy	Parish Church Yard	Nov. 16, 1917
Apoplexy	Parish Church Yard	Nov. 23, 1917
Hardening of Arteries	Parish Church Yard	Jan. 9, 1918
Tuberculosis	Elmwood Cemetery	Feb. 1, 1918
Tuberculosis	Prince Frederick Ch'yd	Mar. 4, 1918
Tuberculosis	Parish Church Yard	Mar. 27, 1918
Apoplexy	Elmwood Cemetery	Mar. 31, 1918
Old age	Interment in Philadelphia, Pa.	Oct. 1-2, 1918
Abscess on lungs	Parish Ch. yard	Oct. 23, 1918
Spanish Influenza	Parish Ch. Yard	Oct. 23, 1918
"	Elmwood Cemetery	Oct. 27, 1918
Pneumonia	Parish Church Yard	Nov. 30, 1918
Influenza	Elmwood Cemetery	Dec. 4, 1918
Pneumonia	Parish Church Yard	Dec. 6, 1918
Heart disorder	Parish Church Yard	Dec. 9, 1918
Influenza		Nov. 9, 1918
Heart Trouble	Parish Church Yard	Feb. 20, 1919
Typhoid Pneumonia	Parish Church Yard	Mar. 26, 1919
Influenza - Pneumonia	McClellanville, SC	Apr. 28, 1919
Hardening of arteries	Prince Frederick Ch. yard	May 10, 1919
Accident- Burnt to death	Elmwood Cemetery	Oct. 25, 1919
D--- Circulation	Elmwood Cemetery	Dec. 29, 1919
Bronchitis	Elmwood Cemetery	Feb. 9, 1920
Influenza	Near C-- field	Feb. 20, 1920
Pneumonia	Parish Church yard	Feb. 25, 1920
Pneumonia	Parish Church yard	Mar. 12, 1920
Blood poisoning	Parish Church yard	Mar. 28, 1920
	Parish Church yard	Sept. 1, 1920
Angina Pectoris	Parish Church yard	Oct. 27, 1920
Apoplexy	Parish Church yard	Nov. 6, 1920
Tuberculosis of spine	Parish Church yard	Nov. 9, 1920
Hemoraglic Fever	Methodist Cemetery	Nov. 11, 1920
Heart Trouble	Methodist Cemetery	Mar. 9, 1921
Heart Failure	Parish Church yard	Mar. 22, 1921
Bright's Disease	Parish Church yard	May 11, 1921

Full Name	Sex & Age	Last Residence	Date of Death
Lucas, Mrs. Margaret Deas	F about 70	Georgetown, SC	May 22, 1921
Sampson, Mrs. Selina Mortimer	F 68½	Georgetown, SC	Feb. 15, 1922
Hazzard, George W.	M 66	Savannah, Ga.	May 9, 1922
Allston, Charles Petigru	M 74 & 10 m	Georgetown (Windsor Place)	May 30, 1922
Campbell	M 2 hours		Sept. 2, 1922
Simons, Mrs. Josephine Alston	F 73	Georgetown	Oct. 13, 1922
McKnight, Mrs. Lula (Doar)	M 28	Georgetown	Nov. 1, 1922
Morris, Charles E.	M 34	Asheville, NC	Nov. 5, 1922
Wendt	M Baby boy who lived a few minutes		Jan. 7, 1923
Morris, Abigail Gertrude	F 22	Hendersonville, NC	Feb. 18, 1923
Heriot, Mrs. Anna Coachman	F 83	Columbia, SC	Mar. 19, 1923
LaBruce, Eugene F., Jr.	M 9 days	Georgetown, SC	Apl 4, 1923
Rosa, Franz D.	M 62	Georgetown, SC	May 4, 1923
Caines, Robert J.	M 44	"Hobcaw"	May 28, 1923
Smith, David Thomas	M 66	Georgetown, SC	Jun. 21, 1923
Congdon, Mrs. Adrianna Leavey	F 82 10 m.	Georgetown, SC	July 9, 1923
Barnwell, Stephen Elliott	M 82 9 m.	Beaufort, SC	Aug. 7, 1923
James, William Alden	M 55 2 m.	Fellsmere, Florida	June 9, 1923
Cooper, Nelson	M about 62	Georgetown, SC	Oct. 11, 1923
Karnow, Charles	M 63	Georgetown, SC	Oct. 21, 1923
Smith, Herbert L.	M 62	Georgetown, SC	Oct. 30, 1923
Hucks, Florida M. Johnson	F 68	Georgetown, SC	Mar. 19, 1924
Lightbourn, John Smith	M 58	Georgetown, SC	Apr. 3, 1924
Smith, Henry Cuttino	M 70	Georgetown, SC	July 6, 1924
Dorrill, Mrs. Jno. W.	F c70	Georgetown, SC	Sept. 23, 1924
Ernest Grace Grissillo	M 3 yrs	North Island, SC	Feb. 6, 1925
Gilbert Johnson	M 88 yrs	Georgetown, SC	March 11, 1925
Oscar E. Emerson	M 78	Newark, NJ	July 19, 1925
Clara Tamplett (Miss)	F 76	Georgetown, SC	Aug. 13, 1925
Mrs. Freeman Farr	F 82	Columbia, SC	Aug. 20, 1925
John G. Carraway	M 72	Georgetown, SC	Oct. 25, 1925
Mrs. Eddie Payne	F 57	Andrews, SC	Nov. 3, 1925
Mary Alston Wright	F 30	New York City	Nov. 25, 1925
George Reynolds Congdon	M 66	Norfolk, Va.	Aug. 24, 1926
Lucy Munnerlyn Wendt	F 26	Lake Worth, FL	Sept. 23, 1926
Caleb Carmalt Morris	M c65	Georgetown, SC	Sept. 16, 1926
Miss Anne Eliza Atkinson	F 88	McClellanville, SC	Oct. 7, 1926
(Mrs. Wm. E.) Hattie B. Sparkman	F 65	Georgetown, SC	Oct. 20, 1926
William Bond Read	M 72	Atlanta, Georgia	Nov. 1, 1926
(Mrs. Gilbert) Elzy Carraway Johnson	F 70	Georgetown, SC	Dec. 18, 1926
James V. Johnstone, Jr.	M c50	Georgetown, SC	Mar. 3, 1927
John Saville Pyatt, Sr.	M 68	Georgetown, SC	Dec. 17, 1927
John Saville Pyatt, Jr.	M 39	Georgetown, SC	Apr. 19, 1928
Wm. Ervin Sparkman, M. D.	M c70	Georgetown, SC	June 9, 1928
Herman Decatur Beckman, M. D.	M 52	Georgetown, SC	Aug. 25, 1928
Allan P. Hazard	M 73	Georgetown, SC	Nov. 3, 1928
Walter Hazard, Esq.	M 70	Georgetown, SC	Feb. 6, 1930
James Vadonlis (Greek)	M c60	Georgetown, SC	Mar. 4, 1930
Wm. Minott Gaillard, M. D.	M 58	Georgetown, SC	May 27, 1930
Frederick W. Ford, Sr.	M 72	Georgetown, SC	July 6, 1930
Franz Delamar Johnson	M 5 wks	Georgetown, SC	July 14, 1930
George W. Austin	M 72	Georgetown, SC	Oct. 29, 1930
Mrs. Rebecca Elizab. (DeLesline) Croft	F 91	Georgetown, SC	Nov. 14, 1930

Cause of Death	Place of Interment	Date of Burial
Fall, breaking hip joint	Parish Church yard	May 23, 1921
Apoplexy	Parish Church yard	Feb. 16, 1922
Cancer of stomach	Parish Church yard	Mar. 10, 1922
Apoplexy	Parish Church yard	May 31, 1922
	Parish Church yard	Sept. 2, 1922
General C----	Parish Church yard	Oct. 21, 1922
Tuberculosis	Elmwood Cemetery	Nov. 2, 1922
Tuberculosis	Parish Ch. yard	Nov. 8, 1922
	Parish Ch. yard	Jan. 7, 1923
Tuberculosis	Parish Ch. yard	Feb. 10, 1923
	Parish Ch. yard	Mar. 20, 1923
	Prince Frederick Ch. yard	Apr. 5, 1923
Pneumonia	Parish Ch. yard	May 5, 1923
Pneumonia	Burying Gr'd Francis Point	May 29, 1923
	Parish Ch. yard	Jun. 23, 1923
Chronic Endocarditis	Parish Ch. yard	Jul. 10, 1923
Arterio Sclerosis	Parish Ch. yard	Aug. 8, 1923
Heart Failure	Parish Canbery	Jun. 10, 1923
Heart ----	Snow Mill	Oct. 12, 1923
Apoplexy	Cemetery in Conway	Oct. 22, 1923
Angina Pectoris	Parish Ch. yard	Nov. 1, 1923
Angina Pectoris	Parish Church Yard	Mar. 21, 1924
Angina Pectoris	Parish Church Yard	Apr. 4, 1924
Apoplexy	Parish Church Yard	July 7, 1923
	Elmwood Cemetery	Sept. 24, 1924
Collitis	Parish Church yard	Feb. 7, 1925
Old age	Parish Church yard	Mar. 11, 1925
	Elmwood Cemetery	July 21, 1925
Paralysis	Prince George Church yd.	Aug. 13, 1925
	Prince George Church yd.	Aug. 22, 1925
Arterio sclerosis	Prince George Church yard	Oct. 27, 1925
	Service: St. Lukes Ch: Andrews, SC	Nov. 4, 1925
Pneumonia	Prince George Church yard	Nov. 27, 1925
Apoplexy	Prince George Church yard	Aug. 26, 1926
Uremic Poisoning	Prince George Church yard	Sept. 4, 1926
Asthma & c.	Prince George Church yard	Sept. 18, 1926
Old Age	Prince George Church yard	Oct. 8, 1926
Angina pectoris	Pr: George church yard	Oct. 21, 1926
Myocarditis	Pr: George church yard	Nov. 2, 1926
Uremic Poisoning	Pr: George church yard	Dec. 20, 1926
Heart failure	Pr: George church yard	Mar. 5, 1927
Heart failure	Pr: George church yard	Dec. 19, 1927
Blood poisoning	Pr: George church yard	Apr. 20, 1928
Heart trouble	Pr: George church yard	June 10, 1928
	Pr: George church yard	Aug. 26, 1928
General decline	Pr: George church yard	Nov. 4, 1928
Heart failure	Pr: George church yard	Feb. 7, 1930
Heart failure	Elmwood Cemetery	Mar. 5, 1930
Heart trouble	Pr: George Church yard	May 29, 1930
Cancer	Pr: George Church yard	July 7, 1930
Whooping cough	Pr: George church yard	July 15, 1930
Dyssentery	Elmwood Cemetery	Oct. 30, 1930
Old age	Elmwood Cemetery	Nov. 15, 1930

Full Name	Sex & Age	Last Residence	Date of Death
Morgan P. Moorer	M 17	Asheville, NC	Feb. 28, 1930
Mrs. Emily Rutledge Allston	F 84	Waccamaw, SC	Apr. 29, 1931
Mrs. Susan E. J. McNeil	F 67	Georgetown, SC	May 16, 1931
Mrs. Lillie J. Hazzard	F 75	Asheville, NC	Sept. 2, 1931
Edna Ruthven Plowden	F 4 yrs.	Georgetown, SC	Sept. 21, 1931
Mrs. Myrtle Della Ruppert	F 65	Georgetown, SC	Mar. 25, 1932
Miss Isabel Johnstone	F 78	Georgetown, SC	May 13, 1932
Mrs. Thos. S. (Mary) Daggett	F 58	Georgetown, SC	July 21, 1932
Thos. S. Daggett	M 69	Georgetown, SC	Nov. 14, 1932
Miss Catherine Ann Ford	F 87	Columbia, SC	Mar. 14, 1933
Miss Violette Hall	F 73	Home: Catskill, NY visiting in Georgetown	Mar. 16, 1933
Mrs. Elizabeth (Smith) Oliver	F 82	Deland, Florida	Aug. 25, 1933
Joseph W. Grisillo	M c60	North Island, SC	Dec. 28, 1933
Fannie Wright Hazard (Mrs. J. I.)	F 71	Georgetown, SC	Jan. 22, 1934
Catherine Ward Pyatt	F	Georgetown, SC	Mar 5, 1934
(Mrs. Wm. D.) Anetta Detyens Jones	F 52	Wilmington, NC	May 17, 1934
Thomas B. Hamby	M	Jacksonville, Fla.	Sept. 16, 1934
Miss Ruth Hall	F 76	Home: Catskill, NY visiting in Georgetown	Nov. 1, 1934
George Thomas Ford	M 56	Georgetown, SC	Dec. 7, 1934
(Mrs. G. T.) Catherine Deveaux Ford	F 51	Georgetown, SC	Dec. 7, 1934
(Mrs. E. Marion Sr.) Minnie D. Doar	F 62	Georgetown, SC	June 28, 1935
(Miss) Marianne Meade Parker	F 53	Philadelphia, Pa.	Nov. 5, 1935
Arthur O. Atkinson	M 88	McClellanville, SC	Nov. 11, 1935
Edgar Stoney Read	M 62	Bellair, Maryland	Dec. 5, 1935
(Mrs. Jas. R.) Penelope B. Parker	F 79	Georgetown, SC	Jan. 2, 1936
Foster Lawrimore	M 31	Georgetown, SC	Jan. 30, 1936
William Chisholm Lucas, M. D.	M	California	Mar. 16, 1936
(Mrs. T. Cordes) Alice Vaughan Lucas	F 43	Santee, Georgetown Co.	Mar. 28, 1936
(Mrs. E. L.) Maude Farr Lloyd	F 60	Columbia, SC	June 16, 1936
William Henry Johnstone	M 68	Lexington, Kentucky	Sept. 20, 1936

Cause of Death	Place of Interment	Date of Burial
Self-inflicted pistol wound	Pr: George church yard	Dec. 16, 1930
Paralysis	Pr: George church yard	Apr. 30, 1931
Acute indigestion	Cemetery, Marion, S. C.	May 18, 1931
Cerebral hemorrhage	Pr: George Church yard	Sept. 4, 1931
?	Pr: George Church yard	Sept. 22, 1931
Paralysis & Pneumonia	Augusta, Georgia	Mar. 27, 1932
Heart failure	Pr: George Church yard	May 15, 1932
Brain trouble	Pr: George Church yard	July 23, 1932
Heart trouble	Pr: George Church yard	Nov. 16, 1932
Old age	Pr: George Church yard	Mar. 15, 1933
Lobar pneumonia	Pr: George Church yard	Mar. 17, 1933
Uremic poisoning	Pr: George Church yard	Aug. 27, 1933
Heart failure	Pr: George Church yard	Dec. 29, 1933
Heart trouble	Pr: George Church yard	Jan. 24, 1934
Uremic poisoning	Pr: George Church yard	Mar. 6, 1934
Heart trouble	Elmwood, Georgetown	May 18, 1934
Heart trouble	Prince George Churchyard	Sept. 18, 1934
Kidney trouble	Prince George Churchyard	Nov. 2, 1934
Automobile accident	Prince George Churchyard	Dec. 9, 1934
Automobile accident	Prince George Churchyard	Dec. 9, 1934
Heart trouble, Long illness	Elmwood, Georgetown	June 30, 1935
Long illness	Prince George Churchyard	Nov. 7, 1935
Old age	Prince George Churchyard	Nov. 12, 1935
	Prince George Churchyard	Dec. 7, 1935
Pneumonia	Prince George Churchyard	Jan. 3, 1936
Tuberculosis	Elmwood Cemetery	Jan. 31, 1936
Body cremated; ashes scattered	Prince George Churchyard	Mar. 23, 1936
Cancer	Prince George Churchyard	Mar. 30, 1936
	Prince George Churchyard	June 18, 1936
	Prince George Churchyard	Sept. 24, 1936

MARRIAGES

July 20, 1916 at Rectory. Edward B. Cox, widower, age 29, Andrews, SC, and Bessie M. Hardee, age 19, Andrews, SC. Wit: Mrs. John S. Lightbourn, Joseph Ward. Officiating Minister: John S. Lightbourn.

April 16, 1917 at Rectory. Nept Myers (colored), age 22, Waccamaw, SC, and Maggie Grant (colored), age 20, Waccamaw, SC. Wit: Charlotte Grant, John Mazyck. Officiating Minister: John S. Lightbourn.

May 21, 1917 at Rectory. Joseph H. Webster, age 21, Andrews, SC, and Ida Turner, age 17, Andrews, SC. Wit: Bride's Mother, Rutha Skipper, and others. Officiating Minister: John S. Lightbourn.

December 29, 1917 at Prince George Winyah Ch. James H. McKnight, age 25, Haxtun, Colorado; Parents: C. P. McKnight and Lula (Cuttino) McKnight; and Lula Mary Doar, age 23, Georgetown, SC; Parents: E. Marian Doar and Mary (Detyens) Doar. Wit: E. E. House, Sadie Bourne. Officiating Minister: John S. Lightbourn.

Thursday, October 10, 1918 at Bride's Residence, Georgetown, SC. Leonard James[?] Ravenel, age 24, Florence, SC, and Alice Elizabeth LaBruce, age 24, Georgetown, SC. Wit: Bride's Mother, Brothers and sister. Officiating Minister: John S. Lightbourn.

Wednesday, July 2, 1919 at the Rectory. George C. Scurry, age 23, Georgetown, SC, and Thelma D. Porter, age 20, Georgetown, SC. Wit: Mrs. John S. Lightbourn, Miss Edna Doggett. Officiating Minister: John S. Lightbourn.

Monday, November 24, 1919 at the Rectory. James O. Scott, age 28, Washington, DC, and Mary Emily Perry, age 18, Georgetown, SC. Wit: Mrs. John S. Lightbourn, Mrs. H. W. Young. Officiating Minister: John S. Lightbourn.

November 28, 1919 at the Rectory. Chester A. Comlin, age 32, Georgetown, SC, and Kate C. Hoeneveld, age 35, Vesper, Wis. Wit: Mr. and Mrs. Comlin. Officiating Minister: John S. Lightbourn.

Wednesday, April 14, 1920 at Prince George Church. Belton O. Brockinton, age 26, Georgetown, SC; and Bertha Lauretta Emerson, age 20, Georgetown, SC; Parents: E. V. Emerson and Annie (Young) Emerson. Wit: The parents, numerous relations and large company of friends. Officiating Minister: John S. Lightbourn.

May 14, 1920 at Prince George Church. Willis S. Williams, age "over 35," Minneapolis, Minn., and Myrtle (Johnston) Currie, widow, age "over 22," Minneapolis, Minn. Wit: Mr. and Mrs. George S. Clark. Officiating Minister: John S. Lightbourn. See License #2319 for this unusual method of stating ages. J. S. L.

Wednesday, November 17, 1920 at Bride's Residence, 1020 Front St. Frank Williams Wolfe, age 25, Charleston, SC; and Margaret Amelia Collins, age 19 years 2 mos., Georgetown, SC; Parents: Mrs. W. J. Collins. Wit: parents of bride and groom and a large company of friends. Officiating Minister: John S. Lightbourn.

December 17, 1920 at the Rectory. James McR. Lowe, age 29, Newbern, NC; and Elizabeth DePraetere, age 25, Belgium. Wit: Mrs. John S. Lightbourn, Mrs. W. W. Munnerlyn. Officiating Minister: John S. Lightbourn.

Wednesday, January 12, 1921 at the Bride's home. Eugene F. LaBruce, age 29 years 20 mos., Georgetown, SC; and Grace Marian Dennis, age 20 yrs, 8 mos., Georgetown, SC. Wit: Brides parents, relations, and friends. Also many relatives and friends of the Groom. Officiating Minister: John S. Lightbourn.

Thursday, September 22, 1921 at Prince George Winyah Church. Mordecai S. Witherington, age 26, Goldsboro, NC; and Alice LaBruce Ward, age 23, Georgetown, SC; Parents: Col. S. Mortimer Ward. Wit: in the presence of the bride's father, many other relatives and friends. Officiating Minister: John S. Lightbourn.

Thursday, November 24, 1921 at the home of the bride. John Herman Carraway, age 40, Georgetown, SC; and Esther (Richardson) LaBruce, widow, age 37, Georgetown, SC. Wit: the families of both parties, about 25 persons. Officiating Minister: John S. Lightbourn.

Thursday, December 15, 1921 at Prince George Winyah Church. Marion Carlish Green, aged 26, of Balsam, NC; and Ruth Carraway, age 23, Georgetown, SC. Wedding in presence of bride's parents, relatives and a large number of friends. Officiating Minister: John S. Lightbourn.

Wednesday, January 4, 1922 at Prince George Winyah Church. William Sander Mahon, age 28, Spartanburg, SC; and Alice Marie Haselden, age 22, Georgetown, SC. Wit: in the presence of the bride's parents, groom's relations, and a very large company of friends. Wedding at 7:30 p. m. Officiating Minister: John S. Lightbourn.

Saturday, 8 p. m., Feb. 26, 1922 at Prince George Winyah Church. Adelbert T. Wendt, age 27, Georgetown, SC; and Lucy Middleton Munnerlyn, age 23, Georgetown, SC. Wit: in the presence of the bride's mother, groom's mother, brothers of the bride, sister of groom, other relatives and many friends. Officiating Minister: John S. Lightbourn.

April 20, 1922 at Prince George Winyah Church. Thomas W. Higgins, age 37, Georgetown, SC; and Maria Jane Carraway, age 36, Georgetown, SC. Wit: in the presence of the bride's parents, other relatives and large number of friends of both parties. Officiating Minister: John S. Lightbourn.

Wednesday, April 26, 1922 at Prince George Winyah Church. Edwin Ruthven Plowden, Jr., age 37, Georgetown, SC; and Edna Tillman Doggett, age 30, Georgetown, SC. Wit: parents of both bride and groom and very many friends. Officiating Minister: John S. Lightbourn.

June 28, 1922 at Prince George Winyah Church. Francis Marion Connor, age 29, Cordele, Ga.; and Eleanor Clyde Doar, age 21, Georgetown, SC. Wit: parents of both parties, other relatives and friends. Officiating Minister: John S. Lightbourn.

August 25, 1922 at the Rectory. Alfred Thomas Baker, Jr., age 21, Andrews, SC; and Daisie Elizabeth Stephenson, age 18, Andrews, SC. Two witnesses. Officiating Minister: John S. Lightbourn.

November 15, 1922 at Prince George Winyah Church. George A. Grille, widower, age 62 years 11 months, Dawson, Ga.; and Mrs. Annie M. Lucas, widow, age 47 years 9 months, Georgetown, SC. Wit: The bride's sister, niece, nephew, and about eight other persons. Officiating Minister: John S. Lightbourn.

June 28, 1923 at Prince George Winyah Church. Francis Perry Sessions, age 33, Greensboro, NC; and Emily Murphy, age 27, Georgetown, SC. Wit: Parents of the bride and groom and many friends. Officiating Minister: Alfred James Derbyshire, Rector, St. Timothy's Church, Columbia, S. C.

Saturday, September 1, 1923 at Prince George Winyah Church. Eugene C. Ward, age 34, Asheville, NC; and Alice Johnston Hazzard, age 33, Asheville, NC. Wit: many relatives and friends. Officiating Minister: John S. Lightbourn.

Saturday, December 1, 1923 at the Rectory, Prince George Parish. Henry Dewitt Smoak, age 26, Orangeburg, SC; and Mary Catharine Gardner, age 18, Georgetown, SC. Wit: James A. Gordon, Olin Gardner, Gladys Martin. Officiating Minister: John S. Lightbourn.

February 9, 1924 at the Bride's Home, King St. Julian L. Johnson, age 25, Columbia, SC; and Louise Delamer Rosa, age 22, Georgetown, SC. Wit: Bride's mother, aunt, uncle and other relations. Groom's mother, brothers and other relatives. Officiating minister: John S. Lightbourn.

May 15, 1924 at the Bride's Home, Prince St. Edward Haselden Carraway, age 29, Georgetown, SC; and Ellen Greer Smith, age 28, Georgetown, SC. Wit: J. H. Carraway, O. Mc.G. Carraway and others. Officiating minister: Rev. C. W. Boyd per H. D. Bull.

October 27, 1924 at Georgetown, SC. Robert Arthur Clyburn, age 25, Winston-Salem, NC; Parents: dead; and Nellie Johnston, age 21, Georgetown, SC; Parents: James V. Johnston, Mrs. J. V. Johnston. Wit: J. V. Johnston Jr, L. M. Rosa, Mrs. P. T. Munn. Officiating minister: H. D. Bull.

November 19, 1924 at All Saints, Waverly Mills, SC. Benjamin Munnerlyn, age 23, Georgetown, SC; Parents: Mrs. Munnerlyn; and Margaret Elizabeth Springs, age 23, Georgetown, SC; Parents: Deceased. Wit: W. Wilson Munnerlyn, Chas. Douglass Springs, Phillip Lachicote, Mrs. T. J. H. Williams and many others. Officiating minister: H. D. Bull. Bride & Groom communicants of Prince George, Georgetown, S. C.

December 30, 1924 at Prince George Church. Louis Lindo Overton, age 25, Georgetown, SC; and Katherine Parkhill Fraser, age 22, Georgetown, SC; Parents: Hugh W. Fraser, Mrs. W. H. Fraser. Wit: Bride's parents, Brothers of the groom and many other witnesses. Officiating minister: H. D. Bull.

June 11, 1925 at 51 Montague St., Charleston, SC. Charles M. Moore, M. D., age 31, Georgetown, SC; Parents: both deceased; and Helen Ellis, age 22, Charleston, SC; Parents: mother deceased, father present at ceremony. Wit: Matt S. Moore, M. D., Mrs. M. S. Moore, McKenzie Moore, Miss Sarah Moore. Officiating minister: H. D. Bull.

December 13, 1925 at Rectory. Harold Kaminski, age 39, Georgetown, SC; Parents: Mrs. H. Kaminski; and Julia Bosard Pyatt, age 25, Georgetown, SC; Parents: Mr. & Mrs. Jno. S. Pyatt. Wit: Gertrude C. Bull. Officiating minister: H. D. Bull.

January 25, 1926 at Prince George Winyah. Harold Weber Barker, age 28, Raleigh, NC; and Helen Elizabeth Battley, age 23, Hamlet, NC. Wit: C. L. Levy of Andrews, S. C., R. W. Smith, Marguerite Skinner. Officiating minister: H. D. Bull.

May 7, 1927 at Rectory. George A. LaBruce, age 25, Georgetown Co., SC; Parents: dead; and Clothilde K. Geisendorfer, age 18, San Francisco, Cal. Wit: Walter H. McDonald, T. W. Higgins. Officiating minister: H. D. Bull.

October 30, 1928 at Prince George Winyah. Frank R. Bourne, age 22, South Island, SC; and Emilie Payne, age 30, Guyencourt, Del. Wit: Joseph Gales Ramsay, Mrs. J. T. Bourne. Officiating minister: H. D. Bull.

June 10, 1929 at Kensington, Georgetown, SC. Johannes Vilhelm Nielsen, Jr., age 25, Charleston, SC; Parents: J. V. Nielsen, Sr., Mrs. J. V. Neilsen; and Virginia Doar, age 23, Georgetown; Parents: J. Walter Doar, Mrs. J. W. Doar. Wit: Frances Black, Charles A. Nielsen and others. Officiating minister: H. D. Bull.

July 6, 1929 at Parish Church, Georgetown, SC. Alfred Muller, age 20, Baltimore, Md.; and Elizabeth Betz, age 20, Baltimore, Md. Wit: J. L. Bull, Grace L. Betz, Mildred E. Houk, and others. Officiating minister: H. D. Bull.

July 9, 1929 at Prince George, Georgetown, SC. Julian Shepherd Albergotti, age 26, Charlotte, NC; Parents: T. McKewn Albergotti, Mrs. T. McK. Albergotti; and Myrtle DeMichel Hucks, age 24, Georgetown; Parents: Dr. H. M. Hucks, Mrs. H. M. Hucks. Wit: Mrs. Sam C. Lattimore, McKewn Albergotti, Eula Sheppard Albergotti, H. M. Hucks and many and others. Officiating minister: H. D. Bull.

October 8, 1929 at Prince George Church. Bacot Allston Wayne, age 34, Charleston, SC; and Lucile Meggett King, age 24, Georgetown; Parents: Mr. & Mrs. Richd T. King. Wit: Theo King, Mrs. Paul Fraser, Hugh S. Wayne, Stephen W. King, C. A. Carton. Officiating minister: H. D. Bull.

October 27, 1930 at Rectory. Wm. Allen Lively, age 27, Chapel Hill, NC; and Celia Clarke Moulton, age 30, New Bern, NC; Wit: Mrs. H. D. Bull, Mrs. C. C. Phillips. Officiating minister: H. D. Bull.

February 20, 1931 at Rectory. Wm. J. Woodbury, widower, age 40, Georgetown, SC; and Edith P. Dusenbury, widow, age 30, Conway, SC; Wit: Edward L. Clerc, Gertrude C. Bull. Officiating minister: H. D. Bull.

June 23, 1931 at Prince George Church. Benjamin James Berry, age 27, Chicago, Ill.; and Virginia Bernice Haselden, age 28, Georgetown, SC; Parents: E. Capers Haselden, Mrs. E. C. Haselden. Wit: Mr. & Mrs. E. C. Haselden, Mr. & Mrs. Jas. W. Wingate, Mr. & Mrs. Louis L. Overton and many others. Officiating minister: H. D. Bull.

October 8, 1931 at Prince George Church. Rev. John Adams Pinckney, age 26, Allendale, SC; Parents: Frank D. Pinckney, Sr., and (Mrs. F. D.) Mary A. Pinckney; and Hilda Witherspoon Emerson, age 29, Georgetown, SC; Parents: E. V. Emerson, Mrs. E. V. Emerson. Officiating minister: Rt. Rev. A. S. Thomas, D. D., and Rev. H. D. Bull.

February 9, 1932 at Res: Graves Station, SC. James Moore, age 21, Georgetown Co.; and Alberta Carter, age 17, Georgetown Co.; Wit: Parents of Groom, Mother of bride and others, Chas. C. Jones. Officiating minister: H. D. Bull.

September 2, 1932 at Prince George Church. Olaf Johann Tobias, widower, age 23, Andrews, SC; and Sarah Gladys Lowther, age 42, Athens, Ga.; Wit: Gertrude C. Bull. Officiating minister: H. D. Bull.

April 6, 1933 at Prince George Church. Derrick Goude, widower, age 43, Georgetown; Parents: deceased; and Vernelle Jacobs, widow, age 29, Georgetown; Wit: Mr. & Mrs. B. F. Fraser, Mrs. H. D. Bull, Mrs. C. W. Boyd, Miss Julia A. Gantt. Officiating minister: H. D. Bull.

June 13, 1934 at Prince George Church. Saltus S. McClary, age 27, Georgetown; Parents: Mr. & Mrs. McClary; and Rosa M. Hucks, age 26, Georgetown; Parents: Dr. Herbert M. Hucks, Mrs. H. M. Hucks. Wit: Parents of bride and groom, brothers & sisters and many friends. Officiating minister: H. D. Bull.

April 20, 1935 at Home. Morrisville, Georgetown Co., SC. Roscoe M. Hinson, age 22, Kingstree, SC; and Virginia Rhem, age 20, Morrisville, SC; Parents: Mr. Louis Rhem, Mrs. Louis Rhem. Wit: Parents of bride, Mr. & Mrs. M. M. Thomas, Mrs. J. M. Carraway, Mr. & Mrs. J. H. Carraway, Mr. & Mrs. D. D. Rhem, and many friends. Officiating minister: H. D. Bull.

August 15, 1935 at Home, King St., Georgetown, SC. Lee Cannon Ballard, Jr., age 24, Georgetown; Parents: Lee C. Ballard, Mrs. L. C. Ballard; and Agnes L. Emerson, age 21, Georgetown; Parents: E. V. Emerson, Mrs. E. V. Emerson, nee Young. Wit: Families of bride and groom. Officiating minister: H. D. Bull and Rev. John A. Pinckney of Allendale.

August 31, 1935 at Prince George Church. John S. Rhem, age 27, Rhems, SC; Parents: Mrs. Rhem; and Rhetta P. Skinner, age 22, Georgetown; Parents: G. Thos. Skinner, Mrs. G. T. Skinner. Wit: Mr. & Mrs. G. T. Skinner, Miss Louise Skinner, Miss Ethel Bellune & others. Officiating minister: H. D. Bull.

April 14, 1935 at Prince George Church. A. Beauregard Betancourt, Jr., age 25, Charleston, SC; Parents: A. Beauregard Betancourt & wife; and Bessie Lesesne Fraser, age 27, Georgetown; Parents: Benjamin P. Fraser (Mrs. B. P.) Bessie F. Fraser. Wit: F. E. Shaw, G. w. Rosa, B. P. Fraser, A. Beauregard Batencourt, Mrs. A. B. Betancourt. Officiating minister: H. D. Bull.

September 19, 1936 at Arundel, Georgetown Co., SC. John Eldred Simkins, age 30, Beach Island, SC; and Esther R. LaBruce, age 26, Georgetown; Parents: J. L. LaBruce (deceased, Mrs. J. Herman Carraway. Wit: J. H. Tiller, Leroy H. Simkins, P. H. Dunbar. Officiating minister: H. D. Bull.

September 20, 1936 at Georgetown, SC. Chas. A. Holland, Jr., age 26, Florence, SC; and Mabel V. Wingate, age 25, Georgetown; Parents: Jas. W. Wingate, Mrs. Jas. W. Wingate. Wit: C. A. Holland, Fred W. Young, J. W. Wingate, Ethel Holland, Myrtle Y. Wingate, Harriet Carroll, Mrs. F. H. Young, Pauline McCown, Mabel Helen Carraway, H. A. Barnes, Myrtle Helen Carraway. Officiating minister: H. D. Bull.

[The following is found at the end of the volume]:

Diocese of St. John's Church, Florence, S. C., October 12th, 1835. The undersigned hereby certifies that Mrs. Vera Pitcher is a Communicant in good standing of the above-named Parish, and is at her request transferred to the Pastoral care of the Rev. H. D. Bull, Rector of Prince George Church, Winyah, Georgetown, S. C. (Signed) Wilmer S. Poegnor.

INDEX

Index prepared by James D. McKain

(Jacobs), Gertrude Bourne 132
  J. Elliott 132
  Katherine Elliott 132
  Marietta 85
  Mary 118,236
  Mary A. 29,33
  Mary Ann 32,79
  Mary Etta 32,56,81
  Ruth 140
  Vernelle 149
  W. Napoleon 126
  William 32
  William Napoleon 116,126,136
  Willis 79
Jacobus, Melancthon W. 39
James, 94
  George Edmund 1
  James Washington 99
  Judge 1
  Mary Elizabeth 112
  Robert Wilson 99
  William A. 57,84
  William Alden 71,142
Jamison, C. P. 119
Jane, 17,25
Jannike, 64
Jayroe, Richard Bruce 130
  W. H. 130
Jean, 54
Jeannerette, Edw. N. 35
Jefferson, Amesby 84
  Anesly 87
  Anseley 82
  Ansley 36
  Emily[?] 112
  Thomas 21,25,36,37,55,69,103
Jenkins, Esther Wayne 132
Jennerett, E. N. 39
Jennings, David 27
Jeppson, John 140
Jepson, Alice 77
  Henry 77
  Nancy Ann 76
Jerrett, H. B. 49
Jervey, Louise S. 42
  Maria F. 42
Jim/Jimmy, 2,64
Jinny, 4
John, 10,66
Johnson, A. O. 50
  Anna 22
  Arthur O. 48,50,59,89
  Arthur Oliver 71
  Caroline White 24
  David Tooker 128
  Elisa 25
  Ella 28,49,100
  Elsie 39
  Elza Eveline 85

Elzy Carraway (Gilbert) 142
Elzy E. 87
Elzy Eveline 58
Florence 48
Franz Delamar 142
G. Lester 110
Gabriel Ross 32
Gabriella 24
Geo. H. 77
Gilbert 47,49,51,58,85,87,140,142
Gilbert Lester 58,85,87
Harriet 54
Helen Louise 130
Jane Oliver 50
John M. 51
Joseph 24,55
Joseph Allison 130
Joseph B. 128
Josephine 30
Julian L. 118,128,130,148
Julian Lester 126,138
Kate 50
Kathryn 48
Lester 45
Louise/Louisa 33,48
Louise (Rosa) 126,130
Louise R. 128,130
Lucien Green 28
Marion Pearl 50
Mary Katharine 48
Matilda P. 51
Nancy 63
Nellie 113
Nellie Geraldin 134
Pauline 48
Peg 42
Rhoda 30,32,33,100
Ross 30,32,33,68,100
Sam 67
Stepney 68
William 94
Johnston, 140
  Albert Nicholson 113
  Andrew 122
  Anna 140
  Anna Catharine 50
  Anna M. 49,51
  Eleanor (Nicholson) 122
  Elise Moore 45
  Elizabeth 49,50
  Francis Elliott 50,122
  G. H. 58,112
  Geo. H. 48-50
  J. V. 148
  James V. 148
  James Vance 136
  Joseph 64
  Lois Leona 136
  Mary 48

(Thomas), Thos. Burrington 95
V. 27
Virginia 35,55
Virginia C. 35
Virginia Caroline 10,78
Virginia E. 21
Washington 96
Wm. Henry 124
Thompson, Anna Malvina 101
Lizzie 75
Thorden, Frances 80
Theodore 80
Thorsen, Frances 69
Julia Ann 30,100
Julia Ann Sellard 30
T. 30
Theodore 68
William Julius 30,100
Thrall, E[?] B. 75
John Asa 74
Thurston, 5
E. 27
E. E. 27
Emily 23
Jane 3
Jane Cogdell 64
Maria R. 25
Maria Reese 80
Robert 67
Samuel Isaac 2,54
Samuel J. 93
Sarah 80
Tiller, J. H. 150
Tilton, A. C. 35
Adelle 56
Amelia C. 34,42,80
Amelia Catherine 106
Charles M. 35
E. M. 37
Edward M. 34,104
Edwin M. 80
Edwin Nathaniel 34
Ella F. 42
Jane A. 42
Jane Anne 56,81
Lillian Constance 59,89
Lillie Adelle 69
Lilly/ie A. 35,36
Mary L. 69
N. O. 37
Nathaniel B. 36
Nathaniel Baker 69
Rebecca A. 39
Robert Allston 102
Robert Morris 36
Theodore Wilson 68
Tober 12
Tobias, Olaf Johann 149
Tom 17,96

Tom Happy, 97
Toomer, C. 9,17
Charlotte 7,54
E. C. 3
Esther 63
Mary 54
Mary Warham 64
Trapier, A. Dehon 51
B. 24,55
B. F. 20
B. Foisin 3
Ben Allston 18
Benjamin F. 2,4,11
Benjamin Foissin 2,20
Charlotte 18,55,80
Charlotte I. 22
E. 21
James H. 21
E. M. 5
Elizabeth 19
Elizabeth S. 99
Emma Heyward 100
Hannah 2,4,23,25
Hannah Mary 4,101
Hannah Shubrick 2,99
Henry 101
J. H. 23
James Heyward 2,99
Julia 20
Maria H. 9
Marion Heyward 104
Mary Thomasine (Ford) 100
Paul 13,98
Paul H. 19
Paul Horry 22
Richard S. 27,106
Sarah A. 29
Sarah Cruger 98
W. W. 3,9
William H. 18,22,66,80
William Shubric 102
William Windham 95
Windham Theodosia 2
Trenholm, Alfred G. 116
Trim, E. N. 38
S. E. Jennerett 38
William 38
Troy, Rosanna 64
Truesdell, Joseph A. 71
Trust, Martha 28
William 28
Tryall, Peter 13,15,65
Tucker, 44
Ann Allston 4
Ann/a Jane 112
Ann/a Manigault 71,140
Annsley 56
Benjamin 21,98
Benjamin Daniel 14

www.ingramcontent.com/pod-product-compliance
Lightning Source LLC
Chambersburg PA
CBHW061735270326
41928CB00011B/2244